THE MURDER OF SARA BARTON

THE MURDER OF SARA BARTON

ISBN 978-1-7348877-2-3
Published by Bond Publishing

This book is a work of fiction. Any similarities to any person living or deceased to a character in the novel are purely coincidental.

Typesetting and Cover Design by FormattingExperts.com

THE MURDER OF SARA BARTON

LANCE MCMILLIAN

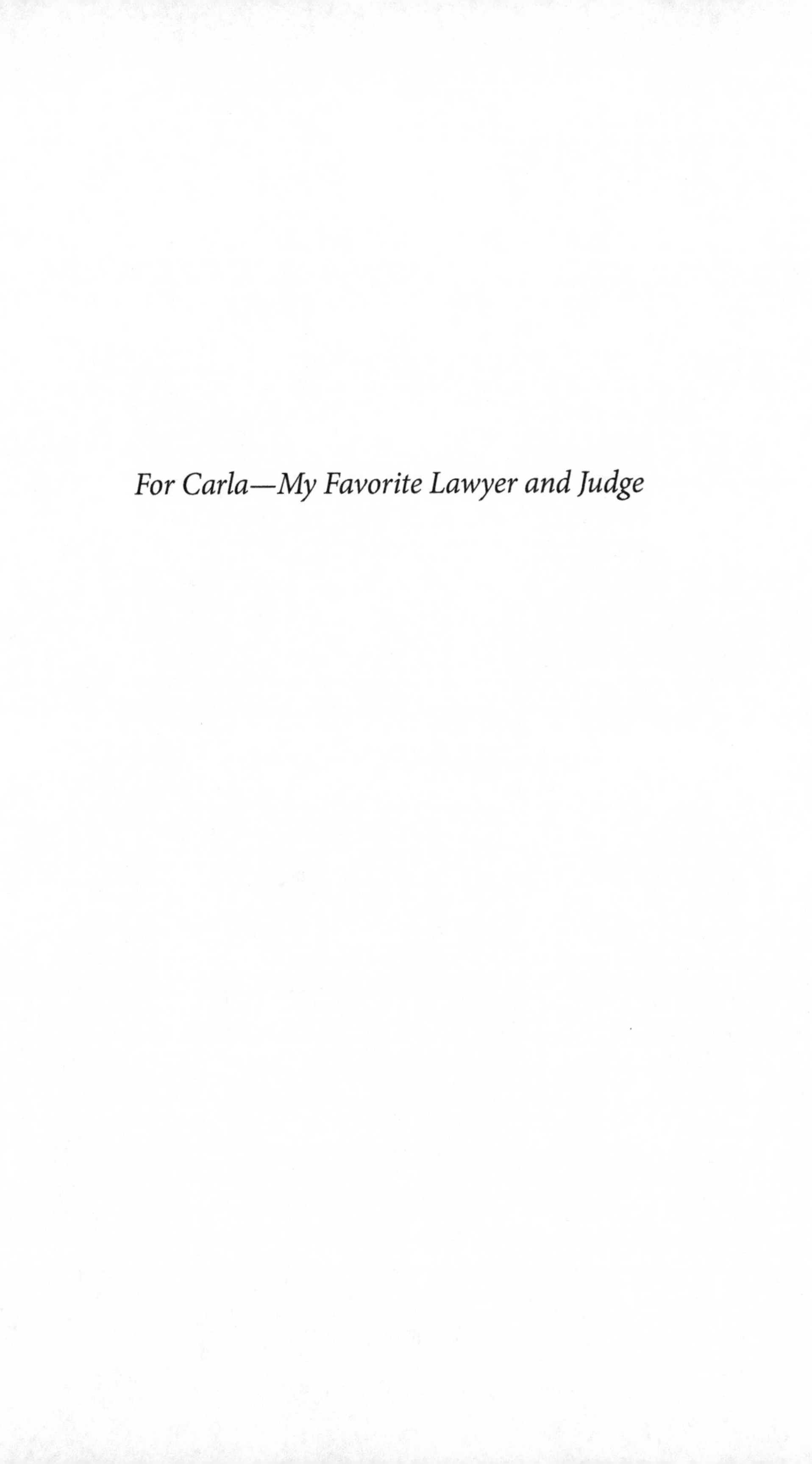

For Carla—My Favorite Lawyer and Judge

1

Sleep eludes me. Lying in bed allows the mind to roam free, but my untamed thoughts know only one destination. Amber and Cale—my dead wife and my dead son. And when I think of them, I think of him. Mr. Smith—the unknown man who murdered my family two years ago. The name is my own invention. When the case failed to close quickly, I needed to personalize my hatred. And Mr. Smith was born.

Because of my position in the District Attorney's Office, the investigation into the murders of my wife and child spared no expense. The trail is now cold. The mystery of Mr. Smith's identity leads to the mystery of his motive. Speculation eats at me. One thought terrifies me above all others—that Amber and Cale are dead because of me, because of who I am, what I do. That fear is why I cannot sleep. The weight is too much.

Escape is the only salvation. Ever since the killings, work is my refuge—nights, weekends, holidays. I never vacation. Chasing murderers shields me from the pain. Some people drink. Some choose drugs. Some hunt sex. I work. I figure to disappear into work for a few years, wake up one day, and find myself cured. But that is a lie. If you run long enough, you eventually come back to the place you started.

***

The phone rings. It is my friend, Detective Scott Moore. He wastes no time. "We have another one."

"Where?"

"A residence in Virginia Highlands. High profile. You're going to want to see it."

He gives me the address. The time is 1:14 a.m.—another sleepless night that I devote to the dead. As the deputy district attorney for all homicides in Fulton County, visiting murder scenes falls well outside my job description. I'm a lawyer, not an investigator. But lately I voyage out at all hours to stare into the faces of the newly condemned and imagine what terrors seized them as they took their last breaths. I ponder Amber and Cale's final, desperate thoughts. Despite my wish to flee from the past, the nature of my work keeps me on a short leash. Death abounds, and I take a strange comfort in its arms.

I believe in God, in Jesus. But I don't talk to God anymore. I have nothing to say. Not that I blame Him for what happened. God didn't kill my family. Mr. Smith did. He made a choice to pull that trigger. Free will is a weapon of mass destruction, and the collateral damage left in its wake falls like poisoned rain from the sky. So I still believe; I just don't feel. Faith in my God survives in the head, but the heart is dry of emotion. I am empty.

***

I arrive at the scene. Virginia Highlands is an upscale section of Atlanta, close to downtown. The house is old with character, typical of the neighborhood, expensive, but not flashy. Scott meets me as I mount the front steps. I ask, "What do we have?"

"I'll let you see for yourself."

I follow him to the kitchen and see a female body dead on the floor. The body's face stops me cold. I turn to Scott, who grins like a happy father watching his children open presents on Christmas morning.

"Is that—"

"Her twin sister." Scott flashes a smile of triumph at my expression of surprise. I turn again to analyze the body. Staring back at me is the spitting image of Lara Landrum, one of the most famous actresses in the world. The lifeless figure is soaked in blood from an apparent gunshot wound to the chest. She died quick.

Scott supplies me with the remaining particulars.

"Vic's name is Sara Barton, 36. Married to Bernard Barton, a lawyer. Know him?"

I shake my head.

"Well, we can't find him. No children. No other family besides her famous sister as far as we can tell. Initial estimated time of death between 9 and 10 p.m. Neighbors did not hear gunshots or see anyone at the house but heard arguing in the street, time uncertain. No signs of a break-in. The victim's divorce lawyer discovered the body and called 911 at 10:03 p.m."

"Divorce lawyer?"

"Weird, huh?"

"What's the lawyer's name?"

"Sam Wilkins."

"Really?"

"Know him?"

"Yeah. From law school."

Non-lawyers cannot understand the sense of kinship forged among law students. No matter how far we drift away from one another in subsequent years, the closeness remains. I call it the bond of survival. Sam's moment of truth came in Professor Ryan's Civil Procedure class. When called on to discuss the famous case of *Pennoyer v. Neff*, Sam completely imploded, botching even the most basic questions. Ryan's parting shot left a mark: "Mr. Wilkins, save your parents some money. Quit law school now. Don't delay the inevitable." Afterwards, a despondent Sam prepared to quit. I talked him back off the ledge. Now, he is a successful divorce lawyer, who apparently makes late night house calls to visit his clients. I don't like it.

"Is he here?"

Scott nods, and we descend to the basement. There sits Sam, wearing the look of the damned. Scott dismisses the police officer standing watch. When Sam sees me, his whole demeanor changes from dread to relief.

"Thank God you are here, Chance."

"Good to see you, Sam." We shake hands. For a second he seems close to hugging me but stops at the handshake. Before Scott and I even say another word, Sam launches into defense mode.

"I know it looks bad. What lawyer visits a client's house this late? But

Sara wanted to file her divorce papers tomorrow morning, and she had to sign the verification to the complaint before we could file. She didn't like meeting at the office, so she told me to come over at ten. I wouldn't normally do that for a client, but there is a lot of money to be made on this case. Or there was. Now she's dead. I can't believe it."

Scott and I look at each other then turn back to Sam. He leaks nervousness. I tell myself that if I were innocent and in his spot, then maybe I would be filled with anxiety, too. But something about him still smells off. Sam gives me a peculiar look, and alarm bells clamor. A memory stored in an unused warehouse of my brain stirs from the distant past. Something significant just happened, but I have no idea what. Sam launches into another monologue.

"I knew I shouldn't have come over here. I should've insisted that she drop by my office. I didn't want to come. I told her. I asked about her husband. She said he had to work and would not be back until after midnight, if at all. She was persistent like that, and I came over against my better judgment. The client is always right and all that. I rang the doorbell. No answer. I knocked. No answer. I tried the door. It was unlocked. I walked in, said hello, anybody here. Everything's quiet. I went to the kitchen and there she was. Lying on the floor. It was awful. I cannot believe this is happening to me." He pauses before adding, "I didn't kill her."

Scott gives Sam a disbelieving look, and Sam wilts in the glare. Giving up on Scott, he turns toward me on the verge of tears.

"You gotta believe me. I didn't kill her."

Sam is embarrassing himself at this point. A lawyer should never ramble. Scott and I have yet to ask him a single question, and still he cannot shut up. Our silent treatment is by design. Most witnesses become uncomfortable with the quiet and rush to fill the void. Talking takes the place of the silence that judges them.

Sam complains, "Are you guys going to say anything? I'm in the hot seat here."

Scott and I continue our quiet vigil. Sam pivots to Scott and then back my way, his anxious eyes begging me to speak. Watching him, the mysterious thought trapped deep in my subconscious emerges in full force. The implications click in an instant—the ghost of Becky Johnson rises again.

I drift back to the first year of law school at the University of Georgia. One Friday night, our circle of friends went to hear a new band play at the Georgia Theatre. Sam begged out at the last minute. We assumed that he ditched us to be with his girlfriend Natalie until we observed her partying on the front row. The next day, Sam explained to me that he had decided to study at home instead of going to the show. As he spoke, his face revealed an odd assortment of conflicting messages—uncertainty, nervousness, guilt, fear. The taint of deceit was unmistakable. I cross-examined him with bloody determination to force his confession—the only thing Sam had studied the night before was Becky Johnson, a third-year law student.

I turn to Scott.

"Can you leave us alone for a few minutes?"

Other detectives would balk. Not Scott. He knows that I will later tell him every word that will pass between Sam and me in his absence. Sam's sense of relief as Scott leaves the room is physically palpable. I study my old friend with mute detachment and allow the quietness of the room to do its work. Sam's discomfort grows. He speaks first.

"What? Why won't you say anything?"

I wait a few moments before replying, "I'm trying to figure out what to do with you." Memories of law school again beckon from the past. Our group of friends preferred poker to studying. Sam was the resident ATM, losing money to us with the regularity of a steady paycheck. Strategically, he knew the correct plays, but his facial expressions and body language betrayed him when it mattered most. Even then I wondered how Sam would ever handle delicate negotiations. Tonight's conversation confirms that some things never change. Sam still flinches when the stakes get too high.

Sam again breaks the quiet and asks in utmost seriousness, "Do I need a lawyer?"

"Did you kill her?"

"No!"

"Then you don't need a lawyer."

Sam looks unconvinced. He studies his folded thumbs and teeters on the edge of regressing into a barely-responsive cocoon. I recognize the signs. The soft touch won't work with him anymore. I need to give him a push.

"Sam, I want to help you, but I cannot help someone who refuses to help himself. You can't lie to the police without repercussions. You're part of a murder investigation. There's a dead body in the kitchen. The good news is that Scott and I are close friends. I can fix what has happened in this room up to this point. You can start over fresh. Clean slate. But the truth needs to start coming out of your mouth. Now."

Without even looking at me, he says, "I don't know what you're talking about."

"Becky Johnson."

The name confuses him for a moment. Then our eyes register mutual understanding, and he accepts my accusation without challenge. But I still need to hear the truth from his own lips.

I emphasize, "I swear to God that if you lie to me now, I will prosecute you for obstruction of justice myself."

Sam straightens up and nods. Fear gives way to resignation. He asks, "Does Liesa have to know?" Liesa started law school a year behind Sam and me. I attended their wedding. I make no promises but allow that I'll do what I can. He emits a heavy sigh. "Please try. You don't understand. I can't lose her." Two seconds later, he realizes the tragic awkwardness of his words. I know exactly what it means to lose a wife. But I barely take notice. I'm immersed in the case. Sam offers a plaintive "sorry." I retrieve Scott to restart the interrogation.

2

"Scott, Sam has something he wants to get off his chest."

Sam confesses that he and Sara Barton had been romantically involved for the last six weeks. The affair started shortly after she sought him out for divorce advice. The two had never met before.

The story ends. Sam sits there satisfied with himself for coming clean, but he has only touched upon the facts at a high level of generality. The particulars matter. Scott dives in. How many sexual encounters? Thirteen. Where would the two meet? Sam's office. Sara's home. A few times at a hotel. Who else knew about the affair? No one. Really? Yes, Sam insists.

Scott next tells Sam to describe in detail the first time he and the victim had sex. Confused, Sam asks, "What do you mean?"

"It's like this. One day you're the attorney, and she's only a client. Let's call that Point A. Then, lo and behold, the next day the two of you are naked together under the sheets. Let's call that Point B. My question is simple. How did you go from Point A to Point B? Who made the first move? When did you know that the two of you would have sex? Where did the sex take place? What sexual positions did you use that first time?"

I stifle a laugh. That last question reflects Scott's visceral dislike of the witness. Sam looks bewildered and embarrassed. He turns to me for help and asks, "Why on earth does this stuff matter?"

I explain, "It tells us something about the deceased." The answer is true enough. Suppose Sam and Sara Barton first had sex in a restaurant bathroom. That would be useful information—the victim liked risk and probably had a propensity for recklessness. Facts like that matter for understanding all the contours of the case. Each murder presents its own puzzle, and every piece of the puzzle provides an added degree of clarity.

Sam begins to give an answer. "Mrs. Barton invited me over to her house—"

Scott interrupts, "Mrs. Barton? I think you knew her better than that, didn't you?" Sam pauses and then continues.

"She invited me over to talk about the divorce. Her husband was gone on a business trip. When I got here, she was wearing lingerie. I knew that being here was a bad idea. I told her, 'I need to leave.' She told me to grow up and have a drink. I sat on the couch, she brought a drink over and sat right next to me. Then she put her hand on my leg. I told her that I was her lawyer and that I was married and that I couldn't do this. She said, 'Don't be a baby.' One thing led to another. We had sex on the couch. And I left."

Scott's face contorts with confusion. Experience tells me that deep skepticism and sarcasm will follow.

"Let me see if I understand this correctly," Scott starts. "This beautiful and sexy woman—Mrs. Barton—lulls you over with the pretense of discussing a legal matter. Yet unbeknownst to you, she really has seduction on her mind. When you arrive, she is practically naked and throws herself at you, overcoming your heroic resistance in the process." Scott shakes his head for dramatic effect. He continues.

"Stuff like that never happens to me, which is a shame. But here's my question: why you? I mean, no offense, but I think we can all agree that she was a little out of your league, right? Why you?" Scott stops and gives all indications that he expects an answer. Sam gives him one.

"I don't know. Maybe she was depressed and lonely, and I was someone she trusted."

Scott pounces, "You mean you abused your position as her attorney to take advantage of a client in her emotionally-vulnerable state? Now that I can believe."

"It wasn't like that. I didn't seek this out. I don't know why me. I was there. She was there. It just happened. I wish it hadn't."

Silence.

I study Sam closely. I think I believe him. Likely he is exaggerating his level of resistance, but the rest of it rings true. Scott's question, though, still lingers. Why Sam? Figuring out the answer would give us a glimpse into the woman lying dead upstairs. My initial instinct sees this as a case that will not solve itself overnight. If true, the first thing we must examine is the victim herself.

Who was Sara Barton?

One thing requires clearing up. I ask, "Why did you really come over tonight?"

"She told me yesterday I could be with her this evening. But I did need her to sign the complaint. Here it is."

He hands the unsigned divorce complaint over, and I read the name of the case: "Sara Landrum Barton vs. Bernard Allen Barton."

Weariness and helplessness line Sam's face. The hour is late. The gravity of his troubles is not lost on any of us. His client is dead. His marriage and career teeter on a cliff of his own making. He is a person of interest in a murder investigation—the adulterous lover of the murdered woman and the person who discovered her body. That's a heavy load for any man—innocent or guilty—to carry.

Scott follows up, "Had your lover told the husband about the divorce?"

"I don't think so. She never said she did."

A knock sounds on the door, and a uniformed officer informs us that Mr. Barton has arrived home. I check the clock. The time reads 2:43 a.m. Where has the husband been? Scott instructs the officer to keep Mr. Barton waiting and to refrain from telling him the news of his wife's death. Sam's time in the box is reaching its end.

Scott bluntly asks, "Did you kill her?"

"No."

"Who did?"

"I don't know."

"The husband?"

"I don't know."

Scott accepts Sam's lack of knowledge and points him to the door.

Sam nods and shuffles out of the room to an uncertain future. I ask Scott, "What do you think?" After a moment's reflection, he says, "I don't think he is a murderer, but I've been wrong before."

***

Bernard Barton does not cut an impressive figure. He is short, rotund, and devoid of a single hair on his head or face. As Scott and I enter the room, Barton booms, "I demand to know what's going on here." I take an immediate dislike to him. He's surly, and I've never cared too much for surly folks.

Scott doesn't allow Barton to hurry him. He has kept Barton in the dark up to this point because he wants to see the husband's reaction to the news of his wife's death. Scott makes the introductions and says, "Mr. Barton, I'm sorry to tell you that your wife is dead."

This precise choice of words is intentional. "Murder" goes unmentioned. Scott wants to see whether Barton asks how his wife died.

Barton asks, "What happened?"

If he murdered his wife, he avoids Scott's trap. No matter. All killers make mistakes, and murder never takes place in a controlled environment. The prying eyes of a snooping neighbor, the patrol car that passes at the wrong moment, trace DNA evidence—all are capable of sending even the cleverest murderer to death row.

Scott gives only a partial answer to Barton's question: "She was murdered." But Barton again fails to take the bait. He responds, "How?" Scott inspects him with a keen eye, no doubt curious as to Barton's coolness and serenity. Even after Scott informs him that his wife was shot, Barton fails to display a readable emotion. The room settles into a tense quietness. Scott and Barton stare at one another with a mixture of indifference and disdain, daring the other to speak first. I feel invisible. Scott at last breaks the deadlock and goes straight to the question of the hour, "Mr. Barton, may I ask where you have been all night?"

"No."

"Why not?"

"I'm a lawyer. I know my rights. No more questions until my lawyer is present."

Scott sounds a scornful chuckle—first Sam, now this. He gives Barton a determined look as if to say, "You and I will meet again." Unfazed, Barton's contemptuous stare conveys its own message, "I am better than you." Seeking a way to break the stalemate, I interject and ask Barton an innocuous question.

"Where do you work?"

A confused Barton turns toward me. Whether he is surprised that I am there or merely that I spoke is unclear. But he does answer the question.

"Marsh & McCabe."

I know the firm—quite corporate and well-to-do. My friend, Jeff Yarber, is a partner there. He attended law school with Sam and me. I will call him later today to get his read on things.

Barton announces, "I'm leaving now." The statement is a declaration and not a request for permission, presenting a clear challenge to Scott's authority. Legally, Scott could probably detain Barton longer, but little reason—apart from spite—exists in doing so. I also have an idea percolating that will only work if Barton is released. Scott looks at me out of the corner of his eye for advice, and I slightly shake my head.

Scott responds, "Okay. But before you go, can you look around the house to see if anything is missing?" Barton hesitates. The mental wheels turn hard in his head. He doesn't want to cooperate but knows that the request is a reasonable one. Barton nods grimly, and another officer prepares to escort Barton through the house. As they leave the room, Scott warns, "Don't touch anything." Barton looks back in silence before skulking out behind the officer, already regretting his agreement to help. With the husband gone, Scott looks at me and comments, "Lawyers."

"I have an idea."

"Kill all the lawyers?"

I ignore the provocation and continue, "Have someone follow him when he leaves. It might be interesting to know where he goes at this time of night."

Scott agrees and offers me a compliment of sorts, "Good thinking. That's why I keep you around." He makes the necessary arrangements with another detective before Barton comes back with the results of his search. Nothing appears to be missing, which lessens the chance that we're looking at a robbery. With his assignment complete, Barton requests to pack a suitcase of clothes to take with him. Scott nips that plan in the bud.

"No. Nothing can be moved. I'm not through with the crime scene."

An exasperated Barton asks, "Can I at least get my cell phone? I left it at home and have been without it all day."

"No."

Barton waits a moment but realizes that the battle is lost. He leaves without another word. An unmarked car follows Barton down the road from a discreet distance.

Little else remains to be done at this point. As I get ready to leave, Scott observes, "You know, he never asked who murdered his wife. Don't you think that is strange?"

"Left his cell phone here all day yesterday, too."

The police can track the movements of a suspect through the travels of his cell phone, but only if the suspect keeps the phone on his person.

Scott says, "Yep. He seemed to want to make sure that we knew that little tidbit."

It's 4:11 a.m. on the dash when I start the engine for the drive home. I haven't mourned Amber and Cale since receiving Scott's call. Three hours from now, I will be hard at work in my office.

This is my life.

3

It's 7:30 a.m., and I am in my office, a desktop full of files in front of me. District Attorney Bobby Lewis—my boss—breezes in without knocking. Not someone to arrive at the courthouse early, he must know about the Sara Barton case. Bobby is a politician and, like all politicians, he loves the sound of his own voice on the evening news, especially during an election year.

Bobby deploys a plastic smile and declares, "Chance Meridian—my favorite prosecutor in the office." False flattery is a favorite leadership tactic of his. He gets to the point.

"Lara Landrum's sister. That's big. First thing off the bat, the election. The murder of a prominent white Atlantan has a way of getting people interested in the goings on at the courthouse. They start paying attention, and we have to make sure that they like what they see. Do we have any suspects? Please tell me a white person killed her."

I admire his candor. As a black Democrat, Bobby's electoral position should be safe. But the subterranean issue of race always sits close to the surface in Atlanta. Bobby wants a white defendant because a white defendant is a no-lose proposition. The black community will applaud his vigorous pursuit of a white suspect for an attention-getting crime. The white community will be relieved that the murder is not the work of violent gangs terrorizing the city. Everyone wins.

Bobby realizes I won't have much to tell him at this point, but I give him what I've got.

"Unless something has changed in the last three hours, no suspects yet. The husband is a jerk, was out late, and refused to talk to us, but that may just be his personality. No signs of forced entry are apparent, and the husband says nothing is missing from the house. Based on that, I don't see a robbery or home invasion."

"You think we can eliminate the possibility of gang involvement?"

"That's my best bet."

Bobby leaves me to my work. He and the police chief will no doubt soon have a joint press conference. Cameras are like heroin to them.

***

Scott gives me an update later in the morning. I hear him smile over the phone. He says, "That idea to follow the husband hit pay dirt."

"How so?"

"Well, we now know where his girlfriend lives. My guy follows him to Southern Towers. Barton goes in, but my guy has no idea which condo. He goes to the security guard's desk, and what do you know, the security guard is my guy's former partner, retired with the pension, just working on the side. He asks him about Barton, and the guard says Barton is there all the time visiting Monica Haywood, who is a lawyer with Barton's firm. He also says Barton is an arrogant ass."

"That does sound like someone we know."

"No kidding. My guy asks if Barton was with his little girlfriend last night. The guard didn't come on duty until midnight, so he doesn't know. But he says he can provide my guy all the surveillance footage for the past twenty-four hours, which he does. My guy takes the video back to the station, watches, and voila, discovers that Barton left Southern Towers alone at 7:38 p.m. and did not return until my guy followed him back."

"Did the girlfriend leave at any time?"

"My guy thought of that, but he didn't know what she looked like so he couldn't check yet."

"Tell him to pull up the Marsh & McCabe website. She'll have a profile page with her picture."

I digest the new information. Barton has a girlfriend, he wasn't with her at the time the murder was committed, and the first thing he does after learning about the murder of his wife is to go back to the girlfriend's place. These revelations hardly make him a murderer, but they do him no favors. Like a hunter closing in on his prey, I feel a tingle of excitement at the commencement of the chase.

Scott's last item of business leads me to cancel my afternoon plans. Lara Landrum is between films and staying at her Atlanta house. She wants to meet with police. Scott asks if I want to be there.

I take him up on the offer.

***

Jeff Yarber, Sam, and I used to be thick as thieves in law school. Now Jeff makes seven figures a year as a Marsh & McCabe partner. I call him, hoping to learn more about Bernard Barton. The news of Sara's murder is already a hot topic around his office. He gives me the low down.

"Bernard is an acquired taste. He rubs a lot of people the wrong way. Arrogant. Difficult. Aggressive in court. Yet brilliant. Can be charming when he's in the mood. Wins his cases. Clients love him. His opponents hate him. The staff is terrified of him. His partners tolerate him."

I inquire about the Barton marriage.

"Bad. Real bad. Cheating on all sides. Bernard has always been a shark. He has hit on every pretty new associate to join the firm in the last twenty years. A few of them have succumbed to his advances. We've had to settle some harassment claims. He's been warned repeatedly to no avail. Like I said, the clients love him, and that means everything in this business. What are you going to do?"

This mindset is why I hate big corporate law firms. Money rules. I keep these thoughts to myself. Instead I ask, "How serious are Barton and Monica Haywood?"

"You know about that already? You guys work fast. Honestly, I don't know much. I've heard the rumors. All of us are pretty numb to it by now. It's consensual. They're two adults. I doubt it will end up being a long-term relationship."

I know the Barton type. Every workplace has its own version. I move on to Sara, "You mentioned cheating by his wife?"

"Yeah, she's having an affair with an associate in the firm named Brice Tanner. Or was, I guess."

I process the information. Jeff doesn't know about Sam and Sara Barton, which is just as well. But that's two lovers and counting for my murder victim. I wonder, "How do you know they were having an affair?"

"There's a video."

"Really? A video?"

"Yeah, it's crazy. I'll send it to you. We had a firm party at the High Museum a few months ago. Sara came with Bernard, but they didn't spend much time together. Instead, Sara glued herself to Brice, and the two of them started dirty dancing in front of everybody. They then went off by themselves to have sex, but the security cameras caught them in the act. A security guy made a copy, raised hell about it with one of my partners, and threatened to call the police. The partner gave the security guy a couple of hundred bucks in exchange for the video. The partner shared the video with one or two people, and it spread like a virus from there."

"How did that go over with Barton?"

"Here's the thing about Bernard. He never shows weakness. That's his persona. To get upset about the tape would mean revealing he cares. He won't do that. Indifference is the best revenge. Indifference to Sara, Brice, and those making fun of him tells them that they are not worthy of his time. That's how he thinks. Now is he really okay with it? Doubtful. He's too proud. But he'll never admit it."

I ask Jeff one last question, "Do you think he is capable of murder?"

"Aren't we all?"

4

Hell.

Visions of that place of eternal damnation differ based on the person. Some see fire. Some see a funny looking devil with horns and a pitchfork. Some refuse to acknowledge the possibility at all.

I see the Fulton County morgue. Death and finality permeate the pores of every crevice and corner of the Dungeon, the name given long ago to the basement room that stores the dead. The air hangs with hopelessness. The coldness, the artificial light, the shadows, the smell—all contribute to the sense of nothingness, a place where color goes to die and life dare not show its face.

Barton stands awkwardly in the basement hall outside the Dungeon. Scott and I watch from a respectful distance. We're all waiting on the coroner.

Dr. Cecil Magnus views punctuality with disdain and instead operates on his own unknowable clock. I don't begrudge him this conceit. Born in the segregated South, Cecil became the first African-American coroner in the country a few years before I was born. Living through those times, he feels no need to toe anyone else's line now.

Cecil arrives, and we all enter the Dungeon together. Barton gives a slight shiver in response to the cold.

"Which one?" Cecil barks.

"Sara Barton," Scott responds.

Cecil grunts and heads to the bank of small silver doors that contain all of his dead bodies. Finding the one he's looking for, he turns the latch and pulls out the long cold table. A gray bag with a zipper down the middle sits on the slab.

Cecil asks, "Next of kin?"

Scott points his head in Barton's direction. Cecil waves Barton over.

Scott and I arrange ourselves to get a good view of Barton's face. Cecil continues with the ceremony.

"Name?"

"Bernard Barton."

"Relationship with the deceased?"

"She was my wife."

Satisfied with this answer, Cecil begins to unzip the bag. The sound of the zipper's descent down the center of the body magnifies in the absence of any other noise. The zipper stops midway, and Cecil parts the bag at the top. After the coroner steps aside, Barton offers a quick glance before looking elsewhere.

"That's her."

"Sara Barton?"

"Yes."

Cecil nods, zips up the bag, pushes the slab into its hole, and locks up. Scott and I escort Barton from the Dungeon and out of the building. The sunlight shines bright.

Scott says, "Mr. Barton, I know the timing is terrible, but we need to talk. This is a murder investigation. Time is of the essence."

"No."

"Don't you want us to catch your wife's killer?"

Barton heads to his car without another word and drives off.

"Chatty fellow," Scott observes.

"I don't think he likes you."

***

Scott and I ride together to Lara Landrum's house. I update him on the sex tape of Sara Barton and Brice Tanner. He relays how he got Barton to identify the body.

"We need to ID the victim, right? Barton's the obvious choice, and I want another crack at him. Two birds with one stone. But I can't call him, you know, because we have his phone. I know from my guy, though, that he is still shacking up with the mistress. I call over there, the mistress answers, and I ask to speak with Bernard. All I get back is 'umm,' some muffled voices, and 'he's not here.' But I know he is. So, screw it, I'm going over there myself."

Scott's phone rings. He answers and talks for a few minutes. I received his call about the murder a little over twelve hours ago, and now I'm about to meet Lara Landrum. The case is moving fast. Scott hangs up and picks up the thread.

"Where was I? I go over to Haywood's place myself and bring three uniformed guys with me just to throw some intimidation around. Ring the doorbell, and the mistress answers. Again, I ask, 'May I speak with Bernard Barton?' Again, she answers, 'He's not here.' I say, 'Ms. Haywood, I know he's here, and I know he has been here since 4 a.m. this morning.' She looks at me, looks at the uniformed guys behind me, and you can see the panic. 'Can I come in?' She nods yes, and we're in. She goes back to the bedroom. Barton emerges, ready to battle. 'We need you to ID the body,' I announce. That gets him. He was ready to go all lawyerly on me, but he can't refuse that request. I have him. He agrees to come. I offer to drive him to the morgue, but he drives himself. You know the rest."

"We still don't have much. He hasn't really given anything away."

"But he knows we know about his mistress, and he knows we know where he's been keeping himself today. We get inside his head, then he starts making mistakes."

We arrive at the house and see hordes of press and television trucks. Unreal. We had seven murders in the county last week, and no one cared. But Lara Landrum's connection to the case has brought out the wolves.

We park in the street. A uniformed officer guards the driveway and waves us through. We hear the clicks of the cameras behind us, capturing our every step. Scott rings the doorbell, and Lara herself cracks open the door to usher us in. She is all alone—no handlers, publicists, friends, hangers-on. Even under these horrible circumstances, her beauty breaks through. Most famous people look pedestrian in person. Lara Landrum is the real deal.

We offer condolences and ask Lara about her sister. Calmly and determinedly, she explains why she wanted to meet with the police. "Bernard did it. He killed her."

That accusation changes the mood. One of the most famous women in the world just told us that her brother-in-law murdered her sister in cold blood. Unfazed, Scott asks, "Why do you say that?"

"Sara was going to divorce him. He wanted to control her, and she wasn't going to let him do it anymore. She had already made a fool of him by having an affair with that boy. That enraged him. After he found out, he flat-out told her he was going to kill her."

I speak up, "Did you hear him say that?" The potential trial is on my mind. If Barton told his wife he was going to kill her, I face a hearsay problem since Sara can no longer testify about anything Barton said to her. But if Lara heard the comment herself, the statement qualifies as an admission of a party opponent, erasing any hearsay worries.

"No. I didn't hear it. Sara told me."

Scott asks, "What affair are you referring to?"

"Brice Tanner."

Lara proceeds to describe the details of Sara's involvement with Brice. The affair was a revenge ploy to make her husband look like a fool for his serial adultery. Except Brice took matters more seriously, even speaking of marriage and a new start in a different city. Sara dismissed such sentiments as youthful folly.

Scott asks, "Are you aware that your sister and Brice Tanner were filmed having sex together?"

Lara dabs a tear that slowly exits one eye. We let her have her grief. A silent interlude passes before she speaks up, "Yes. Bernard was infuriated when he found out. He texted her and called her a whore. When he got home that night, he hit her. You know about the 911 call, right?"

We don't but keep our ignorance to ourselves. Instead, Scott nods and asks, "Why don't you tell me what you know about the call?"

She responds, "They had a big fight the day he learned about the video. Bernard punched her in the back. She locked the bedroom door and called the police. He banged on the door the whole time, threatened to kill her. The police arrived. Sara decided not to press charges. She didn't show them the bruises on her back. The police left. Sara showed me the bruises the next day. I took a picture."

The crying starts in earnest. I hand her a box of tissues, thinking about that picture. When the tears slow, Scott gently continues with his questioning, "Why did she stay with him?"

"Why does any abused woman stay with her abuser? I don't know. I tried to get her to leave. She said she didn't have the energy. Her life was dark, full of disappointment. She was trapped in her unhappiness and didn't see a way out. I should've been more insistent."

Things linger for a bit until Scott nudges forward again, "Thank you for answering our questions during this difficult time. You are being a tremendous help to the investigation. But I have to ask you another question that may upset you. Did Sara have any other affairs besides Brice?" Given what we know, Scott cannot avoid this topic.

Lara fires back, "What do you take my sister for, Detective Moore?" Based on the video with Brice and Sam's description of Sara, I have a pretty fair guess how Scott would answer.

"I have to ask."

Lara sits in stony anger. I jump in.

"Ms. Landrum, let's assume that Bernard murdered your sister. We go to trial. With his life on the line, he will throw the kitchen sink at anyone and everyone he can. He will attack your sister's character. The gloves will be off. The more we know at the outset, the better we can handle whatever Bernard throws at us. At trial, knowledge is power. Detective Moore is right. We have to ask this question because Bernard's lawyers are going to go around town asking it."

I often use this tactic when questioning friendly witnesses on uncomfortable topics. I reference the defense team, make them out to be the bad guys, and tell the witnesses that the bad guys are going to ask them some terrible questions. I then ask the witnesses the terrible questions. The witnesses still don't like being put on the spot, but they blame the ruthless lawyers on the other side, not me. I count that outcome as a double win. My messy questions get answered, and

I build a sense of solidarity with my witnesses.

Lara accepts my explanation, "I'm sorry I overreacted. The answer is no. My sister didn't have any other affairs."

She doesn't know about Sam. The answer portends caution. Sara did not share everything with her sister. What else is out there about which Lara does not know?

Before we leave, Lara texts each of us the picture of her sister's blackened back after Barton hit her. The photo speaks for itself. Barton didn't hold back. I hate him already.

***

Back in the car, I ask Scott, "What do you think?"

"She's hot."

"You've always had a weakness for blonds and that wasn't what I was talking about."

"I think I want to hear that 911 call."

***

Scott and I meet up again early evening. He has promised his ex-wife that he will not miss his daughter's softball game, and time is short. He first plays a recording of the 911 call. The incident occurred a few months ago. Sara screams into the phone, "My husband is trying to kill me!" I hear loud banging on a door as Barton tries to get into the room. Sara pleads, "He has already hit me. Please hurry." The final sounds on the call tell the story without words—more thunderous banging on the door, yelling, a woman crying. The line goes dead.

The call is chilling but evidentiary gold. I ask why Barton wasn't arrested. The story is familiar. By the time the officer arrived, things had settled down. Both Barton and Sara were calm, and Sara did not want to press charges. No outward signs of physical abuse were present, which makes sense since Sara's bruises were on her back. The officer departed, filled out his incident report, and left Barton and Sara alone to resume their dysfunctional lives.

Scott announces, "Bernard Barton speaks to my policeman's gut."

"The current does seem to be pushing that way."

"One more thing before I go. Here's the traffic cam data from the closest camera to the scene, about a mile away."

Scott hands me a list of the 500-plus cars that crossed that intersection last night between 8:30 and 10:30 p.m. and says, "Third page, in the middle." A Chrysler minivan owned by Sam Wilkins passed through the traffic light at 9:51 p.m.—away from the direction of the Barton residence. No minivan was parked on the street when I arrived at the murder scene. Scott adds, "Sam Wilkins drove a Volkswagen Passat to the victim's house." I nod. The minivan must belong to Sam's wife, Liesa.

Scott says, "I'm late. Has to be the wife, right? It's a busy road, probably nothing. You know her. Want to take the first crack at following up on this?"

"Sure."

***

The phone is ringing off the hook when I walk into my house. Only one person calls me on my home number—my mother. I remember the camera crews on the street outside Lara Landrum's house. Mom always calls when she sees me on television in the vain hope that the publicity will push me into politics.

My father's death accelerated this desire to see my career advance. A long time ago, Daddy was lieutenant governor. He shocked everybody when he passed up a near-certain opportunity to run for the top spot. He once explained himself to me by quoting Shakespeare: "To thine own self be true." Mom was not so philosophical. Having sacrificed for years as a political wife, she felt cheated when her husband walked away a step short of the Governor's Mansion. Now she lives her life vicariously through her two sons. My brother is a preacher, meaning Mom sees me as the one to be the governor that my father never was.

Except that I do not want that position or any other political office. The courtroom is my home. Mom knows my stance and rejects it. At the end of our call, she notes, "You will be really well-known after this case. It could open up a lot of doors." Her words fall flat.

To thine own self be true.

5

Amber.

I cannot sleep. Lying in bed, my wife invades me. She establishes a foothold and refuses to retreat. I try to resist. I analyze the Sara Barton case. I think of Bernard Barton, Lara Landrum, Sam Wilkins, everyone. The effort fails. Amber chases me down like a runaway locomotive. Faced with her determination, I allow myself to look at her.

Love at first sight is a myth. You cannot love someone you do not even know. Claiming otherwise is an act of projection. We see someone and create in that person's smile and face an ideal we wish to exist—a fictional cut-out that places on the living the burden of expectations not of their own making. No matter. I loved Amber the moment our paths crossed as college sophomores. The intensity of that love was both the silliest and most serious thing in the world.

Knowing her transformed me, particularly my relationship with God. I was a believer, of course. Everyone is washed in the blood where I'm from. Yet my faith was cultural, not spiritual. Not so with Amber. She lived out her walk, daily seeking God's will because He was the most important thing in her life. She taught me to turn my fear over to Jesus. My selfishness waned, and I strived to be a man after God's own heart. Amber made it clear that sex before marriage was out of the question. My friends thought her crazy. But I waited, we married, and then I didn't have to wait anymore.

Now I question whether my faith was fraudulent all along. I ask Amber but receive no answer. She is gone.

***

The woman in my life these days is Ella Kemp, an assistant district attorney. Our relationship is unspoken, but the affection we have for one another is a living, breathing thing. The problem is me. Two years have passed since Amber's murder, and I'm still not ready. The life I want—the life I had—is gone from me forever. What's the point of starting over?

But Ella *is* special—smart, attractive, determined, compassionate, fun-loving. We've clicked since the day she joined the homicide team in the D.A.'s office. I taught her the ropes and soon we were trying cases together as trial partners. Romance was never on the table when I was married, yet my affection for Ella felt adulterous in the aftermath of Amber's murder. The lingering guilt infects my relationship with Ella to this day.

There's something else, too. Amber's hold on me remains an anchor to my sanity, an enduring link to my former life. I still want to be the man she wanted me to be—abstinence and all. Starting a relationship with Ella figures to upset that balance, and rejecting that part of Amber's example paralyzes me into inaction. At least for now, being alone is the safest cure.

***

The funeral is a media event. Scott and I arrive early, ignoring the cries from the hornet's nest of reporters amassed just outside the church property. Safely inside the sanctuary, we sit down to watch and observe. In a case like this, where the murderer might be someone close to the deceased, the funeral presents a valuable opportunity to gather information. The exercise may prove useless, but that's the thing about an investigation. You never know which avenue of inquiry will bear the most fruit.

The hostility between Lara and Barton underlies a tense atmosphere. She shoots daggers of pure hatred his way. He avoids all eye contact with her and stands off from the crowd, excreting the sense that being here is a distasteful chore. I fail to detect in him a single hint of grief.

Scott gives me a nudge and directs his head across the aisle. I fix upon the object of his gaze and spy Monica Haywood for the first time in the flesh. I recognize her from the Marsh & McCabe website. Incredulous, I say, "The mistress?"

"Alleged," Scott reminds me.

"Sure."

Monica wastes little time making her way toward Barton. They give each other a quick hug. Barton allows his hand to lightly rest on the top of her thigh with the familiarity of someone who has placed his hand there many times. His dead wife's coffin is only a few feet away.

A furious Lara absorbs the spectacle before charging straight for them. She whispers to Barton with force. Monica's nerve falters, and she averts her eyes from Lara's withering scowl. The scene attracts the attention of everyone in the room.

I notice Jack Millwood out of the corner of my eye. I point him out to Scott, whose surprise matches mine.

He asks, "Why is he here?"

His presence is curious. Millwood is my former boss—a giant in the Atlanta criminal bar. I pegged him as a prosecutor for life, but Bobby's ascension to District Attorney changed the plan. The two never saw eye to eye, and Millwood switched to the world of criminal defense. He asked me to join him. Coming from a father figure whom I greatly admired, the offer was tempting. More autonomy and more money would've followed. Amber urged me to take the job and never look back.

I said no. Bobby offered me Millwood's position as the head of all homicide prosecutions, which helped. But the promotion wasn't the decision point. The work itself bothered me. Nearly all defendants are guilty, and being a criminal defense lawyer means representing a lot of bad people—an uncomfortable truth that I could never get comfortable with. That Millwood made such a smooth transition surprised me. Scott, evincing a cop's contempt for defense lawyers, felt personally betrayed when one of his favorite prosecutors went over to the bad guys. He has barely talked to Millwood since. And now Millwood sits across the way at Sara Barton's funeral.

Scott's next question shows that he and I share the same thought, "Do you think that he is representing Barton?"

The explanation makes the most sense. Millwood and Barton might have some sort of personal association, but interaction between the criminal bar and the civil lawyers who populate Atlanta's biggest law firms tends to be limited. The two worlds occupy separate solar systems. As the service begins, I text Millwood to ask why he is here. I watch him shift, glance at his phone, and look around until our eyes meet. He types a reply, and the incoming text reads: "We'll talk later."

The response does nothing to quell my interest. I answer back and ask if he is representing Barton. The return text reads: "We'll talk later."

Millwood's greatest strength as a trial lawyer is his extraordinary patience. He reveals information only on his own terms. Like a great general, he plans out every detail, saving his strongest move for the precise instant when it will have its maximum impact. Disclosing whether he represents Barton is apparently of the same cloth. He'll tell me when he is ready and not before.

We have never opposed one another in the courtroom—the teacher versus the student. Given the work we do, the confrontation is inevitable. The possibility fills me with nervous excitement. Millwood holds a place second only to my father in teaching me how to be a trial lawyer. With Daddy gone, no one's approval means more to me.

One of Sara's friends—a tennis partner—shares some remembrances of their time together. The lack of a personal connection is obvious, and I lose interest. I scan the crowd. A shaken Brice Tanner—Sara Barton's sex tape co-star—sits near the front. Lara told us that Brice was in love with her sister. I wonder if he knew that Sara was also making time for Sam on the side. It would give Brice a motive. Murder can originate from love as easily as from hate.

I search for Sam and find him in the back of the sanctuary. The eyes are tired, the face withdrawn. He stares ahead as if hypnotized. I follow his line of sight to the object of his focus—Lara Landrum. Whatever spell he is under continues for some time. I have yet to follow up on the traffic cam evidence about Sam's minivan from the night of the murder. I could ask Sam, but his wife Liesa seems the better bet. Sam cannot drive two cars at once, which means that Liesa is the witness holding the information we need. Sam figures to be livid—betrayed even—if I go behind his back to interview his wife. That's unfortunate, but the man lied to police during a murder investigation. I'll go talk to Liesa, and Sam can deal with the fallout.

***

The bishop delivers a perfunctory message about the meaning of death. I get no sense that the bishop actually believes anything that he says. The scene plays out every hour across the world. People perish. We attend their funerals, fake listening to the worn sayings of the tired religious leaders who speak at such events. We go home and push away the gnawing sense of unease about what happens when we die. The next morning we wake up one day closer to the end, always with the foreboding that death's march proceeds unabated.

I used to be afraid of the grave. Not because I lacked faith but because I feared missing out on the lives of my wife and son yet to be lived. My jealousy recoiled at the thought of another man taking my place—touching Amber's body, putting Cale to bed at night, calling him "Son." Those experiences belonged to me and me alone. In these anxious moments, the flip side of the mortality equation never entered my contemplation. I never dreamed that I would be the one having to live without them. But here I am.

My faith teaches that there will be an eternal reunion in Heaven for all who are saved. I will be with Amber and Cale again. Because of that promise, death's hold over me has lost its grip. I'll keep living my life, but I won't fear the end. Sometimes, often late at night, I hear the echo of faint voices inside of me sowing doubt about God, Jesus, and everything in between. But I still believe. I have no choice.

***

The service ends, and the mourners slow-foot their way outside. Reporters emit a distasteful buzz in the distance. Scott and I camp out to the side and maintain our watch. Lara appears next to us and launches into Barton.

"Did you see his whore here?"

The question is rhetorical. No one failed to notice Barton and

Monica together. Tears bubble in her eyes.

"I know she didn't decide to come on her own. He wanted her here. He wanted to prance her around in front of everybody. He is poking his finger in the eye of my sister's memory. It's disgusting."

From afar, Barton eyes the three of us talking. I point out his interest to Lara and Scott. Lara responds, "He's scared." She walks off to stand by herself next to her sister's hearse. Lara's parents are both deceased, and Sara was her only sibling. I look at her now and see someone terribly alone. Maybe I'm projecting my own troubles onto to her, but I don't think so. Lara Landrum is an unhappy woman.

6

The autopsy report sits on my desk when I return to the office. The front page reads:

SUMMARY OF CONCLUSIONS

> Body is presented to the County Morgue in a black body bag. The body is that of an adult Caucasian female, 65 inches tall, weighing 123 lbs., and appearing the stated age of 36 years. Livor mortis is present posteriorly and rigor mortis is present to a slight degree in all joints. The hair is blonde. The eyes are partially open; the irises are blue and the corneas are transparent. The nose, ears and external auditory canals are unremarkable. The mouth is partially open and the teeth are natural. Wisdom teeth are not present. A tiny hypertrophic scar is present on the northwest quadrant of the left breast. Evidence of a gunshot injury is found present in the left upper chest, 12 ½ inches below the top of the head, 2 inches to the right of the left breast nipple. There is no gunshot residue on the chest, no charring of the wound, and no gunshot residue in the depths of the wound track. The overall direction of the wound is front to back and downward with a slight right to left deviation. Estimated time of death is between 9 and 10 p.m.

The information confirms what we know. I flip through the autopsy photos with an eye toward their use at trial. I've seen worse, but they'll do the job of inflaming the jury's passions. I throw the whole report into my briefcase for bedtime reading.

***

Millwood calls later that evening to confirm his representation of Barton. He makes the usual pleasantries, his way of probing around to see how I'm doing these days.

He asks, "Still burning the midnight oil, huh?"

"You're the one who called me."

"Yeah, but I'm getting paid $500 an hour to work late."

"Well, you know how it goes. So many murderers, so little time."

"Ha. My offer still stands. You can come and work with me. I'll make you a full partner and you can start making money for all that work you put in. A change might do you some good, too. Give you a fresh start."

I decline. Any chance I would ever do criminal defense died with Amber. I'm a prosecutor for life. I refuse to defend men who kill.

Millwood responds, "Have it your way. Back to business. On behalf of my client, I'm giving formal notice to you and the police that he is not to be questioned in any way, shape, or form without my being present. Mr. Barton is invoking all of his constitutional rights, including his right to remain silent and his right for counsel to be present during police questioning. In other words, keep Moore away from my client."

"You used to love Scott."

"I still love him. He is just too good at his job."

I refrain from the usual spiel about the benefits of cooperating with the State in an open investigation. Millwood taught me that script verbatim. Barton's dug in and he's gonna stay dug in until we slap an arrest warrant on him.

Instead, I say, "It's always the husband. You once told me that. Barton should confess now, and we can make a deal."

"Ha. Not biting. You know where we stand."

***

The next day I make an unannounced house call to see Liesa Wilkins. Her kids should be at school, and I hope to catch her alone. She opens the door. I haven't seen her since Amber's funeral, and her haggard look suggests the onset of hard times. After a quick hug, she informs me that Sam is not home. When I explain that I came to see her, the fragment of a concerned shadow crosses her face. She invites me in, and I tell her my business.

"I'm sorry to disturb you. An issue has come up, and because we are friends, I wanted to talk to you about something off the record."

True enough. Liesa and I are old friends. She started law school the year after Sam and me, met Sam during orientation, and married him two years later. Through Sam, she became one of us. Our law school circle bonded over softball leagues, football games, poker nights, Barrister's Balls, a weekend in Vegas, a trip to Wrigley Field. In the process we transformed from a group of strangers into our own insular, tight community. Seeing Liesa now, my half-agreement to shield Sam's indiscretions from her seems misplaced. Maybe I put my loyalty on the wrong horse.

I explain, "It's about the Sara Barton case."

I let the words breathe to assess any reaction. Nothing. The hint of concern is gone. Unlike Sam, Liesa's poker face doesn't betray her in the moment of truth. But the lack of a reaction is itself a tell. Something is amiss. I switch gears. Playing coy won't work with Liesa.

"I'll cut to the chase. We know Sam found Sara Barton's body at the murder scene around 10 p.m. and that he drove his Volkswagen to the Barton house. The police also did a traffic cam search of all the cars in the area at the time. Your Chrysler minivan went through a nearby traffic light at 9:51 p.m. Since Sam found the body, we have to check this out and tie it up as a loose end. Because you're a friend, I volunteered to ask you directly. Were you driving the minivan that night in the Virginia Highlands area?"

She ushers me to a seat—the veneer of hospitality giving her more time to think. She then answers my question with a question, "You said that this meeting was off the record. What does that mean exactly?"

Here's the thing about Liesa. She's really smart. She seizes on the squishiness of approaching her this way. I'm not a journalist, and talking with her "off the record" has no legal significance whatsoever. Her quick insight is no surprise. A running joke among our friends centered on the clear intellectual gap between Sam and his wife-to-be. We pegged Liesa for greatness as a lawyer until she quit the law to be a stay-at-home mom. Sam begged her to reconsider, but Liesa walked away. But I still recognize the score. She is smarter than me, and we both know it.

"To tell you the truth, I don't know. Look, we've been friends a long time now. I don't want police officers to have to come interview you in your home if it is not necessary. I'm here as a courtesy."

"I'm still confused. Are you here as a friend or a prosecutor?"

Being a lawyer is part performance art. Words are my stock in trade, but words alone only tell half of the story that I am trying to sell. Body language tells the other half. I droop my shoulders and make myself smaller to convey the message that I am not a threat.

"Liesa, you're overthinking this. Sam discovered the body. Your car was in the area. We need to ask you why. That's all. It's a box that needs to be checked off. There's nothing more to it than that. If we thought it was a big deal, someone other than me would be doing the asking."

Once more, she follows up with a question, "Where exactly was the car?"

I name the intersection, which is about a mile away from the Barton residence.

"Which direction was the car going?"

She should be the one answering me. I play along anyway, trying to keep a non-aggressive tone, and tell her the vehicle was coming from the direction of the Barton home toward her house.

Liesa stays neutral but is not as clever as she imagines. I could have been out of here in five minutes. Now, I'm latched on to her scent. A mystery connected to my murder exists here. Her next words only add to my growing unease.

"Do you think Sam killed her?"

I contemplate her with genuine puzzlement. Murder is my life. I bear its weight each day, wrestling with the cynicism that flows from constant exposure to violent death. The toll grows. I make more mistakes than I used to—sometimes read the wrong angles. To compensate, I work harder and sleep less. Trial victories keep piling up, but the infection spreads in steady drips.

Sitting in the living room of my law school friends, the rising concern that I have misread the murder of Sara Barton triggers the wrong response. I get mad. Angry at myself, angry at Liesa, angry at the world—I don't know. Whatever the origin, composure gives way to irritation.

"Why on earth would he do that, Liesa? Was he having an affair with her?"

The words are regrettable, but the outburst manages to finally pry some information out of Liesa's iron grasp. Her reaction says it all—hurt, not surprise. She already knows. Did Sam lie about that, too? Bastard.

Liesa's eyes water. She fights with her whole being the urge to cry. She hisses at me through clenched teeth, "Why are you really here?"

Weary of the entire scene, I quietly answer, "The car. I'm here because of the car."

"I don't have anything to say."

That position won't get her far. Now the police—probably Scott—will be back to ask the who, what, when, where, and why of this second car business. I make one last attempt to reach her: "The police are going to have to come and talk to you now."

"I don't have anything to say to them or to you."

Driving away, I reflect that while she told me nothing, I educated her plenty. She now knows the police can pin her exact whereabouts at 9:51 p.m. on the night of the murder. That's valuable information. I kick myself. Liesa played me the same way I played Sam on the night of the murder. Acting like a friend instead of a lawyer led me to do most of the talking.

But while Liesa admitted nothing usable as evidence in court, her behavior exposed her all the same. Defensiveness of the sort she exhibited means she's hiding something. Her certain knowledge of

Sam's affair is important. Whatever she hoped to accomplish, Liesa just placed a huge target on her back.

The whole encounter upsets everything I thought I knew about the case. I wonder if Barton is really my man after all.

***

Later that night, uninterested in working and too afraid to attempt sleep, I channel surf. Television stories on the murder have dwindled. With nothing fresh to report, the crime shows divert their attention elsewhere. I keep flipping, longing for a distraction. I breeze past the Celebrity News Channel, only to go back when a passing image of Lara Landrum catches my eye. The broadcaster promises, "More to come after the break." I put down the remote.

The report begins: "Breaking news out of Hollywood tonight. Lara Landrum, still recovering from the shocking murder of her sister Sara Barton, has decommitted from all her future movie projects, citing the need for personal time. Insiders also tell us that Landrum has become withdrawn in the wake of her sister's murder, and friends worry about her present emotional state. Landrum intends to stay in Atlanta for the immediate future to be closer to her sister's memory. The murder of Sara Barton remains unsolved."

The rest of the segment features the suntanned host interviewing gossip reporters for their reaction to the news. The reporters pretend to possess special knowledge about the situation, but the generalities they peddle betray their ignorance. The whole exercise is vapid. I switch off the TV and head to bed.

An hour or so later, my cell phone rings. The clock shows 2:26 a.m. I don't recognize the number. I prep for bad news.

I answer, "Hello?"

"Chance Meridian?"

"Yes?"

"I shouldn't have called. It's Lara Landrum. You gave me your number the day you and Detective Moore visited my house. Did I wake you?"

I bolt upright—the President calling from the Oval Office would've been less surprising.

"I'm awake. What's wrong?"

"That's the thing. Nothing is wrong. I just wanted someone to talk to. I keep thinking of Sara. She is my twin. Now she is gone. I feel so alone. I thought you might understand what I'm going through."

Of course. A simple Google search would reveal the painful particulars of my past. Dead wife. Dead son. The killer still on the loose. Unsolved murders haunt the families left behind in murder's wake, and I'm the poster child.

I respond, "I'm not sure that I make the best grief counselor."

"I just want to talk."

"Are you hungry?"

***

We meet forty-five minutes later at Waffle House. In the dead of night, we have the place almost to ourselves. I'm a regular.

We order and make small talk. Country music plays in the background—the modern variety, not the good stuff. When the food arrives, the conversation turns to death. Lara again apologizes, "I shouldn't have called."

"No, it's okay."

"I need to know. Does it get better?"

"That's what they say."

"You don't sound convinced."

I shrug my shoulders, unsure what I can add. Two years have passed, and I still suppress most memories of Amber and Cale just to ward off the darkness from taking over. My coping mechanism for grief is to run from it.

Lara presses forward, "The murder does not feel real. I expect to see her any day now. The phone rings, and I expect it to be her. It never should've come to this. I remember her wedding day. She was so happy and beautiful."

"Still think Barton did it?"

"Definitely. Who else?"

* * *

We stand outside—two hurting people marking time with each other. As we walk to her car, Lara asks one final thing, "Will you bring my sister's killer to justice?"

Thoughts of Mr. Smith—the unknown murderer of Amber and Cale—hover in the back of my mind. But families of victims often ask this question. The standard response I give promises diligence but never results. The future is always obscure. This time—whether because of the lateness of the hour, emotional weakness, or the person doing the asking—I avoid lawyerly platitudes. I say just one word.

"Yes."

She kisses my cheek and drives away. I lurk in the parking lot for a spell and breathe in the night air.

7

The next morning Sam barges unannounced through the door of my office, startling me from my work.

He demands, "What do you think you're doing?"

A saying among trial lawyers goes like this: if the facts are on your side, argue the facts; if the law is on your side, argue the law; if neither the facts nor the law is on your side, bang the table. Sam is banging the table.

"Sam, a lot of deputies around here with loaded guns get skittish when they hear loud disturbances in these offices. You might want to lower your voice a little."

"Don't patronize me."

"Close the door and sit down." He smarts for a bit but does as he is told.

"What's the problem?" I ask.

Sam leans forward, and in an elevated whisper, airs his grievance, "You went to my house and talked to Liesa behind my back. You surprised her and scared her and threatened her. You told her about me and Sara after you promised you wouldn't. Liesa won't talk to me now and is threatening to get a divorce and to report me to the state bar. I could lose everything. You should have come to me first before talking to her. You owe me that. I could've given you whatever information you need. You didn't have to be such a prick, Chance."

"Is that it?"

"That's enough."

I ask myself how I want the rest of this meeting to go. Sam and Liesa are now both persons of interest in a murder investigation, and I have to approach things in that frame of mind. The open question is whether I proceed with an attitude of cooperation or confrontation. I choose the latter. The velvet glove has yet to work with the Wilkins family.

"Sam, let's get one thing straight. I don't need permission from you to do my job. Got that?"

He chews on that a bit before acknowledging the truth of my statement. His eyes avoid mine and look past me out my window, a telltale sign of weakness. I script out my next words. Time to bring the hammer.

"Let's talk about how things stand. First, Sara Barton was murdered. Second, you found the body, putting you at the scene of the crime around the time of the murder. Third, you were having sex with the murder victim whose body you found. Fourth, you lied about having sex with the murder victim. Fifth, if your sexual relationship with the murder victim were revealed, your marriage and career would be ruined. Sixth, no thanks to you, I learned that your wife is also in the vicinity of the Barton home at the time the murder is committed. I think you probably knew that, and you didn't tell me, which is a lie by omission, another strike against you, which is the seventh or eighth point or whatever number I am on now. Next, I go as a friend to talk to Liesa, hoping to put the issue of her whereabouts quietly to bed. But no. Liesa refuses to answer even the simplest of questions and acts guilty as hell about something. Finally, you insist that Liesa didn't know about your affair with Sara Barton before I talked to her, but she did already know. Why are you lying to me about that?"

I don't ask this last question in a way that expects a response, but I pause a moment on the off chance he volunteers an answer. He remains quiet. I continue.

"I look at this entire litany, and I start thinking. Did Sam kill Sara? Did Liesa? Because from where I sit, you two have a lot of explaining to do. That's the lay of the land, and you barging in here to play tough guy is not going to change any of that."

I allow him time to digest my words. His discomfort is obvious, the bravado all gone. He will either talk or clam up. I want him to talk. I give him another push.

"Well, what do you have to say for yourself?"

"We're friends," he offers meekly.

"Come on! This is a murder investigation, and I can't give you any more benefit of the doubt. Stop relying on our friendship to save you and start acting smart. If you and Liesa are innocent, you need to explain yourselves before your stupidity backs you into a murder indictment. If you're guilty, don't say another word and go hire the best lawyer you can afford once you leave this office. You're going to need one. The choice is yours."

To my surprise, he stands up and heads for the door. I try a final tactic.

"Do you know what Liesa asked me?"

"What?"

"She asked me if you killed Sara Barton. Why would she do that?"

Sam looks genuinely perplexed.

"I didn't kill her."

"Did Liesa?"

He leaves without answering. I pick up the phone to call Scott.

***

Scott obtains a search warrant from a judge shortly after getting off the phone with me. Less than three hours after Sam leaves my office, Scott and his team scour the Wilkins home. Another group of detectives picks apart Sam's office. Scott's methods are thorough, and the searches figure to take a few hours. Wrapping my head around the possibility that Sam or Liesa might be a murderer disorients the rest of my day. I remember the law school years of our youth. We were young, full of energy, ready to take on the world. From where I now sit, the world won.

***

Late afternoon, I hear back from Scott. He says, "We might have the gun in the Barton case."

"You found the gun at Sam's house?"

"No."

Scott tells me the full story. Two days after the murder, a neighbor found a gun in a playground down the street from the Barton residence. The neighbor called the police to collect the weapon, but the officer who answered the call failed to see the potential connection between the gun and our crime. The gun was slated to go to storage when the sergeant processing the weapon put two and two together. Scott received the message about the gun while searching Sam's house.

"Gun trace?"

"We ran the serial numbers and came up with nothing."

"Prints?"

"Don't know. They're testing now. Ballistics after that. Maybe the murderer will fall into our lap."

Here's hoping. We have the prints of Barton, Sam, Brice, and Liesa all in the fingerprint database. All attorneys must get fingerprinted before obtaining a license to practice law. If any of their prints show on the gun, we'll know it.

"How did the search go?"

"Nothing. We dusted some prints and will run them, but I wouldn't hold my breath. The wife is a piece of work, a real Ice Queen. Read every word of the search warrant. Grabbed her purse and tried to get into her car to leave. I told her she couldn't touch the car until we searched it. She asked how was she supposed to get around. I told her she could walk anywhere her legs could take her, but that I would drive her to the station if she had something to say."

"How did that go over?"

"She started walking down the street without another word—proud as a peacock. But the search was a bust. I talked to my guys who searched Sam's office. Same story. Nothing. Sam sulked in a corner and looked like he was going to cry. I know who wears the pants in that family. I'm surprised he had the nerve to fool around on her."

"I'm sure Liesa shares your surprise."

"We didn't find any files related to the Barton divorce, which seems strange. They have to be somewhere."

"You're not supposed to read those anyway. Attorney-client privilege. It's kind of a thing."

"Don't tell me stuff like that. I like to have deniability on whether I know something's allowed or not."

We talk some more about the potential murder weapon. A playground is a strange place to dump a gun. The woods or a sewer would be better for making a gun disappear. A fleeing murderer would also want to remove the weapon farther away from the house—unless the murderer didn't flee the scene.

I think again of my friend Sam.

***

Despite the fast-moving events of the day, Lara Landrum's innocent kiss on the cheek consumes more than its fair share of my mental energy. That the touch of those lips to my face would get me thinking untoward thoughts about her doesn't surprise. I'm not dead yet, and Lara is a beautiful woman. I instruct my mind to change the channel. The impossibility of the situation means meeting her again off the clock is a non-starter. Prosecutors and witnesses don't mix.

***

My cell sounds later that night while I'm still in the office. I smile at the caller ID and wonder about the mood on the other end.

I answer, "Hello?"

"It's Sam."

"Long day?"

"Shut up. You proved your point. You're a big man with a lot of power. I get it. I still don't want you talking to Liesa. I'm her lawyer, and you and the police are forbidden from talking to her outside of my presence. But that's not why I called. I have something for you. Can we meet?"

Sigh. The thought of meeting with him again makes my head hurt. Needless drama bores me, and Sam seems intent on shoveling it out in spades.

"What do you have for me? I don't have time chasing some fool's errand."

"It's worth it. I promise. The Varsity in 30 minutes? We can grab a bite to eat."

Sam's promises don't hold much weight with me at the moment, but the mention of The Varsity reminds me that I'm hungry. His suggestion of such a public place also lessens the possibility that he has completely snapped and intends to harm me.

I nevertheless ask, "You're not going to shoot me, are you?"

He laughs.

"Man, I've never fired a gun in my life."

"Good. I'll see you there."

8

"Why are we here, Sam?"

The Varsity stays busy, and tonight reflects that norm. Sam and I sit in the back room with all the windows, affording us front-row seats of the cars charging along the interstate. The room is the only one in the restaurant without a television blaring sports. The mood here is quieter, more private. Sam pulls out a thick file from his briefcase and slaps it down on the table.

I ask, "What's this?"

"My investigative file on Bernard Barton."

The file is thick. Sam now has my full attention, and the interest on my face pleases him. Transparent as ever, Sam's eagerness to now cooperate shows that he is up to something. I remain cautious.

He says, "I knew you would be interested. You think it's the husband, huh? I do, too. I want you to have the file. Use it in whatever way you wish."

We take the measure of each other across a cafeteria-style booth. Three chili dogs sit on Sam's plate, a large Coke to the side. My greasy bacon cheeseburger and cup of water look healthy by comparison. Sam takes a big bite.

I don't reach for the file quite yet. Evidence is my stock in trade, but this isn't going to be some quid pro quo. Sam can turn over the file if he wants, but I'm not buying if he's looking to sell.

"You can give this to me, and I'll gladly take it, no strings attached. But you are still on the suspect list. Liesa is still on the suspect list. If either of you killed Sara Barton, I'll nail you. That's a promise."

"I've known you long enough to know all of that."

"Good."

With the terms understood, I move the file away from Sam to my side of the table. Consuming the file will take hours of work, and the thought fills me with a manic joy. I ask, "Why don't you give me a preview of what I can expect to find in here?"

While chewing, Sam taps the file with his index finger as he washes the food down with the Coke. Fresh mustard snails its way down his tie. He gives me the low down.

"Well, in lucrative divorces I always like to get a private detective working on the case. You never know what will shake out. Some of the stuff I've discovered over the years, you wouldn't believe. My go-to man is good. Ex-cop. You'd like him. Seems like our Bernard likes to gamble, except he's not very good at it. Goes to Vegas every few weeks, always taking his mistress, Monica Haywood. Well, the losses keep adding up, $763k at last count. Now Bernard makes good money, about $1 million a year, but he doesn't take home near that much because of Uncle Sam, so he's struggling. There's something else. The Bartons had life insurance policies on each other. Bernard stands to collect $5 million now that Sara is dead."

My reaction borders on disbelief. The treasure trove Sam has laid upon my lap sounds too good to be true.

"How do I know everything in here is on the up-and-up? Maybe you're just feeding me a bunch of bull to cast suspicion elsewhere."

"I'm not playing you. It's all documented. Subpoena the casinos. Check flight records. There's a paper trail."

I believe him. Part of this meeting is no doubt a hustle. Sam wants to direct my focus to what's behind door number one and away from doors two and three. I'm not blind to the ulterior motives working in his brain. But the information figures to stand on its own two feet. I have another question.

"The search of your home and office didn't turn up any files on the Barton divorce. Where were you hiding this?"

"A safe place."

His proud smile tells me that this non-answer is as far as I'm going to get. This version of Sam presents better than whiny Sam, slippery Sam, or angry Sam. By acting like a lawyer again, he is at least playing the right game. But I'm curious about the reasons behind the change.

"You seemed to have regained your wits about you. What changed since this morning?"

"I talked to Yarber."

That Sam would reach out to Jeff Yarber, Barton's partner at Marsh & McCabe, makes sense. Yarber is a friend to both of us and has been doling out levelheaded advice since grade school. I wish Sam had sought his counsel sooner.

Sam continues, "I needed a disinterested opinion. You know sometimes you get so close to something that you can't see the forest for the trees? That was me. After our argument and the police search, I was on tilt. Liesa was livid. I was livid. It was dark, man. Then Yarber's face just popped into my mind. Out of the blue. And I'm like, 'I need to call him.' And I did."

"And what did Yarber tell you?"

"He said, 'Sam, you've known the guy a long time. He's not going to back down. He isn't some opposing counsel in a two-bit divorce case who you can bluff with a bunch of huffing and puffing. He prosecutes murderers and sends really bad people to death row. Don't fight him.'"

"Good advice."

"Yeah, well, you're still a jerk."

Sam can blame me until the day he dies. He's the one who lied to the police, he's the one who slept with a client, he's the one who cheated on his wife. His wounds are self-inflicted.

We stand to leave. Our business transacted, lack of interest in small talk is mutual. We loiter together outside on the sidewalk, estranged friends who just negotiated an uneasy truce. The lights from inside give me a good view of his face. Good old Sam. His inability to lie convincingly—whether about Becky Johnson or in poker—seizes on me.

"Did you kill her, Sam?"

He winces in mental pain, a helpless expression of disbelief that I keep pushing. Yarber told him I would. I told him the same. I won't back down. I see Sara Barton's lifeless body on her kitchen floor. I see Amber and Cale, too. Hurt feelings are unfortunate, but my first loyalties are to the dead.

Sam pauses before replying, but the hesitation means nothing. His words are irrelevant—the face is the thing. I see the answer before he says a word.

"Man, no."

He's telling the truth. He just is. We stare at each other, unsure of what to make of the person in front of us. Law school seems so long ago. I ask the next question.

"Did Liesa?"

He shakes his head slowly and slumps away toward his car. I stand there, watching him until he drives off. I look up at the obscured stars, their brightness failing to bring clarity to a city masked by its own artificial light. Sam is a bad liar because his eyes betray him at that critical moment of deceit. Now is no different. He thinks Liesa may have killed Sara Barton.

Confused, dumbfounded, sad—I take Sam's file home with me and halfheartedly work through it during the night, thinking of Liesa the whole time.

***

The doorbell shakes me out of my lethargic review of the Barton file. I peer through the window shade and spy Scott's car in the driveway. It's 2 a.m. We do this dance all the time.

He says, "I had the lab guys working overtime. No prints on the gun."

"Wiped?"

"Looks that way."

"Maybe it wasn't the murder weapon."

"I think it is. There were fingerprints on the remaining bullets in the gun."

Ah yes, the bullets in the gun. Even smart criminals forget about the bullets in the gun. The shell casing itself—the remainder of the cartridge that ripped through Sara Barton's chest—does us no good as fingerprint evidence. The heat generated from the firing of a gun obliterates any prints that exist on the bullet prior to discharge. The unfired bullets, though, that's something else entirely. Prints on those can be pristine.

"And do we know who those fingerprints belong to?"

"Yep."

"Who?"

Revelatory moments like now normally make me happy to be a trial lawyer. The process of putting together a murder puzzle ignites the logical side of my brain. Transforming that two-dimensional puzzle into a three-dimensional story taps the creative half. But tonight I face the real prospect of prosecuting a friend. The truth scares me.

Scott continues to hold his cards close to the vest, hoping to extract a little more urgency from me. My atypical lack of enthusiasm throws him off a bit.

He asks, "What's your guess?"

"Liesa?"

"Liesa Wilkins? No. Why her?"

"Then who?"

"Bernard Barton, attorney-at-law."

Relief floods my body. I actually smile. I can prosecute Barton with full vigor. Liesa not so much. I need an enemy, and Barton fits the bill.

"Did you arrest him?"

"I think you would've heard about that. I want to talk to you about it first."

We talk and both agree that the gun has to be the murder weapon. Has to. The timetable on getting confirmation from ballistics is five days. Monica Haywood and Brice Tanner are scheduled to be interrogated by Scott at police headquarters in the interim. An arrest could disrupt those plans, especially the interview of Monica. We need to pin her down while she remains willing to cooperate. Waiting to arrest is the choice.

I bring him up to speed about my night with Sam and my suspicion of Liesa.

He mocks, "His eyes? You saw it in his eyes? Because you played poker with him fifteen years ago? You're killing me here."

"You don't understand. A lot of history exists between us. I can read him."

"You're right. I don't understand. But I do understand fingerprint evidence. Barton is our guy. He loaded that gun. His gun."

Maybe I am wrong about Liesa, after all.

Sam's file on the desk takes on a new, hurried meaning in light of Barton's fingerprint match. In the excitement of the evening, I never get around to telling Scott about my pre-dawn meeting with Lara Landrum.

***

The next morning, Bobby asks, "Where are we on Sara Barton?"

I dole out the latest.

"Is the husband our guy?"

"Stands to reason."

"Let's arrest him now. We have enough."

"Maybe. But we're better off being patient. Just because it's his gun doesn't mean he fired it, and we still haven't confirmed it is the murder weapon. Too many people watching for us to be wrong. We'll have him in a few days when ballistics comes in."

Bobby's election year nerves are on full display, and every day without an arrest makes him twitchy. But electoral sensitivities can't outrun the case. Impatience makes fools of us all.

Bobby counters, "I still don't like him being out there on the loose. What if he runs? He has the money. The press would kill me for that. Do the police have his passport?"

"If he runs, he makes our case that much stronger. He's not so rich that he could simply disappear, not someone like him."

He snorts his displeasure. To help him sleep better at night, I concede, "Your point about the passport is a good one. I'll talk to Millwood about it." That excuse also allows me a chance to feel out my mentor on the case against his client.

***

I'm on the phone with Millwood in minutes. Without going into the particulars of the case, I convey the official concern that his client might bolt the country to escape the reach of justice and that everyone on my side of the fence would sleep easier if Barton would surrender his passport. Millwood absorbs the news in that contemplative way of his.

He asks, "That bad, huh?"

"That bad."

"What can you tell me about the evidence you think you have against my client?"

"Nothing. Any alibi your client wishes to share with the authorities?"

Millwood grunts and doesn't answer the question. We parlay back and forth a little longer, but our hearts aren't in it. The real battle will be in the courtroom. We're both too experienced to give the game away in a telephone call.

"I'll let you know about the passport," he concludes.

"Make sure he doesn't run."

9

Brice Tanner sits alone in the police interrogation room, wearing an expensive suit and a scared look that mocks the confidence of his clothes. I watch him through the glass. He glances at his watch and steals a quick look toward the two-way mirror facing him, not knowing I'm on the other side. The building runs warm, and small droplets of sweat form around his temple. Scott enters to face his prey, carrying a folder and notepad.

"Mr. Tanner, my name is Detective Scott Moore. Nice to meet you. You know why you're here."

Brice nods, but looks down to avoid eye contact.

"Anything you want to say before we begin?"

"What am I supposed to say?"

"Anything you want."

Scott throws out the bait to see if the fish will bite. Sometimes people want to get things off their chest and will reveal information you wouldn't even have dreamed to ask them about.

Brice responds, "I don't have anything to say. I just want to answer your questions and get out of here."

Scott opens the file with a slow turn of the page and organizes his notepad. He begins, "Let's get the distasteful stuff out of the way first, okay? Did you murder Sara Barton?"

"No!"

"Do you know who did?"

"No!"

"Good."

Scott regularly uses this technique. Grab attention right off the bat by starting with the big ask and try to establish an immediate rapport by presenting the question as an annoying formality. The goal is to buy focus and trust with the same transaction. Brice can walk out of here at any point, and Scott does not want to waste time with questions that do not advance the ball.

"How did you meet Sara Barton?"

"At a firm function, maybe a Christmas party or something like that."

"This is Marsh & McCabe?"

"Yeah."

"When was this?"

"Last year. I had just started at the firm out of law school."

"Why was Mrs. Barton there?"

"She was with her husband. He's a partner in the firm."

"Makes sense. Tell me your story."

Brice does so. He and Sara met on the night of that initial firm function. Bernard Barton ditched his wife once the two of them arrived at the party, spending all his time with Monica Haywood instead. Brice and Sara hit it off, but nothing happened between them at first. The two continued to see each other periodically at other firm events. Some flirting transpired on these occasions, but nothing more. Five months ago, Sara showed up at his apartment door out of the blue. The affair immediately commenced.

When Brice finishes, Scott observes, "You left out the part about the sex tape."

"What is there to say? The whole world knows about it at this point. We were recorded without our knowledge. It was an invasion of privacy as far as I'm concerned."

"You were at the High Museum."

Brice shrugs.

"And this scene at the High Museum was after she showed up at your apartment unannounced?"

"Yes."

"What was Sara's reaction to the video going around?"

"Scared. She warned me that Bernard was steaming mad and I should be careful."

"Did Mr. Barton ever retaliate against you?"

"We never talked about it."

"Why weren't you fired? Sleeping with your boss' wife at a company party would seem to be a sackable offense. It would get me fired."

The mental picture of Scott having sex with the police chief's septuagenarian wife crashes my mind. That would be the world's worst sex tape.

Brice answers, "Bernard's a partner but not really my boss. I don't actually work with him. Other partners don't like him at all. They protected me, I guess. I never heard anything about him trying to get me fired."

"Don't you see him in the halls?"

"Yeah."

"How does that go?"

"It's uncomfortable, I guess, but nothing's ever come of it."

"Except now his wife is dead."

Brice digests Scott's words. They don't go down well. He looks at his watch.

"I have a meeting I need to make. Am I free to go?"

"Who do you need to meet?"

This simple question catches Brice off-guard. He does not even try to answer. He wants out. Good. When witnesses wish their questioning to be over, impatience leads to mistakes. Brice's sweating quickens. He looks like someone who would pay $100 to take off his jacket. But taking the jacket off would signal a longer interview, which Brice wants to avoid. He sweats it out instead.

"I have some more questions to ask."

The authoritative tone creates the impression that Brice is not free to go. Scott carefully avoids those precise words, and no law exists against creating an impression. Brice is not in custody and can leave when he chooses. But Brice does not know his rights—a predictable badge of ignorance for a corporate lawyer from one of Atlanta's mega firms. No one has to talk to the police. Three years of legal education, and Brice knows less about his rights than your common criminal. Scott resumes his questioning.

"Where were you on the night of the murder?"

"At home. Working."

"Where's home?"

"I live in an apartment next to Piedmont Park."

I estimate that Brice lives roughly a mile from the Barton residence. Cutting through the park on foot could cover most of that distance with minimal detection.

"Can anyone vouch for you?"

"No."

"Ever been to the Barton residence?"

A pause. "Yes."

"Ever walk over there from your place?"

Another pause. "Yes."

"How would you describe your feelings for Sara?"

"I loved her."

"Did she love you?"

"Of course."

Doubtful. Sara Barton was over a decade older than Brice, married to another man, and having frequent sexual intercourse with her divorce lawyer. I'm not getting the picture of a woman madly in love with the person on the other side of the glass.

"When was the last time you ever saw Sara Barton alive?"

"The day before she died."

"Where?"

"At her house."

"Did you walk over there?"

"Yes."

"Why?"

"I usually walked in case I needed to make a quick getaway."

He sounds like a criminal and realizes it. Scott uses the moment to write something down on his notepad. He assesses what he wrote, pondering, and then writes more. Probably a grocery list. Brice is scared out of his wits. I'm struck as to how young he looks. The ten or so years that separate us in age seem like a lifetime.

"I really need to go."

"Yeah, your meeting. Just a few more questions."

Scott again consults the deep mysteries of his notepad. The sweat starts to soak through the front of Brice's shirt. His armpits must be flowing rivers by now.

"What did you talk about the last time you saw her?"

"Our future. She was getting a divorce. We were going to be together."

"Did you sleep with her that night?"

"Yes."

Scott makes a disapproving smile. Brice shows shame.

"Was she sleeping around with anyone else?"

The shame evaporates. The wounded animal before me bares his teeth. The rage startles. He does not seem so young now.

Unfazed, Scott continues, "Besides her husband, I mean."

Through clenched teeth, Brice responds, "No. She wasn't like that."

"How do you know?"

"I know. We loved each other."

"Do you know Sam Wilkins?"

The question defeats him. The anger dissipates. Hapless Brice makes a less than triumphant return. Looking at the wall, Brice says, "No."

"That does not sound convincing."

"The answer is no."

I don't believe him, but the questioning is over. Brice studies his watch for the third time, contemplates it, and begins to push his chair away from the table.

"I have to go."

Maybe he knows his rights after all.

10

Scott and I are plumb shocked that Monica Haywood agreed to an interview. Yet there she sits in the same seat that Brice occupied yesterday. Scott enters the room, carrying the familiar notepad and folder.

"Miss Haywood, my name is Detective Scott Moore. We met briefly at your apartment the day after Sara Barton's murder. I was looking for Bernard Barton. You said he wasn't with you, but he was. Remember?"

"Yes."

"Why did you lie to me?"

"Bernard's wife had just been murdered. He was grieving. He wanted privacy."

"Are you going to lie to me today?"

"No."

She shows poise. Her conservative business suit gives her the veneer of seriousness. The composed picture before me is hard to square with her relationship with a low-grade philanderer like Barton.

"Let's get the distasteful stuff out of the way first, okay? Did you murder Sara Barton?"

"No."

"Do you know who did?"

"I have a theory."

"You have a theory? I love theories. Let's hear it."

The guess is her theory does not implicate Barton, but I'm open to being pleasantly surprised.

"Brice Tanner. He was obsessed with her. Something must've happened, then bang bang. She's dead."

Juxtaposed with the composure and sophisticated dress, her nonchalance at the death of another human being cools the warm air. Scott responds, "Brice? You think? I buy him as dopey lover type, but

I don't see him as a murderer. I don't know."

"He was arrested for stalking his girlfriend in college."

The change in the shoulders would be imperceptible to anyone who doesn't know him well, but I discern Scott's tense reaction to this previously unknown information. Scott likes springing surprises in his interrogations. He doesn't like surprises being sprung on him.

"His record doesn't show anything like that."

"It was expunged."

"Then how do you know?"

"He is still required to report the arrest to the state bar examiners in his application to practice law."

She's right, and I have a high level of confidence that she speaks the truth about Brice's stalking arrest. The puzzle of her readiness to talk to Scott clarifies. Monica is here to divert our noses away from her boyfriend to Brice. But the prints on the bullets still point to Barton.

"I'm curious. How do you know what is in Brice's bar application?"

"I prefer not to answer that."

I pull up the members of the Board of Bar Examiners on my phone. One familiar name jumps out—Bernard Barton. Mystery solved. The interrogation goes forward.

"You're Bernard Barton's girlfriend?"

"Yes."

"Two of you going to get married now?"

"I hope so."

She and Barton are a pair. Both share a contempt for the basic expectations of polite society. I remember the spectacle at the funeral, where Barton and Monica paraded their affair mere feet from the coffin of Sara Barton—Lara Landrum's scowl choking on the gratuitous vulgarity.

"Where were you on the night of the murder?"

"I got home from work around six-thirty and stayed there for the rest of the night."

"Can anyone vouch for that?"

"Bernard was with me the whole time."

Bang bang. She just shot herself, and she doesn't even know it. We have the surveillance footage. We know Barton left her apartment at 7:38 p.m. She's lying, and we have direct video evidence proving that lie. I shake my head. Fabricating an alibi is clumsy and stupid. That's the problem with arrogant people. Convinced of their own superiority, they never question their own judgment.

Scott now has the weapons to carve her up into little bits, but I don't want her exposed just yet. I send him a text: "Don't trap her. Wanna talk. Take break." His buzzing phone alerts him to my message. He reads it and sets the phone aside.

Scott continues, "Did he spend the night?"

"You know he didn't. He left for home about two-thirty in the morning."

Barton arrived at his house at 2:43 a.m., his dead wife's body still in the kitchen. Assume he killed her at 9:30 p.m.—that's five missing hours. His cell phone conveniently cannot help us, and no hits show up from either his credit cards or the keycard to his office building. Add it all up, and we have zero. Barton's movements during this critical time constitute a giant black hole.

Scott asks, "What did the two of you do from the time you arrived home until the time Bernard left?"

"What do you think?"

"I have no idea. That's why I asked the question."

"We had sex if that is what you want to know."

"I see. Did it bother you later to realize that you were having sex with a woman's husband at the same time she was being murdered?"

"No. I'm glad I can provide him with an alibi."

"Interesting."

Holding up his phone, Scott says, "I need to step out for a minute and check something in another case. Sit tight. I'll be right back."

He exits before giving Monica any opportunity to object. When he joins me in the observation room, he crows, "We got her dead to rights. I'm going to bust her with the video."

"Don't."

"Are you crazy?"

"Keep your eyes on the prize—Barton. We bust her now, then he knows what we know less than one minute after she leaves here. What's he going to do? Start work on a new alibi, one that we cannot as easily disprove. Instead, let's continue to play stupid and see how far the two of them run with this story. Maybe Barton will start saying that he was with her the whole night, too. I'd much rather catch him in a lie than her. Let's give him the chance to lie to us."

We watch her through the mirror. The composure remains intact—the weight of lying to the police in a murder investigation brushing off her like a feather.

Scott concedes, "I see the logic. How would you handle the rest of the interview?"

"Get her to sign an affidavit verifying under oath everything she has told you today. When the time comes, probably at trial, I'll pop her with it. I can prepare the affidavit right now."

"Hop to it."

Within the next half hour, Monica signs the affidavit, cementing herself as a perjurer. The affidavit safely in his hands, Scott has a few more questions.

"You and Bernard go to Vegas a lot?"

He surprises her. She makes calculations in her head. The police already know the truth, might as well admit it.

"We love Vegas."

"Who doesn't? Bernard has run up a lot of gambling losses, huh?"

Fidgeting. Monica came here prepared and delivered her lines on cue. But this detour is off-script. The mental wheels work furiously to try and land on the answer Barton would want. But he's not here. She's on her own now.

"I wouldn't know about that."

"You never saw him gamble?"

"Some. Look, I've patiently answered your questions, but I need to go."

"Yes, you've been very helpful, and I appreciate your willingness to aid the investigation. I know you're a busy person, and I value your time. Just a few more minutes, I promise."

Scott Moore—the most reasonable man on earth. You want to help, you've helped, and all I'm asking for is just a little more help. Can't you give me that? For someone who wants to appear cooperative, the offer is a hard one to refuse.

"My sources tell me that Bernard owes nearly $750,000 to a bunch of casinos. Have you ever heard him talk about that?"

I love Scott's wording. He has *sources*. That detail will give Barton and Monica something to chew over during dinner. The wide eyes from the witness confess her surprise. Whether the surprise originates from the size of the debt or the thoroughness of the investigation is unclear.

She answers, "No."

"Did you know that Bernard has a $5 million life insurance policy on his wife?"

"News to me."

Maybe she's lying, maybe not. But the safest course for her in these uncertain waters is to play dumb. She's not going to tell us anything else of use today. Scott senses it, too.

"Okay. Again, you've been very helpful, and I thank you for that. If you want to later clarify anything you've said today, please don't hesitate to contact me, day or night. If you learn something about Bernard's possible involvement in his wife's death and want to talk, let me know."

"Bernard was with me at the time of the murder."

"Yeah sure."

They look at each other knowingly for a few seconds before Monica gets up to leave. I'm guessing she regrets signing that affidavit right about now.

11

The arrest warrant for Bernard Barton sits on my desk, armed and ready to be presented to a judge. The only unchecked box is the ballistics report. Scott's contact in the Georgia Bureau of Investigation promised to e-mail the report over directly—results still unknown. The warrant declares that Barton's gun fired the bullet that killed Sara. If the GBI tells us something different, the papers will head to the shredder, and we'll re-examine the case with fresh eyes.

Scott and Ella Kemp wait with me in my office. Every ding of Scott's phone brings expectant looks yearning for news. The shake of Scott's head deflates the balloon each time. A case this big and explosive is virgin ground for all of us. Being on the brink of publicly naming Barton as the murderer feels like our Super Bowl. Quietness pervades the room.

"I hate waiting," Ella fumes. She's cute when she's impatient, and I reflect on how much I care for her. To upend the silence, Ella starts tapping her foot to a steady beat. I rock in my chair to the same rhythm. I hate waiting, too.

The ding we're looking for arrives at last, and Scott reads the report with practiced calm. When the moment is to his liking, he announces, "In the considered expert opinion of the Georgia Bureau of Investigation, the gun belonging to one Bernard Barton fired the projectile that killed the late Sara Barton."

I add everything up in my head one more time—the sex tape between Sara and Brice, the 911 call, Sara Barton's bruised back, Barton's threat to kill her, the fingerprints on the bullets in the murder weapon, the gambling debts, the $5 million in life insurance, the girlfriend and her fabricated alibi. Motive. Means. Opportunity. We got our man.

Scott and Ella rush downstairs to get the warrant signed. Once the arrest is made, official responsibility for Barton transfers from the police to the prosecutors. My part in the drama is about to go live. I head over to deliver the good word to Bobby. The lunch hour is near. If we time the arrest right, Barton's bail hearing will have to wait until tomorrow morning, and he'll be forced to spend the night in jail.

The thought of Lara Landrum leads to a smile. Millwood always taught me to keep the family of the victim at arm's length and that the pursuit of justice should never be personal. Arm's length went out the window with Lara ever since that meeting at the Waffle House. Even though I refuse to meet with her again under similar furtive conditions, thinking about her does no harm. The case is personal, and I want to win it for her.

***

The logistics of arresting Barton now take center stage. When reputable lawyers like Millwood represent the arrestee, we often allow their clients to turn themselves in voluntarily. Not this time. The press attention here makes this situation a different animal. Bobby wants his perp walk. The voters of Fulton County need to see the impartial administration of justice, and the video of affluent white guy Bernard Barton in handcuffs does just that. The footage will also go well with Bobby's inevitable press conference to announce the arrest.

Bobby, Scott, and I gather in Bobby's office in the afternoon to discuss the mechanics. The key ingredients for super-sizing the impact of the perp walk consist of picking the right location for the arrest and leaking to the media the time and place.

Scott says, "My guy trailing Barton says he is at work now."

Bobby asks, "Marsh & McCabe is at Peachtree and 14th Street. That's perfect, right in the middle of Midtown. How much lead time you need to give the media?"

"Forty-five minutes," Scott responds.

"Do it."

Scott leaves. Bobby smiles, opens a closet in his office, and analyzes his different suits with the concentration of a nuclear physicist splitting the atom. The press conference will be in a few hours. Dark colors look better on television, and the available wardrobe choices in the closet reflect that. Brights work better in the courtroom, but Bobby hasn't tried a case in years. His closet reflects that, too.

As I head back to my office, Bobby instructs me, "Don't lose this."

"I haven't lost one for you yet."

***

Scott's face dominates the national news. Footage of him leading Bernard Barton in handcuffs into a waiting police cruiser plays on an endless loop.

He brags, "I'm famous."

"You might be able to get a date now."

"Look who's talking."

The arrest couldn't have gone any better. Caught unaware, Barton looked wild-eyed and surly as the cameras rolled. Better still, the 24-hour news cycle guarantees that the video will keep playing again and again and again.

Scott explains, "Best perp walk of my life. You know I hate lawyers. I enter the office and walk right past the receptionist. She protested, 'You just can't walk back there like that.' I hold up the warrant and say, 'This says I can.' I get to Barton's office. He's on the phone. I take the phone from him and hang it up. 'Bernard Barton, you are under the arrest for the murder of Sara Barton. You have the right to remain silent, so on and so forth.' Put the cuffs on. Walk him through the office. Lawyers, secretaries, paralegals—everyone is watching. Get this, a few of them are even smiling. I've seen a lot, but I ain't ever seen that. It's like they were cheering me on. We get to the sidewalk and begin the march. I parked the car down the block to make the walk longer. And the media is going nuts. Cameras and microphones in our faces. 'Bernard, did you kill your wife?' 'Why did you do it, Bernard?' 'Bernard this, Bernard that.' And he looked terrible, like a crazy man. Everybody in America is going to bed tonight knowing that he is our guy."

"Did he say anything?"

"Nah."

"Millwood called me, disappointed we did not give Barton a chance to turn himself in."

"He would've done the exact same thing we did."

"Yep."

"Traitor."

***

Bobby's press conference announcing the arrest emphasizes that justice is colorblind in Fulton County. Ella and I watch in my office. Bobby's performance shows him at his best—funny, charming, appropriately serious. The camera loves him, and the pundits gush about his record as a hard-hitting, yet fair, prosecutor. He does not say a single substantive word about anything, only platitudes about justice, fairness, mom, and apple pie. But he dazzles.

Ella observes, "You gotta hand it to the guy. He's good."

"He is that."

"Wanna grab some dinner?"

"Not tonight. I'm going home."

Disappointment sags in her face. She's perfect—attractive, smart, fun to be around. Ella could make me happy if I would only give her a chance. But love leads to pain, and I'm still overdrawn from the last withdrawal.

"You know, it can be just dinner," she says.

"It's not that. I'm really tired."

"I thought you never sleep."

"That's why I'm tired."

"Fine. But one of these days I'm not going to take 'no' for an answer."

We walk together to the parking garage and go our separate ways.

***

Being alone and loneliness differ, and the heaviness of the latter affects me more than at any other time I can remember. Once at home, I check my phone for messages that aren't there. The thought of Ella beckons me. Should I call her? I almost answer yes. Maybe tomorrow.

I lounge on the couch and take an inventory of my surroundings.

The house is as it was at the time of the murders. I cleaned the blood off the floor but left everything else the same. I study the painting of Thomas Jefferson above my mantle. Before me is a man of complexity, a person at war with himself and the times in which he lived. My father revered Jefferson and passed his love of history on to the next generation. Because of this upbringing, the past has always spoken to me. But now I scan around at a house frozen in place and feel the danger of too much looking back.

Cancer killed Daddy a year before I lost Amber and Cale—the three most important people to me gone in quick succession. I picture them together in Heaven, joy-filled and laughing just as they were in life. I'm of different cloth. Like my mother, I am sharp-tongued and judge the world with cynical doubt. These days, my worst tendencies consume me. No one is left to soften the hard edges.

I close my eyes.

***

Knocking on the door, followed by a doorbell, startles me awake. I don't know how long I slept. My mind re-focuses, and I stumble to the front entry hall. Only Scott would come over this late. I open the door without checking.

The voice outside says, "Hi."

Still recovering from the effects of waking up mid-dream, I stare at Lara Landrum dumbly, unsure of the situation. I wonder if someone else died.

She says, "I wanted to say thank you."

I stand there mute, fighting the cobwebs. Both body and mind feel heavy and slow-footed.

"May I come in?"

"Yeah."

We stand together awkwardly just inside the door, close to one another. Too close. The proximity breaks me out of my stupor. I'm afraid to retreat and give her more ground. She is the first woman to be alone with me in this house since Amber. The unfamiliar territory scares the hell out of me.

She asks, "Can we sit down?"

"You shouldn't be here."

"Well I'm here."

Lara brushes past me, struts into the living room, and sits down. I follow her from a safe distance, but continue to stand. She wears form-fitting jeans and a purple tank top. I'm pretty sure she is not wearing a bra. The effect on me is no different than it would be on any man. I sit down next to her, but not too close.

She asks, "What happens next with Bernard?"

She wants to talk about the case. This whole setting is wildly inappropriate. I answer anyway.

"He will try for bail tomorrow."

"Will he get out?"

"Maybe. Probably."

"He's a murderer."

"It happens."

She shifts closer and puts her hand on my leg. The old nerves spring up from a place long dormant. She rubs the leg and then teases her way to higher ground. My heart beats quicker and my blood flows faster, but this cannot happen. Emotions impair judgment, and the chemical reactions her touch stirs within me are a pathway to stupidity. I remove her hand.

"You have to leave. You're a witness in the case."

"No one needs to know."

"I'll know."

We look at each other. Her playful eyes pose a dare. The scene is ridiculous. One of the most beautiful women in the world sits on my couch, offering herself to me. I have no idea what's going on.

I ask, "Why?"

"I like you. You're real. You know pain. Real pain. What it's like to really hurt in the depths of your soul. I feel it, too. We're both wounded animals, and we can help each other get well."

"You know nothing about me."

"I know everything. I know you blame yourself for your wife's death. I know you're scared to let yourself be happy again. I know you hold yourself to impossible standards. I know you haven't made love to a woman since your wife died. And I know you want to make love to me right now."

I kiss her.

But then thoughts of Amber, Ella, Jesus, and the Georgia Rules of Professional Conduct descend at once, a tableau of impressions all with the same urgent message: "No!" I pull away.

She removes her top to reveal the most perfect breasts I've ever seen—generously-sized, chiseled out of marble, unblemished.

I kiss her again. Her bare chest rubs against me, and the last flickers of resistance die a flaming death. I lead her to the bedroom. She pushes me down on the bed, Amber's bed. We lose ourselves in each other. I release all thoughts of history, loss, or pain. The moment devours me, and I love it. Afterwards, we hold each other, and she falls asleep in my arms—just like Amber used to do. I feel like a real person again.

The moment passes. My mind registers the significance of what just happened, and anxiety spreads. I go outside, stand on the back porch, and contemplate. The wind feels good on my exposed skin. The quiet produces a comfortable peace. I think about my faith and the role Amber played in making me a godly man. I think of Jesus' promise to give me rest if I would only submit my yoke to Him. I consider the naked woman in my bed and am forced to look God square in the face.

My faith matters to me—even if I'm terrible at it. To the world, sex between consenting adults is no sin. But I am a fundamentalist. God sets the rules. I obey. I believe in the concept of law so much that I dedicate my life to prosecuting man's law here on Earth.

But making love to Lara reminded me of what it feels like to have joy. The hangover of loss is too heavy. I need to love and to be loved. Lara represents a life preserver to a drowning man, and the prospect of rescue thrills me. I want more.

The air turns chilly. I retreat back to my couch and look again at Thomas Jefferson—slaveholder, freedom fighter, misogynist who used a slave girl for sex, fierce advocate for equality who proclaimed to the world "that all men are created equal."

I ponder the contradictions that animate a man's soul. I peer into myself and negotiate a truce with the darkness. The yoke of sin feels light in the aftermath. I marvel again at the naked woman in my bed. God can wait.

I return to her and sleep better than I have in years.

12

Lara lies by my side when I bolt awake at nine the next morning. The lateness of the hour astounds. Barton's bail hearing starts in an hour. My phone gives notice of a text from Ella: "Where are you?"

"On the way," I text back.

I shake Lara to wake her. Time is too short for a shower. I spray on some deodorant, brush my teeth, and comb my hair. A still undressed Lara sneaks up on me, encircles her arms around my body, and says, "Come back to bed."

"Barton's bail hearing begins at ten."

"You should probably go to that."

"Probably."

I dress, choosing my best dark blue shirt to appeal to the cameras. The clock taunts, but I need to talk to Lara before I depart.

I plead, "You cannot be seen here. I cannot emphasize that enough."

"I'm aware of the delicacy of the situation."

"It only takes one photographer to catch us. Barton could walk free if this thing blows up in our faces. Prosecutors cannot sleep with witnesses."

"I've been dodging paparazzi for years. I know how it's done."

"Your nonchalance worries me."

"Get out of here. I'll see you tonight."

The mention of future meetings makes the situation all too real. In morning's light, the fear of discovery slaps me square on the nose. Before I have a chance to worry, she sends me on my way.

***

The players for the initial appearance take the stage. Millwood will argue for bail, Ella will argue against. A black person accused of murdering

Sara Barton would not possess a snowball's chance in Hell of pre-trial release. As a white, well-respected lawyer, Barton has a shot.

The courtrooms in the Fulton County Courthouse do not look like the sprawling courtrooms you see in the movies—those deep caverns of wood, ancient marble, and majestic windows. Those old courthouses were where I watched my father's trials and what made me want to be a lawyer in the first place. They still exist, but only in small towns scattered across the state. Fulton County's courtrooms are small, clean, modern, and devoid of natural light. The pedestrian setting belies the high stakes.

I shake hands with Millwood before having a seat next to Ella. The media fills the courtroom and the cameras film away, allowing the rest of the world to experience the event live. A ragged Barton, unshaven and wearing the ugly orange jumpsuit of prisoners everywhere, comes in with a deputy guiding his arm. On appearance alone, he should stay locked up. A bailiff announces the arrival of Judge Edwin Lee Lynn, today's duty judge. I groan. Barton's chances for bail just increased.

Ella strides up the lectern and argues, "Bernard Barton stands accused of murdering his wife, Sara Barton, in cold blood. As you know, Your Honor, bail is the exception, not the rule, in murder cases. Based on the murder of his wife and previous incidents of domestic violence, Bernard Barton constitutes a danger to the community. He is also a millionaire with the money and motive to attempt an escape, making him a significant flight risk. Both of these reasons caution against allowing Mr. Barton to go free under the present circumstances."

Judge Lynn pivots to the defense table: "Mr. Millwood?"

"Thank you, Your Honor. Bernard Barton is an upstanding member of the Atlanta legal community. He has never been arrested in his life before yesterday, and he vigorously denies the charges brought by the State. Nor has he ever been arrested for any acts of domestic violence, despite Ms. Kemp's innuendo to the contrary. The evidence against my client is highly circumstantial, and Mr. Barton should not have to sit around in a jail cell while the State bumbles around Atlanta trying to create a case. We ask that reasonable bail be set. Mr. Barton is prepared to turn over his passport to the Court right now to allay any concerns about him being a flight risk."

When Millwood travels back to his seat, Judge Lynn scans over some paperwork and jots down a few notations. Millwood and Lynn attended law school together, and Millwood has a habit of getting his way in Lynn's courtroom. While the judge generally does a good job, his penchant for agreeing with his old friend strikes me as something more than a coincidence. Call it a hunch. The bias is bearable today—at trial is a different matter. But the trial judge won't be picked until after we have an indictment, and the odds of getting Lynn again are small.

The judge announces, "Bail is set at $1 million. The defendant shall surrender his passport. We're adjourned."

Not a surprise. As we pack up our belongings, Ella asks, "Are you okay?"

"What?"

"You seem distracted."

"I'm fine."

I can still smell Lara on my skin, and guilt about what I'm doing to Ella gnaws at me. I grimace inwardly but fantasize about being with Lara tonight.

***

Bobby, Ella, and I congregate after the bail hearing. The next big decision is whether to seek the death penalty.

Capital punishment isn't immoral. You kill, and the State may take your life in return. The rub is the criminal justice system. Innocent people wither away on death row for a variety of reasons. Tough-on-crime prosecutors seek convictions at all costs to impress voters. Police officers miss, misinterpret, or manufacture key evidence. Incompetent defense lawyers make a weak case against their clients seem foolproof. Judges demonstrate bias against the accused. Expert witnesses peddle bad science for a hefty fee. And, of course, race and economics infect the system at its operating core. The death penalty disproportionately falls on those who are black and those who are poor.

Because of these factors, I trust the death penalty in my own hands but few others. I know my heart, and shedding innocent blood terrifies me. Two men I've prosecuted have received the needle of lethal injection—Willie Joe Sawyer and Harry Fleming. Sawyer raped and killed a 5-year old girl. Fleming murdered a hapless store clerk in an armed robbery gone bad. As their execution dates approached, I took a day off to get away and assess the evidence against them one last time, just to be sure. I also watched both executions with the families of the victims. Seeing the life seep out of their bodies gave me no pause at all. Both were evil men.

Does Bernard Barton deserve the same fate?

Not every murder is eligible for the punishment of death. Some type of aggravating factor, defined by statute, must be present. Eleven aggravating factors qualify under Georgia law. The only one we could potentially hang our hat on reads: "The murder was committed for pecuniary gain."

Five million dollars in life insurance is a lot of pecuniary gain.

Bobby probes, "What do you think?"

I answer, "A path exists for us to get there, but it complicates the case. We seek death and get the one squirrely juror who opposes capital punishment, then the whole conviction is in doubt because some crusader wants to make a stand. Enough weirdness will surround the trial already because of the media. I'd prefer to keep it simple."

"Ella?"

"The defendant is not a sympathetic figure. We should avoid giving anyone a reason to make him into one. I always have this fear, too, that jurors hold us to a higher standard in death penalty cases. As Chance said, the trial is going to be a circus as is. We don't need any more volatility in the kettle."

Bobby strokes his chin, no doubt looking at all the electoral angles that might flow from each possible choice.

"All right. Let's take the death penalty off the table. Just make sure you get me my conviction."

Willie Joe Sawyer and Harry Fleming were both black. Bernard Barton is white.

13

After spending another night with Lara, I ponder the logistical problem of how to carry on a secret love affair in a city of six million people. Going to her house is impossible. Someone's liable to be staked out there at all hours. My place is safer but hardly ideal. I have neighbors, and Scott drops by unannounced like clockwork. Hotels are out. Lara is too famous, and every hotel I know has surveillance cameras everywhere. Envisioning myself on TMZ as grainy video of Lara and me plays nonstop doesn't sit well. I'll pass.

The solution grabs me with bittersweet fervor—the condo in Midtown where Amber and I first lived after moving to Atlanta. The real estate crash made it unsellable when we bought our house, so we converted it to a rental. The place now sits vacant after a long-term renter moved out last month. Perfect. I notify the property management company to take the rental listing off the market. Lara and I can escape to the condo whenever we like. Secure underground parking would allow us to come and go in relative anonymity. Even if paparazzi follow her as far as the garage, they still couldn't tell who in the building she would be visiting. No one will ever know.

***

Two days later, I wait for Lara in the condo I once called home. The furnishings that I cobbled together yesterday are sparse—a bed, a couch, some chairs, a table—but enough for its intended purpose. The balcony faces east away from the city. Trees cover the landscape, the exact opposite of the concrete jungle to the west. Stone Mountain rests in the distance.

Like a green teenager on his first date, my pulse quickens when I hear the knock on the door. The nerves stay with me as I tiptoe to the entry way and wave her in before anyone lurking in the hall can see us together. The disguise she wears is not bad—baseball cap, large sunglasses, baggy clothes to hide her figure. Only when she removes the hat and the blond hair comes tumbling down does she resemble Lara Landrum again.

She inspects the bare accommodations and taunts, "I love what you've done with the space."

"I'm a minimalist by nature," I respond.

"You realize I'm accustomed to a certain style, right?"

"That's what you get for associating with a commoner."

The smile I receive in return confirms the wisdom that less is more. I suspected as much. She is not with me because of her taste for the finer things. Our shared experience of loss unites us, and high-priced decor speaks little to those stuck in the valley of pain. The bond we have is simple, raw. Authenticity is the only thing I can give her, and that realness is somehow enough.

Lara sheds the dreary clothes and sits on the couch wearing only a bra, panties, and a playful grin. I stand there dumb, mesmerized by the sight. It's Friday afternoon. All across Atlanta cars battle bumper to bumper to flee the harsh world of the city. But all is tranquil in the condo. Lara teases with dancing eyes and asks, "What are you thinking?"

"I can't believe you're here."

The little remaining natural light left in the eastern sky maneuvers through the gaps in the blinds and produces a black and white effect throughout the room. The blood red of her matching undergarments pops against this shadowy background. I'm afraid to move because the scene is too perfect—the peaceful unreality of a fragile snow globe.

"You can come over and kiss me, you know."

The words snap me out of my daydream. I float over and kiss her, softly at first, testing the reality of the experience.

She says, "For a minimalist, you seem to be wearing a lot of clothes."

I get the hint and follow her lead to the bedroom, becoming more minimalist with each step. Police sirens wail in the distance, and I think about the hold such sounds have had on so much of my life. Like an expert witness who understands the nuances of obscure topics inside and out, I know that the volume level of police response can inform the careful listener. When the noise reaches a certain crescendo, murder again stirs in the Atlanta air. But today I resist its pull on me. Lying next to Lara, the dirges of the outside world whimper out of my consciousness. The focus now centers on life, not death. When she falls asleep later that evening, I stroll out on my balcony and peer deep into the night, marveling at how I landed in this position. The city is quiet, and I welcome the change.

***

One week later, we seek an indictment for murder against Bernard Barton from the Fulton County grand jury. The proceedings are decidedly one-sided. To proceed to trial requires merely a majority vote of the grand jurors. Probable cause, as opposed to beyond a reasonable doubt, is the governing standard of the day. It's a low bar. The rules forbid lawyers for the defense from even appearing, so the prosecutors are the only game in town.

Ella and I start with the 911 recording. The horrified faces of the grand jurors confirm what I already know. The emotional impact of the call packs a powerful punch. The room sits in tense silence as the voice of Sara Barton screams out for justice from beyond the grave.

"My husband is going to kill me!"

"He has already hit me. Please hurry."

The line goes dead, and we let the silence linger before passing around the photo Lara took of her sister's back. Multiple black bruises scar the landscape of the otherwise beautiful white skin. The picture makes the words on the 911 call even more terrifying.

The rest of the morning until mid-afternoon features Scott's testimony about the other evidence in the case. The process is methodical. The crime scene and autopsy photos establish that Sara Barton died from a gunshot wound. The fingerprint and ballistics evidence show that the defendant loaded the bullets into the murder weapon. The gambling debts and Monica Haywood's fabricated alibi demonstrate Barton's desperation before and after the murder.

We also show the sex tape of Sara Barton and Brice Tanner at the High Museum to gauge how that evidence plays in real life. The footage strikes me as a double-edged sword. While the video provides Barton a strong motive for murder, the visuals of the victim atop a younger man on the floor of a museum could lessen a jury's sympathy for her.

One incredulous grand juror asks Scott, "Her husband was there at the party while this was going on?"

"Yes."

"Was this before or after the 911 call?"

"A few days before."

The grand juror whistles, and the others nod in recognition of the almost certain cause and effect. I take note. The video is so bad that it is good—the greater Sara's open and notorious adultery, the greater the rage felt by her husband toward her.

When our presentation is complete, the grand jurors waste little time. The vote is unanimous. Bernard Barton now stands indicted for the murder of his wife.

But first things first.

14

Corey Miller leads a southwest Atlanta gang called the Rattlesnakes. Last year, he executed DeShawn Carter in broad daylight on a pothole-riddled street in Pittsville—the city's most menacing neighborhood. Witnesses to the killing numbered at least two dozen. DeShawn Carter had testified against a Rattlesnake in a small-time drug case and sent Miller's fellow gang member to prison. Miller sent Carter to the morgue in return.

The witnesses to the crime kept their mouths shut. Except one. From behind a curtained window in her house, Tasha Favors, a 10-year old girl, observed the execution in all its awfulness. The police didn't find her. She came to them. Tired of the violence destroying her community, Belinda Favors brought her daughter to the police to report what happened.

The first time I met Tasha remains engraved in my mind. She told her story to Scott, Ella, and me:

"I was doing my math homework at the kitchen table. My Nana was taking a nap in her bedroom. I heard a bunch of noise from the street. I know not to go outside by myself so I just looked out the window. Mr. Corey had a gun in his hand and was yelling at a man on his knees. I was scared and hid behind the curtain, but I could still see. There was a bunch of people standing around, just watching. Then Mr. Corey walked up and shot that man in the head. I didn't see nothing else. I ran to my room and got under my covers and cried."

One grand jury indictment later, I now ready myself to put Corey Miller on trial for murder. But I have a problem.

In America, a criminal defendant has the constitutional right to face his accuser in court. To convict Corey Miller, I must put Tasha on the stand. Miller has already killed one witness and would no doubt murder another one to save his own skin. To guard against such threats, some states allow witnesses to testify anonymously behind a screen or even in disguise when their lives are in danger. Not Georgia. Here, I must name my potential witnesses ten days before trial, and they must testify out in the open. Protecting Tasha under these rules requires hiding her in plain sight.

I make the mandated disclosure to the defense team and report 219 names as potential witnesses—the most I've ever listed. Ninety percent of these names are decoys. I name every adult and child who lives in the vicinity of the murder, every member of Miller's gang, every criminal informant from the area. I disclose Tasha and Belinda Favors as required, but breezing over their names in a list of 219 people is easy. Or so I hope.

***

The pre-trial conference takes place a few days before the scheduled trial date. Outside the judge's chambers, I shake hands with Miller's counsel, Joe Parks. I like Joe. He falls into that great sea of mediocre trial lawyers. No shame exists in being average, and Joe seems content with being who he is and nothing more. We go in to meet the judge.

Judge MacDonald Ross sits before us behind a massive desk, a bored expression dominating his ruddy face. A court reporter sits to the side, her machine ready. Ross wears his robe in chambers, one of the few judges to do so. The conceit is telling. Just like lawyers, judges come in all shapes of good, bad, and mediocre. Ross is a bad judge. He's just not that smart, and I question how he ever passed the bar exam. But he's reliably pro-prosecution, so I live with his shortcomings without much fuss.

The first issue Joe raises is the size of my witness list. Ross' face jumps from boredom to horror when he hears the 219 number. I doubt he can even count that high, much less competently handle a case with that many people testifying. He looks to me for an explanation, plainly hoping I will make the problem go away. I reassure him.

"Obviously, Your Honor, we're not going to call 219 witnesses. But this case is complicated with a lot of moving parts, involving a gang that calls itself the Rattlesnakes. Defendant Corey Miller is the gang's leader, and he murdered a police informant in front of a large crowd of people to teach the neighborhood about what happens when they cross the Rattlesnakes."

I pause here to build drama for the next point—my ace in the hole that I doubt even Joe knows about.

"People are scared out of their minds down there, Judge. And they have reason to be. One of the people on the witness list, Tavon Munson, was shot and killed on Sunday. I turned the list over to Mr. Parks on Friday."

The judge turns his head to look at poor Joe, who based on his reaction had no idea about Munson's murder.

Joe responds, "Well, I didn't kill him."

Ross pivots to me for help.

I ask Joe, "Did you show your client the list?"

"Maybe."

The response earns a dubious look from Ross. I press forward with my argument.

"And since Miller has already shown a violent disregard for the workings of the criminal justice system, I would ask for extra security in the courtroom and around the jury." I hesitate before adding, "And courtroom staff." I throw my best somber face at Ross and hope he catches my meaning that Miller might very well kill him, too. He answers me with an acknowledging nod. He's not that dumb.

Joe chimes in, "He can still narrow his list down some out of fairness to the defendant."

I counter, "The case law supports our position, Your Honor. The appellate courts have upheld witness lists of this size. Everyone we're going to call to the stand is on that list, and everyone on that list possesses relevant information. Many on that list frankly refuse to testify because they fear ending up like DeShawn Carter and Tavon Munson. We're hoping to change their minds between now and trial."

Ross has never been reversed on appeal when ruling in my favor. He may not know much about the law, but he knows his reversal stats and that I've always done right by him on that score. He's going to side with me on this one.

Ross says, "The witness list is fine. Let's move on to other things."

The rest of the conference bogs down in the standard stuff. The judge loses interest in most of it. Joe and I do what we need to do, and everything is pronounced ready. The trial starts Monday.

***

Over the weekend, we employ other last-minute measures to keep Tasha safe. Scott floods the neighborhood with law enforcement personnel asking questions of everyone. Police huddle with any members of the Rattlesnakes they can round up, hoping to sow distrust in the gang. Uniform officers make a big show of going to Belinda Favors' front door to ask questions. Belinda emphatically refuses to talk to them, shakes her head back and forth, and slams the door in their faces.

Tasha moved out some time ago to live with an aunt in neighboring Clayton County. Belinda wanted to make the move with her daughter, but we prevailed upon her that moving now would raise too much of a red flag. So she stays put, sweating out the time until Miller is convicted. No one seems to notice that Tasha doesn't live there anymore. I take that as a good sign.

The recently deceased Tavon Munson lived one street over from where Corey Miller murdered DeShawn Carter. No evidence suggests that Munson witnessed the murder or had any other knowledge about the case. I put him on the witness list because he lived in the area. Now he's dead. Did he die because of my strategy to cast a wide net of suspicion over everybody in the neighborhood? I push the question aside. The danger to Tasha leaves me with nothing but bad choices. I do the best I can and live with the consequences. If Miller did order Munson murdered, making sure Miller never walks the street again is the best medicine.

***

The day before the trial finds me at the condo with Lara. I try to savor the moment, knowing that she will board a plane later in the week to handle neglected business in Los Angeles. The timing is as good as any. Trials are 24-hour affairs, so I'll have less time to miss her. The symmetry bites. For two years prosecuting murder has been my sword to ward off the pain of my separation from Amber. Now work will serve the same purpose but with a different woman.

Lara asks, "Are you going to miss me?"

"Of course."

"I don't know. You're going to have a lot of late nights with that sexy assistant of yours."

"Do you sleep with all your co-stars?"

"Of course!"

Her laugh lets me in on the joke. Whether she's truly concerned about Ella and me is harder to gauge. After seeing Ella on TV arguing at Barton's bail hearing, Lara quizzed me about whether the two of us were a thing. She need not worry. Sleeping with a witness is already a dance on the live wire. Throwing the dynamite of another woman into the mix exceeds my tolerance for risk.

Later on, we eat Chinese take-out. I am quiet as I work over the Corey Miller case one last time—the pre-trial habit of a man who has always lived too much inside his own head. Lara notices my detachment as I chew mechanically on my food.

"You're not saying much."

"I'm mentally preparing myself for battle."

"You make it sound like a war."

It is. Law is the price the victors of history impose on the defeated, and a prosecutor's job is to wage war against those who think the terms of peace somehow do not apply to them. Trials may lack the bloody violence of the battlefield, but they are a species of combat all the same. The trial lawyer who doesn't go into trial with the mindset of a warrior starts from a position of weakness.

I explain none of these thoughts, don't give her an answer at all. The conversation dies, and Lara doesn't try to resuscitate it. She leaves me to myself. I sit on a couch and stare straight ahead at the barren, off-white wall—thinking.

My concentration breaks. Lara says something I don't quite catch.

"What?"

She asks, "After this trial, then it's Bernard's turn?"

"Yes, then it's Bernard's turn."

15

Corey Miller sits across the way in the courtroom—contemptuous, defiant, cocky to the end.

I reckon he was a cute kid once upon a time, but all I see now is a monster. The diminishing Christian inside of me recalls that, according to Jesus, being angry toward someone in your heart is the same thing as murdering that person. The anger in my own heart—enough to strike down a mountain—refuses to accept the rebuke. Actions matter. As a prosecutor, my entire career rests on the certitude that the act itself—the *actus reus*—possesses a singular moral significance. The law doesn't punish thoughts. Corey Miller made a choice to kill, and he must reap the consequences.

The bailiff calls the courtroom to order.

***

An uneventful morning of jury selection gives way to the lunch hour. Scott and I share company and some cold sandwiches. Because of security concerns for Belinda and Tasha Favors, Scott plans to stay close for the duration of the trial.

He asks, "Where were you last night?"

"What do you mean?"

"I dropped by your house at midnight, and you weren't there. You weren't in your office, either. Do you have some girl on the side I don't know about?"

An air of ambiguity surrounds the joke, as if the levity is only a subterfuge to fish for information. Proceed with caution, I tell myself. Lara and I use the condo precisely because Scott drops by my house unannounced at all hours. This moment was inevitable. I lie.

"Waffle House. Where else would I be at that time of night?"

"Ugh. I was thinking you might've paid Ella a visit. You should, you know."

Scott often exhorts me to stop keeping Ella at arm's length. I don't dare tell him about Lara. He is a man that plays things by the book, and sleeping with a witness ain't by the book. I make a non-committal noise at the mention of Ella, willing the topic to go away.

Scott says, "You need to start taking better care of yourself. You keep eating at that place you're going to die of a coronary. Too much grease."

Me, I love the grease and the atmosphere. Something joyously democratic surrounds the wayward cross-section of humanity that gathers at Waffle House in the dead of night. I look at the witching hour crowd and see in their different stories my own displacement from society. That my first date with Lara took place there seems fitting—realness birthing something new.

***

The first days of the trial contain no surprises. My opening statement promises the jury the goods. An eyewitness will sit in that empty witness chair and identify Corey Miller as the man who killed DeShawn Carter. No name is named. Having made the vow to produce such a witness to the jury, the entire case now rests on the shoulders of a little girl. But that truth has always hovered over this prosecution. Our proof against Corey Miller begins and ends with Tasha Favors.

The design of our case reflects this reality. Tasha will be our last witness, and every witness is a building block to reach her. Ella handles our law enforcement witnesses and uses them to paint an evocative picture of the murder scene—the victim dead on the ground, his brain half-flapped out on the dirty asphalt of the street. She elicits the phrase "execution-style killing" from one of the testifying police officers, who helpfully provides a visual by touching Ella's temple with his index finger cocked to simulate the nature of an execution-style kill.

As the Coroner for Fulton County, Cecil Magnus takes his turn in the witness box under Ella's guiding hand. He confirms that DeShawn

Carter is dead and that the muzzle of the murder weapon was touching Carter's head at the time of the fatal shot. He also brings his autopsy photos to parade before the jury. I've digested more pictures of dead bodies than I care to remember, and these gruesome beauties rival the worst of them.

Joe's participation in these early stages is more observer than attorney. None of the evidence so far implicates Miller, leaving Joe with nothing to challenge on cross-examination. He just sits there, the courtroom's forgotten man. He is competent, but lacks imagination. A better lawyer would ask questions simply to build a rapport with the jury and establish himself as someone who plays fair with the other side's witnesses. Not Joe. He allows the prosecution to dominate the room.

Scott's role as the lead detective on the case presents a quandary. Any other trial, he would be front and center as part of the State's case. The concern now centers on Tasha. Scott knows her identity—the only potential prosecution witness with knowledge of that closely-guarded secret. If Joe demands the answer of him on cross, Scott will have no choice but to tell the truth. I make the call not to put him on the stand. Softening that decision is that Scott adds little unique value to the meat of our case. His investigation revealed nothing. No one would talk to the police except Tasha. And Tasha can speak for herself.

***

Walking the halls of the courthouse during a lunch recess finds me consumed with thoughts of the trial—the things that happened, the things that didn't. This focus renders me oblivious to the people I pass, much like when I'm driving and suddenly realize that I have no recollection whatsoever of the past minute or so. I never crash in those situations, protected from disaster by some combination of habit, muscle memory, and subconscious awareness of my surroundings. The same dynamic now operates. I manage to avoid running into people even though I don't see them.

The shouting of my name from across the hall awakens me from this particular stupor. I calibrate my brain to pinpoint the source of the noise. The results do not compute—Bernard Barton. He walks up to me and starts a conversation.

"Counselor, good to see you."

He sticks out his hand, daring me to either shake it or not shake it. I'm not sure which. I shake.

I say, "We shouldn't be talking."

Because he's represented by a lawyer, I'm prohibited from having any *ex parte* communications with him. Barton doesn't care.

"I'm a lawyer. I know the rules. I can handle you by myself."

I nod. Sure you can, Bernie. Our eyes lock. I don't say anything because I don't have anything to say. Barton wants to chat.

"I'm here handling a matter on the side for an old friend. Feels good to get out of the house. I expect I'll be right back at it full-time soon enough."

He sells confidence, but I ain't buying. God has yet to create the person who is confident in the face of a murder charge. Marsh & McCabe put him on leave when the indictment came down. Yet here he stands, preening for attention. His act may work to seduce young female associates, but I'm unfazed. I've prosecuted men much worse than Barton. I'm prosecuting one right now. Barton fancies himself invincible, but tough guys don't beat up on women.

He asks, "You here with the Miller trial?"

I laugh at his counterfeit smugness and leave him to his games. Walking away, I ruminate on the sisterly connection that now links the two of us together. The thought bothers me more than it should—as though Barton and I stand as mirror images of each other. The idea sticks in my throat and refuses to go down. I want to vomit it out.

***

Trials have a rhythm that builds to a crescendo. No matter how much you prepare, the beat of work rarely relents. Something somewhere always requires your attention.

The Miller trial is no different. Ella and I work together late into the night. My tie long discarded, our shoes strewn across the floor, and the scattered remains of a rushed dinner littering a side table, we sit in my office—me at my desk, her at the conference table—working side-by-side like we have for five years now.

Amber never displayed a single pang of jealousy about her husband working closely with another woman at all hours. The trust is remarkable in hindsight. The sexual abandon unleashed in me by Lara reveals how close to moral anarchy I always stood. Given the right push, I jumped full throttle into the gorge. Sitting next to Ella tonight, I feel like a different man than the one who used to sit next to Ella. Instead of seeing her as a valued colleague, I imagine the sexual relationship between us that never was. She *is* beautiful.

The fickle trajectory of fate teases me like a court jester. My love life is not my own. It is the product of a predetermined destiny that chucks its meat hooks into my sides and guides me to a slaughter not of my own volition—a dead wife with whom I should have grown old, a clandestine affair with a famous starlet who chose me to give herself to, and a beautiful woman I'm bound to hurt, someone who I could bed tonight, probably this exact moment if I walked over to her right now. That last thought tantalizes. The lust flares up. I push the images away.

Ella catches my stare. She smiles the smile of incipient love—the kind a woman smiles when love is fresh and hopeful, before the hard facts of life whittle the dream down into lukewarm reality. The smile guts me with a jagged-edge machete—the type of tool I used to make trails in the woods where I grew up, the grooves on the edge able to gnaw through the toughest of branches. I break the gaze and pretend to pay attention to my work. Ella asks, "What?" Still smiling that sweet, damnable smile.

I play dumb, "What?"

"Why were you looking at me like that?"

"I was lost in my thoughts."

"About what?"

"Tasha."

"Oh."

The whole tableau is a lie. Ella's reality of who I am and what the two of us might be is a fiction, and she lacks the faintest idea. The real world—the secret world I actively hide from her—mocks her ignorance. I hate her stupidity and hate myself for making her stupid.

We both pretend to work in order to relieve the awkwardness of the moment. I make sure to keep Ella fully clothed in my mind the rest of the night. The focus now rests on Tasha—the last pure and undefiled thing in my life. Maybe Tasha can save me. But first I have to save her by ensuring Corey Miller gets the death sentence his crime surely merits. The high stakes rooted firmly in my mind, I bear down in the ongoing quest to deliver justice to the dead.

16

I call Tasha to the stand. I scrutinize Miller's face and get nothing but blankness for the trouble. The door in the back of the courtroom opens. Heads turn. I watch Miller. He doesn't twitch. Tasha enters, trailed closely by Belinda. The courtroom is compact. The journey to the front is short. I open the gate for Tasha, offering up a big smile, hoping to reassure her. Belinda sits in a seat on the front row, providing mom a clear view of where her daughter will testify on the stand.

Miller finally registers Tasha, and the slight flicker of the eyes betrays his knowledge. I imagine the calculations adding up in his head. He killed DeShawn Carter directly in front of Tasha's house. When Miller notices Belinda, the blank mask he has fronted all trial transforms into a glare of deadly malice. He turns his hand into a gun, points it at her, and fake shoots. God bless Belinda, she absorbs Miller's hostility and returns it with a death stare of her own.

The mask drops for only a few seconds. Joe and Judge Ross both miss the performance, but the distressed face of Juror Number Seven shows that she witnessed everything. White as a sheet, she physically backs up in her seat to get away from the defendant. I grab a file. Juror Number Seven is named Clarissa Simon, a white 37-year old Buckhead housewife. Perfect. Simon will no doubt spread the word to the other jurors at the next recess. I just got my conviction.

The bailiff swears Tasha in. I position myself for the questioning, making a point to block Miller's view of Tasha. The plan is to start easy, make her comfortable, and introduce her to the jury.

"Can you state your name for the record?"

"Tasha Favors."

I walk her through her background. We start with where she goes to school, her teachers, and her favorite classes. Tasha makes straight As, and I bring that fact to light. We talk about church and Sunday school. Tasha sings in the choir, and her favorite song is "How Great Thou Art." I ask her what she does in her free time. Belinda Favors works in a nursing home, and Tasha draws pictures to brighten the days of the residents who live there. I feel like a movie director who requisitioned central casting for a perfect little girl, and they sent over Tasha.

She projects well. We prepped her early and often. But until people get on the stand, you never know how they will perform under the bright lights. With a 10-year old girl, the unknown is only magnified. Tasha is our entire case. If she freezes, Miller walks free. Her poise so far belies her tender years. She speaks in a clear voice. Everything she says screams authenticity. The jury eats her up.

Having created a favorable impression, the questioning turns to the day of the murder. The goal is to get our identification of Miller and hightail it out of here. The nerves in my body penetrate to the bones. That's fine. A lawyer who isn't nervous at trial needs to find another line of work. I ask Tasha where she was at 4:30 p.m. on the date of the murder. She tells the story of how she sat at the kitchen table at her house working on her math homework while her Nana napped.

"What was your math homework about?"

"Fractions."

Little details enhance the credibility of a witness. You build trust with a jury on the small stuff before asking about the big stuff. Tasha is doing great.

"Did something happen to cause you to stop doing your homework?"

"It got noisy outside. I heard a lot people talking loudly, and I went to the window to see."

"What did you see when you looked out the window?"

All eyes focus on Tasha. The only sounds are the clicks on the court reporter's keys. In the silence, the impact of each key strike is magnified far out of its normal proportion.

"I saw a man on his knees in the street. Another man with a gun was talking to him."

"How far was your window from the street?"

"About the distance between me and my mom now."

I direct Belinda to stand. The distance between mother on the front row and daughter in the witness stand is maybe forty feet.

"The man you saw on the street on his knees—had you ever seen him before?"

"No."

Ella moves a blown-up picture of DeShawn Carter into position. I direct Tasha to look at it. She identifies Carter as the man on his knees in the street.

"The man holding the gun—had you ever seen him before?"

"Yes."

"Who was he?"

"Mr. Corey."

Tasha's soft-spoken description of Miller as "Mr. Corey" is powerful. The contrast between the respectful 10-year old and the murderous 21-year old represents the wide gulf between everything that is right with the world and everything that is wrong. And both of them live on the same street. I puzzle at a humanity that can produce such disparate outcomes from the same starting line.

I ask, "How do you know Mr. Corey?"

"He lives in my neighborhood."

"Do you see Mr. Corey in the courtroom?"

I move for the first time to create a sight line from witness to defendant. Tasha looks at Miller and points without hesitation at the man she saw shoot another person in the head. Amazing. She is the bravest person I've ever met in my life. I resume my place to guard Tasha from Miller's glare.

"Let the record reflect that the witness identified the defendant, Corey Miller, as Mr. Corey."

"You testified that you saw Mr. Corey holding a gun and talking to a man down on his knees in the street. What happens next?"

"Mr. Corey put the gun to the man's head and shot him."

Miller's voice, unheard until this moment, suddenly reverberates throughout the small room: "That little bitch be lying!"

The stillness of the courtroom shatters. Deputies move closer to the defense table. The judge's gavel bangs. I turn to face Miller, again making sure that I stand in his line of vision to the witness stand. The hatred in his eyes spits out the rawest emotion I've ever encountered in my life. He scares me, but I can't show it. I match his menace with a scowl of my own, encouraging him to transfer his violent urges my way. Anything to protect Tasha.

Judge Ross speaks, "Mr. Miller, another display like that, and I'll have you removed from the courtroom."

I allow things to calm before resuming. I catch a glimpse of Belinda. Miller's outburst rattled her. Scott puts his arm around her for reassurance. Belinda wants her daughter out of here. The finish line is close.

"You saw Corey Miller shoot a man in the head. What did you do next?"

"I ran to my bed and got under the covers and cried. I was scared."

Suddenly the dam breaks. Tasha cries fast-moving tears. The change surprises me. She has never once cried in my presence. I rush to grab some tissues and take them to her. I hurt for Tasha, but the calculating part of my lawyer brain concludes I couldn't have scripted that breakdown any better. The jury is now as protective of Tasha as I am.

"No further questions, Your Honor. Thank you for your testimony, Tasha. You're a brave little girl."

***

Joe must be careful. Tasha is a sympathetic witness, and he has to treat her with kid gloves. Handling a child witness on cross-examination is a precarious balancing act for a trial lawyer. The lawyer must simultaneously undermine the truth of the child's testimony yet avoid appearing to be a big bully who picks on little kids. With dishonest children, this task is hard enough. With honest children, it is near impossible. And Tasha speaks the truth.

I prepped her for cross-examination, of course. I subjected her to a variety of approaches, some soft, some mildly harsh. Ella did a few rounds with her, too, just to throw Tasha a different look. Our ultimate message to her was twofold—listen carefully to each question and tell the truth. Do that, and everything will be fine.

As Joe readies himself for his first question, Miller hands him a piece of paper. Joe reads it, frowns, and puts it down on the defense table. He begins.

"Hello, Tasha. My name is Mr. Parks. I'm just going to ask you some questions, and I want you to tell me the truth, okay?"

"Yes, sir."

I love the "yes, sir." That type of testimonial genuineness is hard to fake.

"You mentioned where you were living at the time you allegedly saw a shooting in front of your house. My first question is where do you stay now?"

Hell no. I shoot straight up.

"Objection, Your Honor, relevance."

Joe responds, "He opened the door by talking about her living arrangements."

"I didn't open the door on where the witness is living now. That information has no relevance to this case whatsoever. None."

A distracted Judge Ross looks up from what must be his cell phone, oblivious to anything that was just said. He rules, "I'll allow the question."

"Your Honor! Corey Miller is on trial for killing a witness. The State believes that the life of this witness—"

"I've made my ruling."

"Your Honor, may we approach—"

"I've made my ruling, counselor, sit down!"

I throw down my pen on the table in disgust. Ella places her hand on my arm lest I toss something else. Ross stares at me hard, mulling over his next actions. Incompetent bastard. Ella yanks me down, and I sit.

Ross allows the moment to pass without further admonitions to me. Joe asks his question again.

Tasha looks at me confused. I nod. She answers, "With my Aunt Patricia." She then provides house number, street name, city, everything. Belinda's soft sob behind me tortures my ears. My emotions fly right past anger to fury.

Across the way Miller writes down something in the wake of Tasha's answer. Clarissa Simon, Juror Number Seven, observes Miller's action and takes it the same way I do—the transcription of Tasha's current residence. Her stunned face shows that she gets it. Miller has only one use for that address.

Listening proves elusive. My body sits still in my wood back chair, but my insides shake with uncontrollable stress. The clash between the motionless outside and the racing cauldron within demolishes my ability to process information. The physical imbalance takes me back to the night Amber and Cale were killed. The same feelings of wrath and helplessness grip me now. I might explode on the spot.

Joe ends his questioning. Judge Ross is forced to address me: "Mr. Meridian, any re-direct?" I look at Ella dumbfounded. She shakes her head. I look at Ross and shake my head.

"All right. The witness is excused. Court's adjourned until tomorrow." The gavel bangs.

Scott walks with Belinda to the witness stand. Mother and daughter hug. Belinda's tears water Tasha's hair. Three uniformed deputies summoned by Scott encircle the two. Officers tonight will no doubt station themselves outside Aunt Patricia's house where Tasha is currently staying, but Scott will have Tasha and Belinda tucked away safely under police guard somewhere else until the end of the trial.

I attempt to pack away my trial materials, but the numbness in my hands makes grasping papers and pens a struggle. The only thing I feel is the gash to my professional pride in losing control at a critical moment. Ella caresses my arm.

"It's okay."

"Did Joe hurt us on cross?"

"Not even a nick. Tasha did great."

The laborious packing job concludes. I try standing on wobbly legs. They hold. I walk—each step a little firmer than the last. We make it to the office.

I tell her, "I need to take the rest of the night off."

"That's a good idea. I'll hold down the fort."

We part for the evening. I collapse in my office chair—thankful that Lara doesn't leave for Hollywood until tomorrow morning. After the horrible last hour, I need her and no one else.

***

While Lara and I lie next to one another late into the night, firefighters rush to Pittsville to put out an explosion at the one-time home of Belinda and Tasha Favors. No injuries are reported. The previous inhabitants no longer live there.

17

"The defense calls Anthony Wayne."

The defense's star witness shuffles up to the stand. Joe cleaned him up as best he could—jewelry and exposed tattoos out, slacks and a tie in. The rough edges prove harder to wash away. His mother may have named him Anthony, but everyone else calls him Q-Bone. The pre-trial order states that Q-Bone will provide an alibi for Corey Miller at the time of the murder. I'm all ears.

Leery of his own witness, Joe doesn't waste any time and asks, "Do you remember where you were on the day when DeShawn Carter was shot?"

"Yeah."

The lawyer looks at Q-Bone expectantly and gets blankness in return. Each of them waits for the other to speak. Joe blinks first.

"Where were you?"

"Watching TV."

"Was anyone with you?"

"Yeah."

Joe's face sags. He clearly prepped Q-Bone to provide better answers, but Q-Bone is dropping the ball on his end of the performance.

"Who was with you?"

"Corey."

"The defendant Corey Miller?"

"Yeah."

Joe stands behind Miller to give everyone a good look. As identifications go, it's weak stuff. Placing his hands on Miller's shoulders, Joe tries to put lipstick on the pig, "You're sure you were with Corey Miller at the time of the shooting?"

I interrupt, "Objection, leading. This a direct examination, not cross."

"Sustained."

Lawyers don't get to ask their own witnesses leading questions that suggest what the answer should be. Q-Bone is making Joe work too hard, and a visibly flustered Joe wants to take shortcuts.

"How do you know you were with the defendant at the time of the shooting?"

"Corey and me have been boys for ten years. I know who he is."

I stifle a laugh. Whatever rehearsal Joe had with the witness didn't take. Getting testimony out of Q-Bone is like pulling teeth one at a time, tooth by tedious tooth. The work is bloody and unpleasant for everyone.

"That's not what I meant. How do you know you were with Corey when DeShawn Carter was shot?"

Q-Bone still fails to see the light. He stares at Joe for help, but their telepathic connection fails to generate a spark. Dead airtime again hangs in the courtroom between lawyer and witness.

"Say that again," Q-Bone says finally.

"Were you with Corey watching TV when you heard the gunshot?"

"Objection, leading and lack of foundation."

"Sustained. Rephrase."

Joe circles back to his previous question, hoping that Q-Bone can pick up the hint: "How do you know you were with Corey when DeShawn Carter was shot?"

The witness finally understands and testifies, "We was watching TV together when we heard the gunshot."

The answer is so obviously coached that a male juror chuckles. Joe gets the testimony he wants, but the journey to get there kills Q-Bone's credibility. Snake bit by the unreliability of the witness, Joe hustles back to his seat before any more damage can be done. He got his client's alibi on the record, and that is good enough.

"No further questions," he announces with the relief of a man who just escaped from an inferno and lived to tell about it. But I haven't had my turn with the witness yet, and I aim to see Q-Bone burn.

***

"Your friends call you Q-Bone?"

"Yeah."

"You're a member of the gang called the Rattlesnakes?"

"Nah, man."

"You've heard of them?"

"Yeah, man. Them some bad dudes." He laughs, thinking himself to be some kind of comedian. The courtroom is silent.

"You have a rattlesnake tattoo on your arm, don't you?"

I hold a manila folder up in my left hand. Q-Bone's criminal history makes for a thick file. I have pictures of his arm if he wants to get cute.

"Yeah."

"But you're not a member of the Rattlesnakes?"

"Nah. I just like rattlesnakes."

He laughs, but this attempt at humor bombs, too. The awkward void of the quiet unnerves him. He really thought that was a funny joke, and he can't understand why the audience fails to appreciate his winning sense of humor.

Q-Bone's list of priors is prime impeachment material, but attacking his character seems superfluous after that disastrous direct examination. His credibility is already shot. My needs at this point are few—attack the fabricated alibi and grill Q-Bone about the murder of Tavon Munson shortly after he appeared on the witness list. I start with Tavon.

"Do you know a Tavon Munson?"

"Used to."

"The same Tavon Munson that was murdered in your neighborhood two weeks ago?"

"That him."

"The same Tavon Munson that was murdered two days after being put on the State's witness list for this case?"

"Yeah."

"How do you know who was on my witness list?"

It's typically poor form to ask an open-ended question on cross-examination because a cross-examiner should never give a hostile witness an opportunity to explain anything. But every rule has exceptions, and if the witness' answer can't hurt you, an open-ended question here and there can be put to good use. Q-Bone sits there like a stone. The non-answer speaks volumes. I press forward.

"Did Corey Miller tell you Tavon Munson was on the witness list?"

"Nah, not him."

"Did Mr. Parks tell you Tavon Munson was on the witness list?"

Q-Bone looks to Joe for guidance, but I'm having none of that.

"Don't look at him. Look at me. I'm asking the questions. Did Mr. Parks tell you Tavon Munson was on the witness list?"

"Nah."

"Did Mr. Parks give you the witness list?"

I'm still mad at Joe for asking Tasha where she now lives and have no qualms creating the impression that Joe is a conspirator in Tavon Munson's murder. Maybe I'll indict Q-Bone for the killing of Tavon and name Joe as an accomplice for fun.

"I don't remember where I got the list."

"You don't remember?"

"Nah."

"But you got the list?"

"Yeah."

"And Tavon Munson's name was on that list?"

He pauses, again uncertain as to what he should do. He's already admitted he knows Munson was on the list. Walking that back now would be hard for him. He apparently reaches the same conclusion.

"Yeah."

"And Tavon Munson is now dead?"

"Yeah."

"Shot in the gut?"

"Yeah."

"How do you know he was shot in the gut?"

More uncertainty fills his eyes. He wrestles with his brain to spit out some answer that won't lead to his arrest. Struggling, he starts to glance at Joe—

"Stop looking at him! How do you know he was shot in the gut?"

"I just know."

"You just know that Tavon Munson got a bullet in the gut?"

"That right."

The answer satisfies me. He sounds like a man who was at the scene of the shooting. If I push harder on the origin of his knowledge, maybe he says someone else told him about Munson and that does me no good. Jack Millwood, my mentor and now Barton's attorney, taught me, "Always cash in your winnings." I've won this point with Q-Bone. No need to keep sitting at the table and foolishly lose it all back.

I announce, "Let's move on to the DeShawn Carter murder."

It's a statement, not a question. That doesn't stop Q-Bone from blurting out, "Tavon Munson shot that dude." All the energy in the courtroom suspends itself in mid-air, waiting for the other shoe to drop. My heart speeds like a bullet train, but I smother any emotion to make sure my surprise doesn't reach the surface.

"Tavon Munson?"

"Yeah, man. I saw him do it."

God bless America. Q-Bone sits there pleased as punch. His stupid grin proclaims his certainty that he has pulled one over on all of us. He fails to realize that the joke's on him. Out of the corner of my eye, I catch a glimpse of Joe, who looks morose. Miller, for his part, wears his customary scowl.

"You saw him shoot DeShawn Carter?"

"Sure did."

"I thought you were at home watching TV with Corey Miller when the shots were fired."

Q-Bone's smile vanishes. Even he understands that a person cannot be in two places at one time. Or as my Grandpa used to tell me, "You can't ride two horses with one ass." In the heat of the moment, Q-Bone got greedy. Not content with merely lying about being Miller's alibi, he fabricated seeing Tavon Munson kill DeShawn Carter, too. I don't press the contradiction, I'm tempted to sit down right now with the score tilted heavily in my favor. But something tells me that Q-Bone will be the gift that keeps on giving.

"We can't ask Tavon if he killed DeShawn Carter, can we?"

"Don't look like it."

"Cause Tavon's dead?"

"Tavon's dead."

He laughs another solitary laugh, as if the idea of murder makes for good comedy. Everything he says is wrong. The jury loathes him.

"Did you kill him?"

"Nah, man. Not me."

"Shoot him in the gut?"

"Nah, man. Not me."

"Isn't it a fact that the Rattlesnakes killed Tavon Munson before he could come to court to testify that Corey Miller killed DeShawn Carter?"

Q-Bone pauses on this one. He starts to swing his head toward the defense table, but stops halfway when he remembers my earlier admonitions not to look at Joe for answers. Like a trained puppy, Q-Bone now adapts his behavior to what I've taught him to do. I love cross-examination. With no answer forthcoming, I ask the question again.

"Isn't it a fact that the Rattlesnakes killed Tavon Munson before he could come to court to testify that Corey Miller killed DeShawn Carter?"

Truth is, I had no intention of calling Munson to the stand, know nothing about him except that he was murdered, and have no idea if he was even in Georgia at the time of the DeShawn Carter killing. The speculation that Tavon witnessed the Carter murder is based on the thinnest of reeds. If the jury draws the wrong inferences, so be it. I don't care as long as Miller gets convicted.

Q-Bone finally answers, "Nah."

"Isn't it a fact that the Rattlesnakes killed Tavon because they didn't want this jury to hear what Tavon had to say?"

"Nah."

"The Rattlesnakes knew that Tavon's testimony would put Corey Miller away?"

"Nah, man. We didn't do it."

"We? We? I thought you weren't a member of the Rattlesnakes."

His earlier denial of being a Rattlesnake recoils back to bite him hard. Everyone in the courtroom looks to Q-Bone for an explanation of the discrepancy. Joe should object since I didn't actually ask a question, but he looks like a man playing out the clock, waiting for the game to end. The silence marches on and grows in its harshness. I let Q-Bone sweat. I won't be the first to talk. I can stand here all day.

"Man, I was just kidding about that."

"Just like you were kidding about not killing Tavon Munson?"

I don't let him answer.

"No further questions, Your Honor."

18

"I can't find Brice Tanner anywhere," Scott says. We meet for lunch at Harold's B-B-Q, just down the street from the Atlanta federal penitentiary. I have time. The Miller trial is off today because Judge Ross has to attend the funeral of one of his former colleagues on the bench. Harold's isn't located in the best part of town, but the food tastes good. I see two federal judges a few tables down eating over a plastic red-and-white checkered tablecloth. It's that kind of place.

"What do you mean you can't find him?"

"He's vanished. Moved out of his apartment and no longer works at Marsh & McCabe. I tried getting some information from the law firm, but they wouldn't tell me anything except that he doesn't work there anymore. I told them that it was important, but they said that was all they could tell me."

"Well, you did arrest one of their partners in their offices and made sure the news was there to cover it."

"Shut up."

"Hold on."

I take out my phone and find Jeff Yarber's number, my friend at Marsh & McCabe. He answers on the second ring. We catch up first, then I ask about Brice.

"I heard Brice Tanner no longer works for you guys. What happened there?"

"Ah, I doubted this was a social call. You never want to just talk. Yeah, Brice left us a few weeks ago. He came back from some time off sporting a beard, a diamond stud in his ear, and perhaps a tattoo. Reports vary. You met him, right? He was completely clean-cut, clean-shaven, all-American type. Not anymore. He came back, said he didn't want to practice law anymore, and went away."

"Where is he now?"

"I heard the mountains. Brasstown Bald area or something. We have the address. I'll shoot it to you."

I give Scott the scoop. Like everything else about the case these days, I filter the information through the lens of how it will look at Barton's trial. Innocent explanations abound for Brice's retreat into the mountains—the murder of the woman he loved, disgust at working for the same law firm as that lover's murderer, the general discontent that affects almost every lawyer Brice's age who works for the faceless, soulless mega-firms. The problem is Millwood. Brice is a canvas upon which many different stories can be painted, and Millwood is a creative artist. Using Brice's abandonment of his prior life as evidence of a guilty conscience is almost too easy. Scott and I decide to pay Brice a visit in the near future to scout out his mental state.

***

Closing arguments offer no great insights about the Miller case. Joe relies on Q-Bone as an alibi witness—the only game in town for the defense. The same Q-Bone who testified that he was in two different places at the same time when the shooting went down. Joe dances around Tasha and whines about the unfairness of convicting a man for murder solely on a child's testimony. The State must offer more proof, he pleads. Then he sits down.

I start with Tasha. A man was murdered right in front of her house. She witnessed the killing, a visual that will give her nightmares for the rest of her life. Tasha knows Corey Miller well—"Mr. Corey" she calls him. She came to court at great risk to her personal safety and identified him for all to see. No mistake exists here. Corey Miller fired that gun.

We have Tasha on one side, and Q-Bone on the other, one with no motive to lie and one with every motive to lie. Which voice has the ring of authenticity? I invoke the ghost of Tavon Munson. Q-Bone knew Tavon, knew that Tavon was on the State's witness list, knew that Tavon was shot in the gut. I ask the jury, "What did Tavon know about the murder of DeShawn Carter that got him killed?"

Murdering a witness rocks the foundation of the criminal justice system. Corey Miller thinks himself above the law, that killing those who dare to testify against the Rattlesnakes makes him beyond the reach of the police, the courts, and you the jury. Show him he's wrong. Show him that we as a society do not tolerate murder. Show him that he does not get to dispose of DeShawn Carter simply because he pleases. Hold him accountable for his crime.

That's my story, more or less. The waiting begins.

***

Awaiting a verdict stresses me out more than the trial itself. A trial allows no time for reflection. It is a manic sprint from one witness to another, one piece of evidence to the next. Days spent in court bleed into nights of feverish preparation. When the hard work ends, nothing is left to do but sit and wait. Stuck in the purgatory of uncertainty, the mind replays the entirety of the trial, creating a list of everything I did wrong. Experience as a trial lawyer does not make the waiting easier. Even today, despite my record of success in the courtroom, jury deliberations mercilessly taunt my confidence in who I am. Jurors not only sit in judgment of the defendant but of me as well.

I am not alone in my neurosis during this dead time. Ella feels it, too. Her routine centers on pacing around the courthouse like a marathon runner to burn off the nervous energy that afflicts her. Millwood used to chain-smoke. Now he plows through packs of gum. I just sit, rocking back and forth in my chair. Thinking. Thinking. Thinking.

Nothing screams failure like a prosecutor losing a murder case. Juries are not eager to release accused murderers back onto the same streets they themselves walk. "Innocent until proven guilty" sounds nice on a postcard, but juries want to convict. Victory requires nothing more than giving the jurors a reason to follow what they are already inclined to do. Losing when the deck already sits stacked in my favor would mean I'm not very good at my job.

***

Five hours and counting now.

Why is the jury taking so long? The universal rule of thumb is that delay favors the defense. I once had to wait five days for a verdict. By day four, I had already journeyed through the five stages of grief—denial that there was a problem, *anger* at the jury's intransigence, *bargaining* that there was a reasonable explanation to explain the delay, *depression* that I had lost a winnable case, and *acceptance* of my own inadequacy both as a lawyer and a man. A bemused Amber took her husband's shifting emotions in good stride. She always believed in me, even during my dark periods of doubt.

When the jury returned to the courtroom, I strained without success to read their faces for any clues. Nothing. I prepared for the worst and felt almost confused when the foreman called out, "Guilty." Turned out that eleven of the jurors quickly landed on the defendant's guilt, but it took four days to convince the lone holdout.

Amber and I celebrated by taking a short vacation to Jekyll Island to allow me to recuperate. Sitting outside while enjoying a sunset dinner, her radiance overtook me. She had never looked so beautiful. That trip remains one of my best memories. Try as I might to avoid thinking about Amber since her murder, jury deliberations always remind me of those few precious days. Waiting for the Miller verdict is no different. I see her so clearly. On a bicycle. Eating ice cream. Drinking wine. Splashing in the water. Strolling on Driftwood Beach. Wearing a bathing suit that both revealed and hid much. Happy times.

I flash a look of hatred at the clock. Six hours. Still no word from the jury.

***

The news of a verdict reaches Ella's phone first. I straighten my tie and put on my jacket. I splash some cold water on my face to ready myself before finding my assigned seat. I analyze Miller for any sign showing a heightened awareness of the moment and again find nothing. The possibility that I'm more nervous about the verdict than

Miller strikes me as inconceivable, but that appears to be the truth. The callousness with which he treats the lives of others would make a perverse semblance of sense if he likewise doesn't put much stock in his own life. Judge Ross enters the room.

"Bring in the jury," he orders.

I always search the jury for signs of its verdict. This practice is nothing more than alchemy, although it does pass the time. The knot in my stomach tightens.

"Has the jury reached a verdict?"

"We have, Your Honor," responds the jury foreman.

After inspecting the verdict, Ross addresses the defense table, "Will the defendant please rise?" The words are a command framed as a request. At Joe's urging, Miller stands up, annoyed at the effort required to get on his feet. Joe stands next to him, the dutiful attorney to the last.

"Mr. Foreperson, you may read the verdict."

My heart races abnormally fast for a man simply sitting in a chair. Ella gives my knee a squeeze under the prosecution table, a first for her, and a sign that the nerves are eating at her insides, too.

"We the jury, in the matter of the State of Georgia versus Corey Andrew Miller, on the charge of first-degree murder, find the defendant ... guilty."

The pause before "guilty" throws me a little. Was it a pause or a "not"? I ask Ella, "Did he say guilty?" Ella nods and gives my knee another squeeze. I take a deep breath. Thank God.

***

Judge Ross calls the courtroom to order. Miller slumps back down into his chair. Maybe he does care. The jurors look relieved, but their work is not yet done. Next up is the sentencing phase and the determination whether Miller will be put to death for his crime. But the hour is already late, and Ross sends everyone home for the day.

After the adjournment, Joe meanders over to Ella and me. He wants to make a deal.

"I need to talk with my client, but I was wondering about a trade where we agree to life with no parole in exchange for taking the needle off the table."

I answer, "That's the deal I offered you before the trial. Why would we take that deal at this point?"

Joe shrugs his shoulders in response. I pressed him hard before the trial to get Miller to take my offer. I would gladly have traded the death penalty to spare Tasha from testifying. Miller turned it down, and I'm in no mood to negotiate now.

Joe pouts, "You got my client for life. I don't see why you need him dead, too."

"He killed a witness, Joe. We need to make an example of him. He had his chance to avoid the needle. He rolled the dice and lost. Now he has to live with it."

"Whatever," retorts Joe. He slinks off.

Idiot. The death penalty as a tool of leverage for encouraging pre-trial pleas only works if we actually seek lethal injection once we win a conviction. Rejecting the deal must have consequences. Otherwise every murder defendant would take his chances at trial. Miller should've pled.

On our walk back to the office, Ella asks, "Still want to indict Joe?"

"I want to, but I won't. He wasn't involved in any conspiracy. Indicting him would only make him a martyr to the cause within the defense bar," I answer. "But I'll invite him to Miller's execution."

"Ouch," responds Ella.

"He deserves it."

"Let's make sure Miller gets it first."

Someone bumps hard into me forcing my body into a half-spin.

"Watch where you going," huffs Q-Bone. The bump is no accident. Q-Bone flares at me with murder in his eyes. Ella hurries away, no doubt to retrieve a deputy. I stand my ground. I'm in the mood for a fight.

"Big lawyer man. What you got against the Rattlesnakes, lawyer man?"

"I grew up in the country, Q-Bone. I've never been afraid of snakes.

They're small and they scamper away at the slightest little thing. I bet you've never even seen a rattlesnake in the wild, have you? I have. They have a rattle. Big deal. Babies have rattles. Are you afraid of babies, Q-Bone?"

In reality, snakes terrify me, always have, especially rattlers. But Q-Bone doesn't know that.

"Lawyer man is real funny. Were you laughing when your wife and kid got what was coming to them?"

I peer down on him. I'm 6'2 200 pounds. Q-Bone's lucky if he's 5'9 in heels and is so thin he's invisible from the side. Q-Bone gives me his best triple-dog-dare look to encourage me to make the first move. If I respond to his provocation, he wins. But Q-Bone doesn't get to win.

"Q-Bone, have you ever seen a man die by lethal injection? I have. I've sent two men to their death. Your pal Corey is going to be the third. Here's what happens. Men with masks—we don't want the condemned to know their executioners for some reason, so they wear masks. These men with masks strap you down to a table so you can't move. Then they get these big needles—the biggest you've ever seen—and they stab them into your arms and legs."

I play-act the injection of the needles into his body. He steps back and says, "Man, what the—"

"Wait, I'm not done yet. The prisoner is strapped there with big needles digging into his skin, and he starts reacting to the poison. Except the poison hasn't started yet! Both times I've seen it, the dudes are crying out in pain before the bad stuff even begins. That's how freaked out they were."

"Man—"

"Still not done. And then it starts. For real. The poison begins its destructive march through the body. It's crazy, Q-Bone. The civilized world has banned chemical weapons because they're too inhumane, yet the State of Georgia uses chemicals to kill a man from the inside out."

I shake my head in disbelief at this dichotomy.

"Where was I? The poison starts doing its work, and the soon-to-be dead man's eyes start to bug out. The face turns purple, and there is foaming at the mouth. People watching in the observation room start to throw up. It's that disgusting. I'm told the man's genitals—that's your boy parts, Q-Bone—the genitals feel like they're on fire as the poison reaches the veins down there. It's a terrible way to die."

I pause to let the images sink in for a second or two.

"That's going to happen to Corey. You can come watch if you want, you and me ringside seats. Of course, I kinda have a feeling—call it a lawyer man hunch—that you're going to meet the same fate."

His strut is gone. He lost it sometime around the first mention of the big needles. He's too ignorant to recognize that my entire description of lethal injection is make believe. During my monologue, Ella returned with a deputy. A shake of my head kept them from interrupting. I wanted Q-Bone to hear every single word.

The performance scared him, and he knows I know it. In an attempt to save face, he works to re-establish his tough guy credibility in my eyes.

"I don't care what you say, man. That little girl is still going to get got."

"Tasha Favors?"

"Hell yeah, Tasha Favors."

I turn to the deputy, Deputy Besh according to his badge. I ask, "Did you hear him say that?"

"Yes, sir."

"Ella, did you hear it?"

"I heard it."

"I heard it, too," I say to round things out.

A confused Q-Bone fails to appreciate the criminal significance of his words. He knows something is wrong, but he doesn't know what, and he doesn't like it.

He spits out, "What?"

I answer, "Deputy Besh, can you please arrest Anthony Wayne, alias Q-Bone, for making terroristic threats against Tasha Favors?"

"Yes, sir."

Besh takes out his handcuffs and tells Q-Bone to turn around with his hands behind his back. Q-Bone does neither.

"What's this, man?"

People start to gather around. I see an ACLU lawyer I casually know looking at us warily with a phone in her hand. She's not filming yet, but it would only take a couple of seconds for her to start. I don't want this situation to escalate to the point where Besh has to forcefully subdue Q-Bone. I need to talk Q-Bone down off the ledge.

"Q-Bone, you just threatened to kill somebody."

"Nah, I didn't."

"Close enough. We need to take you in. You'll be bonded out and back home tomorrow if everything goes smoothly. But if you resist and everything goes to hell, I will bring the wrath of God down on your head. Okay? Now turn around and put your hands behind your back."

Despite the antagonism between Q-Bone and me, or perhaps because of it, we have a rough understanding of each other. Besh takes him into custody, and a potential crisis is averted. Before Q-Bone is led away, I warn him, "And forget about that little girl." He slumps and gives me a half-nod.

The crowd begins to disperse. Toward the back I see a familiar, unwelcome face—Bernard Barton. We make eye contact, and he flashes his trademark smirk before stalking away. I turn to Ella and announce, "God, I hate that guy."

19

The death penalty phase of the Miller trial starts on a morning brimming with white sunlight. I wear the same purple tie I wore when I convinced the Willie Joe Sawyer and Harry Fleming juries to sentence those men to death. A weird thumping sound repeats on a loop when I enter my garage. The noise originates from an orange and black butterfly flying into a window, trying to reach the fresh air. Over and over again, the scene repeats itself. I shake my head at the futility.

The garage door rises, and the natural light of the day floods even the darkest corners of the space. Yet the butterfly fails to understand the freedom offered by the new light. Instead, he keeps crashing into that window, over and over again. Sigh. I grab one of his spastic wings and hold on for dear life against the power of the furious flaps. I transport the butterfly outside the garage to release him. He flies away and disappears into nature's welcoming arms.

The butterfly's flight into freedom is humbling in its beautiful simplicity. I smile for almost the entire drive to the courthouse. When I realize that saving that butterfly was the first thing I've done in a long time completely free from self-interest, the smile fades, and I feel the emptiness of a life with myself at its center.

***

Twelve hours later, the deputies lead Corey Miller back to his cell as a man condemned to death. The result was inevitable the moment Miller yelled, "That little bitch be lying!" Maybe it was inevitable the day he was born.

The whole proceeding felt perfunctory, like an inconsequential misdemeanor traffic trial as opposed to a hearing to decide on a man's life. Ever his worst enemy, Miller glared angrily at the jurors the entire time. No character witnesses spoke on his behalf, and Joe's efforts for his client were lukewarm, if that. I said what needed to be said, and the jury did what needed to be done. Corey Miller now officially sits on Georgia's death row.

***

Ella and I decompress in my office in the wake of Miller's condemnation by a jury of his peers. Lara remains in California, and I have nowhere else to go. Ella sits before me in a wing-backed chair with her legs pulled under her—shoes and hose off, blouse untucked, beer in her hand. I nurse a bottle of Coke with a gravity it doesn't deserve.

She asks, "What now?"

"All Barton all the time."

"That's not what I meant."

I feign ignorance but know she's talking about us. I stare down hard at my Coke, as if the secret to all of the world's problems rests at the bottom of the glass.

"What are you afraid of?"

Ella's question pulls me back to the here and now. I drag my eyes away from the bottle and look at her with a confused mask, pretending to be stupid. The audience isn't buying the act.

"Don't. You're much too smart to play dumb like this."

I decide to lie.

"We work together. It would be too complicated."

"You don't believe that."

She's right. I could see myself loving Ella under different circumstances. That we've grown close is no surprise. Office romances in the legal profession are as widespread as pollen in the spring. Late nights at work, stressful deadlines that never abate, too much alcohol—the working conditions of the modern lawyer breed intimate familiarity among those who are near. A quarter of the lawyers in town have a former junior associate as a second wife. Don't even get me started on the judges.

"I'm your boss. It's bad policy, sexual harassment even."

Ella laughs, unfurls her long, brown legs from the seat, and stands as a woman on a mission. She glides toward me with much mischief. I couldn't be stiller if a lion stood there eyeing me as its next meal—or more afraid. When she reaches me, she plops down into my lap.

"To hell with policy."

Her lips descend and latch onto my mouth. I don't push her away. She tastes as good as I've imagined. She disengages from the kiss, and we hold each other, forehead resting on forehead, hot breaths hanging in the air between us.

"Spend the night with me."

She feels good. Too good. I close my eyes and remember Lara. I wriggle out from under Ella to gain my feet. She slides into the space I just vacated, startled and amazed by the sudden movement.

"I can't."

"Is it another woman?"

"God, no."

The immediacy of the answer doesn't quell her doubts. Hard, skeptical eyes probe my face searching for signs of deceit. Finding nothing, she tries another tack.

"What is it then?"

"Amber. Cale. Everything. I'm not ready for this. I'll probably never be ready for it. Forget about me."

The lies flow so easily. I amaze myself. The scary part is that I don't really care.

"It's been two years, Chance," Ella argues.

"I gotta go."

"Is it because I'm black?"

That leaves a mark. I stand there with my mouth open, stunned into a long silence. The race issue has never once infected our relationship. Ella's willingness to play that card hurts.

"How could you say such a thing?"

"Well, you are a white guy of a certain age from rural Georgia. I doubt your momma would approve."

"Do you really believe that about me?"

"It would explain a lot."

"The answer to your question is no."

I leave her there in my chair—bewildered and anguished at the man who refuses to love her. I head home, thinking of another woman and placing all my hopes of salvation on her.

***

Monday morning follows an aimless weekend without Lara. I didn't work, didn't shave, didn't leave the house, didn't dwell on the awkwardness with Ella. Freed from the hurry of the trial, the separation from Lara hit me with maximum velocity. I missed her and lacked purpose in the vacuum created by her absence. The only relevant moments of Saturday and Sunday were our brief conversations on the phone. I remember little else. Back at my desk, work doesn't hold the same interest as before, and I'm at a loss on how to go about my day. Lara returns to town tonight.

"Bobby wants to meet us."

Ella's words break me out of my mental haze. Her presence in my office comes as a surprise. I get up slowly and fight the heaviness of my legs. The story is the same after every trial. My body needs time to re-adjust. As the years advance, the recovery period lengthens. The thought of another tiresome meeting with Bobby increases the weight of the walk. Ella leads me through the relevant door.

"Surprise!"

I flinch against the yell that greets me as I enter the room. I look around, gather my bearings, and register various constituencies of the District Attorney's Office. Everyone smiles at me, the apparent guest of honor. Today is not my birthday, not even in the remote vicinity. The meaning behind this gathering mystifies. Ella beams. I see a cake. I smile awkwardly, unsure of what to do.

Bobby emerges from somewhere, carrying a large smile with him, and motions for everyone to gather around. He addresses me:

"We all know you're the hardest working person in the office. You set an example for all of us to follow. You make me look good every day, and I personally appreciate it. We have tough jobs here. We see the very worst of humanity, and the public expects us to make sure that those who are most dangerous do not walk free. It is important work, and you know more than anyone the high cost crime exacts on its victims. Even after enduring a personal tragedy no one should ever have to endure, you didn't give up the fight. You rededicated yourself to the pursuit of justice, and we all draw inspiration from what you do and the professionalism with which you do it. We want to say thank you and to congratulate you on another win at trial. May Corey Miller never see the light of freedom again."

Applause.

The staff finishes clapping, and pats on the backs go around. The attention appropriately humbles me, but the slow shame stings. Public disclosure that I'm sleeping with a witness in the office's biggest case would make everyone in this room look bad. Guilt by association.

Bobby adds, "There is more. Ella, your turn."

Ella moves next to him and starts:

"As Bobby said, we all see how hard you work. We also know that you've been working non-stop without a break for a couple of years now. We think you need a vacation. We all pitched in and reserved you a cabin in the North Carolina Highlands starting Wednesday through Sunday. You can go off by yourself and recharge, but you cannot take any work! You are a great mentor and a friend. You inspire us, and we love you."

She hugs me, wiping away tears from her eyes as she does so. The guilt I feel stabs the heart repeatedly. Everyone applauds again—the praise heaping burning coals on my head.

Bobby emphasizes, "And you have to take the time off! No work! That's an order! We need you rested and focused for the Barton trial."

More applause.

People in the office have long encouraged me to take a vacation. I've always resisted. But things are different now. I put my guilty conscience to the side. I think of Lara and agree to go to the mountains.

***

Before I leave, Scott and I meet to discuss Barton. As part of the investigation, Scott periodically sends officers to stake out the Barton place. Turns out that Monica Haywood has moved in. Apparently, the two lovebirds are engaged.

I exclaim, “What?”

“She is living there. Her condo is empty and for sale. Everything has been moved out.”

“Is he insane? Does he *want* to get convicted?”

“He doesn’t care about appearances, does he?”

“Millwood can’t know. No way he would allow that. The jury will convict Barton for epic bad taste if nothing else.”

Barton’s arrogance continues to puzzle me. He can’t be so stupid. Maybe his sense of superiority is so ingrained that he can’t control himself. I don’t know. But I do know juries, and arrogance never plays well. Once the jury decides it doesn’t like a defendant, the odds of that defendant escaping conviction near zero. Barton is dancing with fire. Millwood would tell him the same.

Scott says, “They finally got you to take a vacation, huh? Good. I had an idea about that.”

“What?”

“You should take Ella.”

“I thought you were going to tell me to take you.”

“You’re not my type.”

I shrug, hoping to deflect further Ella talk. Scott continues to assess me, making clear he wants some kind of answer.

I offer, “I want to be alone. Think about things. It will do me some good. Ella understands.”

“She’s not going to wait forever. You’re making a mistake.”

“I don’t think so.”

20

Lara radiates beauty on the drive to the mountains. A fear gripped me that California would change her back into a famous movie star, too good for someone so pedestrian as me. That kind of worry eats at a person, exposing the fine line between love and torture. On Monday night, I paced around the condo waiting for her with panicked nervousness, watching the slow clock tick. When she came through the door, relief flooded me. She was mine again. Two days later, we make our way to the mountains.

The cabin is perfect—secluded from prying eyes, views that go on for miles, welcoming solid wood. I walk the circumference of the wraparound porch a full three times to bask in the glory. The setting is like paradise, our own little Eden tucked away in the North Carolina hills.

Lara takes the opportunity afforded by the privacy to walk around the cabin stark naked, as if doing so is the most natural thing in the world. I stare stupefied. The planned grocery run will keep.

Entwined together in bed, the random shadows cast by the bright but fading sun draw patterns across our skin. Lara snuggles closer to me, using both my body and the last remnants of the day's allotment of sunshine to keep herself warm. The mystery of light has always fascinated me. I was born a creature of the day, rising farm early, eager to experience the new horizons that burst anew with each sunrise. Somewhere along the way I became a creature of the night. Amber and Cale's murders accelerated the trend, but I blame the city. No one goes outside during the day in the city.

We finally make it to town to stock up on supplies. Lara sports a wig, glasses, and a Braves cap to hide her identity. The transformation works. I don't even recognize her. The charade excites me. It's as if I'm perpetuating a massive heist on an unsuspecting world—the possessor of secret knowledge that belongs to me alone.

Back at the cabin Lara wears the wig even when it's time for bed. "Pretend I'm someone else," she says. "Pretend you're someone else." The thought is a strange one for me. I've never been anyone other than myself. "You can be anyone you want to be," she adds to encourage me. "Who do you want to be?" I consider the question and land on an answer.

I want to be a man who is free from consequences.

Following Lara's lead, I embrace the role and submit to the power of imagination, both mine and hers. From far inside of myself, I see two strangers in the night play out their parts with reckless intensity, the woman firmly in control, slowly kidnapping the man and transporting him to places he has never before been.

***

Friday afternoon arrives. I sit on the back porch by myself, reading a book, enthralled with breathing the mountain air in a carefree environment. Living in the city surrounded by death has worn me down. I should've escaped much sooner.

A voice calls me into the cabin. Lara, the wig long gone, stands in the archway of the bedroom wearing a look of desire and nothing else. "Come here," she says, summoning me with her right index finger. I put the book down and do as I am told.

I dance with Lara on the bed in a series of unscripted movements. The motions are unhurried. Laughter and joy accompany our explorations. I savor each long kiss, thankful to no longer be alone. I lower myself on top on her and begin a gentle rhythm.

The mood in the room changes slightly without warning. My mind picks up on the subtle shift but is slow in sending any messages to the rest of my body. I continue my movement while the woman underneath me focuses on something else.

Lara asks, "Can I help you?"

She is not talking to me, and this detour is not one of her role-plays.

Someone else is in the room. The hairs on my neck stand up in full fear mode. I flash on possible weapons and strike out. I stop, turn, and see her. My first thought surprises me. She's beautiful. The metamorphosis from business dress to casual wear highlights her delightful face and the joyful perkiness of her personality.

She storms out of the room.

"Ella, wait!"

I throw on a pair of boxers and give chase. I make the front door as Ella nears her car.

"Wait!"

The gravel driveway cuts into my bare feet as I step across toward her.

"Ella, please!"

She turns to face me.

"What?"

That she speaks is a relief until I realize I have nothing to say. I just wanted her to stop, for everything to stop, for the world to go back to the way it was a few moments ago.

"What?" Her voice rises.

"I don't know."

She does her damnedest to avoid tears—burying her hurt to keep it below the surface. She resorts to anger instead. The contempt is chilling. She might as well be staring at Corey Miller.

"Look at yourself!"

I don't do it and keep my attention on her. The expression on my face reveals a painful authenticity—no filter, no calculated look, no mask. The message is a mystery to me, but it's real whatever it is. I have no control over anything out here. I'm naked.

"Look at yourself!"

This time I listen and take a self-inventory—no clothes except plaid underwear, goose bumps erupting on my cold flesh, and beat-up feet dying a slow death from a thousand cuts. The picture would be comedic in other contexts. But no one is smiling in this scene. Even worse, what I glimpse on the inside is far uglier than external appearances. I see a man exposed. Ella sees him, too.

She gets in her car, starts it up, and drives away. The tires kick up dust from the gravel, covering me in the grimy residue. I stand there in a sea of helplessness, too stunned to anticipate the myriad different ways the future could break from this point forward.

I drag myself back to the cabin.

21

We drive home from the mountains two days later. With every mile closer to the city, the weight on my chest bears down a little more. Ella's short visit cast a pall over the rest of the weekend. I never got around to finishing that book.

The maintenance of my secret now rests in the hands of a person slapped in the face by my betrayal. The uncertainty of what will happen Monday morning hovers over me like an unannounced jury verdict. I don't wait well. Bobby will run me out of the office on a rail if he learns the truth, and I fear that Lara will not hang around if I cannot deliver the justice I promised for her sister.

Looking over at her as she sleeps against the passenger window, I dive deep into the depths of my feelings toward this woman. Her presence next to me is no accident. Lara spent the week with me in that cabin instead of Ella for a reason. I chose Lara and may even love her. Sometimes things are that simple.

***

"What do you think she is going to do?"

Lara's words jolt me out of a faraway trance. I didn't realize she was awake. The last five minutes driving on dangerous mountain roads are an unrecollected blur. I wince in distress at my slippery grasp on events. Holding the steering wheel tighter, I answer the question.

"I don't know."

"A woman scorned."

"It's more complicated than that."

"That's what you think." Her words carry an authoritative tone that conveys the message that she knows of which she speaks. I wonder what man would ever be fool enough to reject Lara Landrum. I don't dare ask. She continues, "Will the D.A. take you off the case?"

"Yes."

"You better talk to her then."

I nod. Feeling vulnerable, I run my hand down her thigh for reassurance. A hint of a flinch follows, but she allows the hand to stay. I keep it there until the next curve of the road demands otherwise. I feel like a man living on borrowed time.

***

I knock on Ella's condo door shortly after returning to the city.

"It's you."

Her voice conveys no anger, just sadness. I follow her into the living room. We sit on opposite couches—the prosecution and the defense. The apartment's furnishings are sleek, stylish, sexy even. The whole vibe is one of promise and possibility. The contrast with my own furniture stuck to the past strikes me as somehow symbolic.

We measure each other. I pray she'll break the silence, but she's not budging. I taught her well. Make the other party state his position first. I say the only thing I can.

"I'm sorry."

"For what?"

Good question. I'm sorry I hurt Ella, but not for what I did. I'm mainly sorry she found me out.

"Everything."

"Not good enough. You don't get to come in here and offer a sorry-ass sorry and put everything back together again. You have a lot to answer for."

"I'm sorry for the man that I am then. I'm sorry that I'm weak and stupid. I'm sorry I hurt you. I never wanted that. I'm sorry my wife and son are dead. I'm sorry Lara is a witness in our murder case. I'm sorry the world is such a terrible place—me included. Sorriness follows me like a black cloud. I can't get away from it."

The force of my self-indictment knocks her back a bit. Her mood returns to sadness. We mourn in silence, avoid looking at the other, and sink under the feeling of what's unsaid. When our eyes again meet, a single tear runs down her left cheek.

"Why her?"

The answer probably has so many layers that I would never get to the bottom of it if I spent the rest of my life digging for the truth. Lara's own vulnerability played a part for sure—tragedy seeking out tragedy and all that. But I could've been happy with Ella. It didn't have to be Lara.

"I don't know."

She accepts that for a time, then observes, "She's very beautiful."

"So are you."

"She's white."

"*Ella*."

"Maybe you're a racist without even knowing it. How many white people have you put on death row?"

Her words are terribly unfair, but I keep my thoughts to myself. I deserve whatever censure she decides to dole out.

She again asks, "Then why?"

"I don't know."

More tears. Part of me longs to cry with her, but I can't. I didn't cry when Amber and Cale died, and I don't cry now.

"Here's the thing," Ella continues. "I waited for you. I gave you space. I gave you time. I knew you had to heal but believed that we would be together in the end. I felt it. I thought you felt it, too, that we had this silent understanding between us. Now I think everything was all in my imagination, that I was just some dumb lovestruck schoolgirl holding on to promises that were never made. I wasted two years of my life. Am I just a fool?"

"No. I had feelings for you. I still do. Maybe too strong feelings. I had feelings for you even before Amber died. Maybe guilt over that paralyzed me. I don't know. You're asking me to explain actions I cannot explain."

The part about Amber gets her attention—and mine. Not for the first time, pinpricks of conscience needle me, as if I willed Amber dead to begin a love affair with another woman. The feeling is hard to shake.

As if reading my thoughts, Ella reassures me, "You never did anything close to inappropriate. You were a good and faithful husband. You're the most strait-laced, by-the-book person I know, which is why …" She doesn't need to finish. The hurt is not only personal. I also failed her professionally as someone she looked up to.

I transition to the workplace side of the equation.

"I need to know what you're going to do tomorrow when you go into the office."

"I don't know."

The unknown hangs in the air. The beat of my heart reverberates inside my head. I'm here tonight because I want the case. Ella asks, "What should I do?"

"Tell Bobby."

"Your career in the D.A.'s office will be over. Bobby will have to get rid of you and hope the case doesn't get blown to hell."

She searches for wisdom out the window, wrestling internally with herself.

"I'll keep your secret." Agreeing to the falsehood, she becomes smaller and weaker, poisoned by my deceit. She is now my accomplice and not happy about it. I should resign, spare her this pain. But I won't. I can't. I made a promise to Lara.

"There are some conditions. You have to break it off with her. You can't keep sleeping with a witness. You know that. Also, she's my witness at trial. I'll take the responsibility for prepping her and I'll handle her questioning. You're too close to the situation. You need some distance from her."

"Those are reasonable terms."

"I have your word?"

"Yes."

Ella starts to walk me out. She says, "There's something else I need to tell you."

We stop.

"I told Scott."

Damn. I curse the prospect of another painful conversation in my future.

"Anyone else?"

She shakes her head.

We loiter together at the door. She kisses me. The driest, deadest meeting of lips ever. She places her hand on my chest—a touch of regret.

"Get out."

***

The second I enter my house, a knock bangs on the front door. Scott brushes in without so much as a hello.

I ask, "Were you staking me out?"

"Something like that."

He marches to the kitchen, opens the fridge, and grabs a beer from his previous stash. He studies me, takes a sip, and shakes his head. The disgust is plain. He takes another drink, and it begins.

"Anything you want to tell me?"

"I know you know, so say whatever it is you want to say."

"Okay. I'll say it. I've been saying you need to get laid for a while now, but I didn't mean for you to do it with a witness. And not some witness in some random case, but a witness in the most high-profile murder investigation we've ever had together. And not some just random witness in our otherwise high-profile murder, but the most high-profile witness in the case, who also happens to be one of the most famous women on the planet. What the hell were you thinking?"

"How long did you work on that?"

"Shut up! This is serious."

"I understand that."

A stare down commences.

"Well, are you going to explain yourself?"

"What is there to say?"

Driving home from Ella's condo, I took it on faith that Scott would shield me. Now my faith waivers.

He asks, "So you talked to Ella, I gather?"

"I did."

"What did she say?"

I relay the substance of the conversation, including Ella's conditions for me to stay on the Barton case.

He responds, "She changed her tune from when we talked. You must have sweet-talked her good. As worked up as she was the other night, I didn't figure her to keep your little secret. I guess you expect me to do the same?"

"I have no expectations."

He grunts and paces around the room.

Stopping, he swings around and asks, "Did Ella tell you everything?"

"As far as I know."

Examining me closely, he concludes, "I didn't think so."

"What?"

"We slept together."

My heart stops. His eyes dare me to make an issue of it. He itches for a fight I cannot win. I have no claim to Ella, no standing at all, nothing that would make her off-limits to my friends. The mere suggestion is grotesque. But the heart is a funny, ugly thing. Scott's words are a punch to the gut. Stress fills my body, my face flushes, and I lose a little feeling in my hands.

Scott notes the change in me and smirks.

"Calm down, lover boy. I didn't sleep with her, but I should have."

"She wouldn't have an ugly brute like you anyway."

"Maybe she will with you out of the picture."

"That'll be the day."

My breathing returns to normal. Despite my unclean hands, my relationship with Scott would never have been the same had he slept with Ella. I know it. He knows it. The hypocrisy astounds. Jealousy is a green-eyed monster.

The detour into jocularity also means that my secret is safe with Scott. The net of my wrongdoing keeps capturing accomplices. The burden of jeopardizing the careers of Scott and Ella adds to the weight on my shoulders. I tell myself again I should quit the case.

Scott changes the subject, "Have you talked to your girlfriend about Ella's demands?"

"Not yet."

"What if she doesn't want to go along with them?"

"Is there any other choice?"

"No, there isn't."

He points at me for emphasis.

I walk him out. As he stands at the front door, he turns and asks, "So, what's she like in bed?"

"You've got to be kidding me."

"No, seriously."

"Get out."

***

I call Lara afterwards and relay Ella's conditions for staying on the case. I don't mention anything about Scott.

Lara responds, "I'll sleep with who I damn well want to sleep with."

The response starts a longer argument. I explain to her all the reasons why Ella is right. I point out that the relationship risks the case and her value as a witness. I mention the media frenzy that would consume us both if word leaked. I ask her if she wants to see Barton walk free. None of these attempts at persuasion work.

"Look, I will not have other people telling me what I can and cannot do. I still want to see you, and I don't want to be shut out like this. Nothing has changed from before. One other person knows. That's it. She's already agreed to protect your secret. We'll be careful."

This level of resistance throws me for a loop. She's accustomed to getting everything she wants, and being told "no" exposes in her a healthy dose of entitlement. That Ella is the one dictating the terms only makes it worse.

With a note of finality, I dictate, "It's just not possible now. After the trial, we can do what we want."

She answers, "I'm coming over."

She hangs up. Repeated calls back go straight to her voicemail. I consider texting, but decide—like a knowing criminal—that the less in writing the better. I just wait.

When the knock comes, it does not originate from where I expect it. She's at the backdoor. I'll give her that.

"Let me in before someone sees me."

"We cannot do this."

She barges in anyway and plops herself on the couch in the living room. I remain standing.

"Why are you here?"

"Come to me." She pats a spot next to her on the couch. I resist for a few seconds, but eventually relent. The combative person on the phone is gone. The person next to me is all sweetness and light.

She grabs my hand and says, "Look, I love you. I haven't found love in a long time, and I don't want to lose that. Bernard has already stolen my sister from me. He's not going to take you away, too. I want you by my side, and you want me by your side. After everything we've been through, we're entitled to that little bit of happiness."

No one is this good an actress. Earlier in the day, I told myself that I might love this woman. Do I? I don't know. Love is a word of many meanings. Ella asked, "Why her?" The answer eludes me, except that I like the way I feel when I'm around Lara. Is that love? For whatever reason, Ella never pulled me out of the abyss. Lara did. That distinction between the two explains everything.

I say, "I love you, too."

The right decision would be to walk away from the Barton trial. I won't do it. I want the case too much, both for myself and Lara. I'm gambling my relationships with Scott and Ella for her. I'm gambling my career. But the prize in front of me is worth the risk.

We embrace and head to the bedroom.

22

With Corey Miller stashed away on death row, the focus at work turns full bore to Bernard Barton. An upcoming scheduling conference will set a firm date, but my guess is that the trial will occur within the next two months. That sounds like a lot of time, but in a case of this magnitude, no minute will go to waste. My calendar is clear. All other matters have been farmed out to my lieutenants. Barton is my business and nothing else.

Ella and I meet to divide up our responsibilities. We don't mention the other night at her apartment, but its presence occupies the whole room all the same.

As we talk, a subtle shift in the power dynamic between us occurs without specific acknowledgment. I'm still the boss, but her leverage over me affords her all the power. She pushes me on a few points, more than ever before, and I yield. Her tone throughout is business-like, formal, and distant. But we're still working together on the case. I chalk that up as a win.

***

Judge Mary Woodcomb welcomes Millwood and me into her chambers. She sat on the bench for my first trial ever and treated me with much-appreciated gentleness. Sometimes when we see each other away from the courthouse, she reminds me of that trial and congratulates me on how far I've come. She was also the only judge to attend Amber and Cale's funeral. Mary is one of the good ones.

The three of us gather to discuss the scheduling of the Barton trial. Mary's office suite features a little sitting area, and she joins us there for the discussion, eschewing the big desk and other trappings that typically accompany the judicial role. I contrast her with the incompetent

Judge Ross and say a silent hallelujah of thanks that Woodcomb's steady hand will steer the ship of the trial.

"What dates are we thinking, fellas?"

Millwood answers, "As soon as possible. My client is innocent and needs justice sooner rather than later. We're ready to go tomorrow. We'll make a speedy trial demand if we have to."

The judge smiles at Millwood's puffery and directs the next question to me, "What about the State?"

"Tomorrow might be a bit quick, but Bobby told me to go full steam ahead on this one. My calendar is clear."

Mary's knowing nod shows her understanding of the importance of good publicity for a district attorney in an election year. She takes out her calendar and does some mental calculations before writing down a few notes. Then she asks, "Will you guys be ready to start five weeks from now?" We both affirm yes.

"All right, that date is yours. I'm writing it down in ink. Short of a plea, consider this date set in concrete. Speak now or forever hold your peace." She gives us a moment to object, but neither of us takes her up on it. "Okay, we're set. Any chance of a plea?"

Millwood jumps in, "None."

The judge responds, "That was certainly heartfelt. Anything else then?"

I say, "Cameras?"

Mary whistles and asks, "How famous do the three of us want to be? Thoughts?"

"Your courtroom, your rules," offers Millwood.

Woodcomb nods and turns to me expecting my feelings on the matter since I'm the one who brought it up. I shrug my shoulders and say only, "I'm agnostic."

"That's helpful," she retorts. "Is Lara Landrum going to testify?"

"She is."

Mary considers the issue, then says, "Public interest will be high, and I'm of the mind that seeing two skilled and ethical advocates like the both of you will do the public some good. I'll let the cameras in. Let's all put our best foot forward."

I quip, "The nightly crime shows thank you for the ratings boost and the free programming."

Mary groans, "No kidding. I can't watch those things. They're terrible. But I hear Nancy Grace is worth $30 million now, so maybe the joke's on me. Anyway, if the trial is going to be on television, then we don't have to worry about witness sequestration. What about the jury? Should we sequester them?"

Jurors get sequestered to avoid the taint of outside publicity affecting their deliberative process. And this case will be swimming in publicity.

I answer, "If the defendant gets to go home every night, then the jurors should, too."

The thought of otherwise bored jurors talking about the trial at the end of each day doesn't sit well with me. Even a strong case can be henpecked to death over time. I don't need some clever juror going Henry Fonda in *Twelve Angry Men* on me every night.

Mary responds, "What do you think, Jack?"

"That's fine."

Millwood and I stand to take our leave. Before we get out of there, Mary asks, "Is this the first time you two have faced off?"

"Yes ma'am," I answer.

"He's good, Jack. Better watch yourself. I was there for his first trial. He has come a long way."

"He should be good. He had the best teacher around."

"Yep," I say, "My dad was the best."

We all laugh at the joke. Woodcomb knows the long history between Millwood and me. We're all friends here—even as we carry out our very different professional roles.

The meeting adjourns. Five weeks. We'll be ready. As I walk to my office, Mary's confident observation that I'm an ethical lawyer stings me for my duplicity. I'm letting more people down than I even realize. But the die is cast. The only thing I can do now is win.

23

Scott and I decide to pay Brice Tanner a visit. Unable to find a phone number for him, our visit will be unannounced. The drive to Brasstown Bald in the north Georgia mountains should take a couple of hours.

Scott asks, "How you getting along without the actress?"

I wondered if he would broach the topic. I look out the passenger side window to hide my face before answering.

"Fine, I suppose. It never should've happened."

"Do you love her?"

I consider the question and try to calculate the best answer to put the issue to bed.

"I loved sleeping with her."

"I bet you did."

The envy dripping from his voice could fill a lake. My response—purposely couched in the past tense—has its desired effect. He's now thinking about Lara naked. I'll let him bask in the fantasy as long as he wants. I start to visualize her naked, too.

He asks, "How did it happen?"

"How did what happen?"

"How did the two of you hook up in the first place?"

One thing I've learned from a career of studying witnesses is that a good liar never departs more than necessary from the truth. "Keep it simple, stupid" is good advice for whole swaths of life. It is excellent advice for one looking to successfully lie. I tell the truth.

"I think she learned about Amber and Cale somehow. She called me up to talk about how to deal with her grief. We had dinner. One thing led to another."

"She went to you for grief counseling? Could she have made a worse choice?"

The words come out harsher than he intended, but he said what he said all the same. He is not necessarily wrong. I told Lara myself that I make a bad grief counselor. But Scott's impolite words create an opportunity to put an end to the conversation. I feign more offense than I feel—exploiting what happened to Amber and Cale as an artifice to hide my continuing sin.

"I'm sorry about that," he says.

"Just drive."

***

The address we have for Brice takes us along a deserted dirt road deep into the Georgia hills. As we drive further away from civilization, I begin to have *Deliverance* flashbacks.

I ask Scott, "Is your gun loaded?"

"Always."

We finally arrive at a glorified shack. I check the number on the mailbox twice to make sure. It's a match. I shake my head and move to disembark.

"Wait," Scott says.

He opens his glove box and takes out a holster holding another gun. He hands it to me.

"Just in case."

I retort, "You have a shotgun in the trunk? We may need that, too."

"You think so? I can get it."

I'm unsure if he is serious. I strap the holster to my hip, remove the gun, and familiarize myself with it. If you're going to carry a gun, you better damn well know how to use it. Satisfied, I re-holster the weapon, safety on. Scott and I tread lightly toward the house. He leaves the shotgun in the trunk.

Our uneasiness outsizes any risk we have actually perceived. The gun hangs heavy on me. Just knowing it is there makes me itchy. I hope for his sake Brice doesn't emerge with some kind of weapon. He wouldn't survive the encounter. I wonder about the recusal rules when a prosecutor shoots a witness. Millwood would have a field day with that one.

Scott bangs on the front door and yells out Brice's name. No answer. I peek into a dirty window to see whatever I might see. The inside of the building appears to be in worse shape than the outside, as if one of those deranged hoarders on television has lived here for the past twenty years. That we may have the wrong place seems certain until I smell the pungent scent of marijuana. I sniff to make sure.

"I smell it, too," says Scott.

I see an ashtray full of discarded weed on a massive pile of dog-eared paperbacks—mostly Westerns from the look of it. None of the joints in the ashtray appear lit, but the aroma is fresh enough to indicate current habitation.

We make our way around back to check the temperature there, Scott in the lead. A noise arises directly ahead of him. I freeze. I know that sound. Scott does not and asks, "What's that?" I search for the source and locate it two feet from him. Another step and Scott will be in a world of pain.

"Don't move a single muscle."

He's smart enough to know that this is not a drill. He freezes his body immediately in response to my command. He does allow his eyes to trace my line of sight to the object that captivates my attention. The rattle of the rattlesnake continues to warn, indicating that a decision on whether it should strike Scott remains up for a vote.

The gun is in my hand now. I ease into the shot so as not to startle the rattler with any sudden movement. Safety off, I squeeze the trigger. The boom of the explosion shatters the serenity of the otherwise quiet woods. The rattler dies an immediate death. Scott refuses to move for a while out of an abundance of caution. When he finally allows himself to stand down, he unleashes a string of profanity so poetic that it is positively Shakespearean in its lyrical quality.

Upon this scene, a hapless Brice pops out of the woods and scares the wits out of us. We return the favor by pointing our guns at him.

He squeals, "What did I do?"

Thankfully we don't shoot—the day's quota on killing already paid in full. We lower our weapons.

***

The man before us cannot be the same person Scott interviewed at the police station a few months back. For starters, he looks like he has never had a haircut or a shave in his entire life. I didn't realize hair could grow that fast. The only recognizable features are the timid eyes and the high-pitched voice. Those remain. Not for the first time I wonder why Sara Barton set her sights on him. Scott introduces me, and I explain we just want to talk.

Brice says, "Um, I guess we can talk, but you can't come into the house."

"We know about the dope," I answer. "We don't care. That's not why we're here. The reason we're here is to find out why you're here."

"I don't understand."

I search for a place to sit down outside. Like Brice, I want to avoid going into that house. A clearing ahead offers a few chairs—the green metal chairs emblematic of the country. I used to sit with my grandfather in chairs like these, watching him whittle a stick, a routine scene of a happy childhood. I smile at a memory I haven't come across in over twenty years. The chairs are rusted, but still retain their country strength. We all take a seat.

I ask, "Why did you quit Marsh & McCabe?"

"Couldn't do it anymore, man, the whole billable hour thing, keeping track of my day in six-minute increments. It's inhuman. Had to get away."

"How did you end up here?"

"Got a deal on the place."

No doubt. Houses that fail to meet code tend to sell for a discount. Brice probably paid cash, obviating any need for a loan or any appraisals. I don't envision many lenders signing off on this property as good collateral.

"You look different," I note.

"Got tired of presenting myself in the way other people wanted to see me. Life's too short for that. Who says I can't have long hair? Who says I can't grow a beard?"

Who says you can't bathe? Maybe he smokes marijuana to mask his stench. Scott's eyes may roll out of his head. The happy hippie act never gets far with him. Brice comes across as the dumb college student who thinks non-conformity is the way to stick it to the Man. But the performance lacks sincerity. He sounds like someone trying to convince himself of something he doesn't believe.

I say, "Here's the thing, Brice. Bernard Barton is going to say that you quit your job, came up here to get away from the world, and turned yourself into Grizzly Adams because you have a guilty conscience after killing Sara."

This alternative explanation for his self-exile from civilization shakes him out of his stoned dimwittedness.

"I didn't kill her!"

"I know, but the defense is going to make it look like you did."

Brice presents me with a tough decision. He's going to testify at the trial. The question is whether I call him to the stand or whether Millwood does. I don't need Brice to get the video of Sara and him together at the law firm party into evidence. Truth be told, I don't really need him for anything. But I want to avoid the jury thinking that I'm hiding Brice from them. An attorney should almost always deliver his own bad news.

And Brice is bad news. He was the dead woman's lover. He was at her house the night before the murder. He has no alibi. He lived within walking distance of the murder scene. Those are objective, hard facts.

"Do I have to testify?"

"If subpoenaed, yes."

"What if I never accept the subpoena?"

The hint of a bad idea flickers in his face. He considers disappearing. But Barton's money guarantees Brice would not disappear for long. Throw out enough dollars, and those bounty hunters can find anyone. I need to nip these incipient thoughts in the bud. Running away will not end well for Brice.

"Don't even think about it. They'll find you. They always do. Hiding only serves to make you look guilty as hell. There's no upside in it."

Sitting across from him now, the decision I'm debating decides itself. Brice is a bomb that I must detonate myself. I'll soften his rough edges and preemptively take some sting out of Millwood's cross-examination. Brice graduated from Emory Law School and worked for one of Atlanta's biggest law firms. He isn't a total idiot. I can make this work, but first I need some more answers.

Changing the tone of the conversation, I tell him, "You lied to the police about whether you knew Sam Wilkins or not." The comment is a statement, not open for debate.

"No, I didn't."

"Yes, you did," Scott chimes in, marking his first participation in the conversation since sitting down. His silence up to this point adds firmness to his words. Brice contemplates another denial, but knows from the impatience on our faces that we won't be having any of it. He picks another plan.

"What of it?"

Scott responds, "Liars always have something to hide."

"Not me. She was getting a divorce to be with me. He was her divorce lawyer. That's all."

Scott continues the assault, "Was that all?"

Dark clouds gather behind Brice's baby blue eyes. That's the thing with Brice. A lingering hard edge—not quite rage, more like a bubbling seething—reveals itself when you prod the right nerve. With annoyance on his face, he answers, "Don't know what you're getting at. I don't know how the two of them knew each other. I just know that he was her lawyer."

He is lying, and all three of us know it. I tally the potential damage in my head. Brice's lie about Sam is a good lie, as long as he can defend it. Any testimony that Sam was having sex with Sara would blow up the case. That affair is still on the down low, and I pray it stays there. I need Brice's lie to hold.

Scott presses on, "Why did you lie to me in the police station then?"

"I didn't lie. I forgot the name of her lawyer in the heat of the moment. That's all. It's not easy being questioned by the police, you know."

It could work. Millwood faces obstacles showing Sam and Sara Barton were even lovers, much less that Brice knew about the affair.

If Brice sticks to his story and keeps himself emotionally in check if asked about it, his denial should be unimpeachable. At trial, a lie is not a lie unless it can be shown to be a lie. The truth doesn't matter if Millwood can't prove it.

Scott assesses Brice's explanation and decides to let the matter drop. If Brice insists on claiming that Sam was only Sara Barton's divorce lawyer, we gain no advantage in educating him otherwise. But we're not finished with Brice. Sam was just the warm-up act. Brice's arrest for stalking an ex-girlfriend in college—conveniently mentioned during Monica Haywood's interrogation—still demands an explanation. Scott found the original arrest report. Now we need to hear the story from Brice's own lips.

Scott says, "Okay, Brice. Now we need to ask you why you stalked Brittany Wood."

Another nerve exposed. Brice slumps into a pose of defeated disbelief. Not enough weed in the world exists to deaden his pain of hearing that name again. He looks away, far off into the deep forest. I follow his gaze but see nothing but trees. After a couple of deep breaths, Brice finally speaks.

"How do you know about her?"

"I'm a detective. It's my job to find out things."

Brice doesn't appreciate the comment. Scott's glare challenges him to make something of it. The standoff does me no good. I jump in, "Monica Haywood told us." I need Brice to focus his anger in the right direction. For better or worse, we're all on the same team now. Brice considers this new information with great distaste.

"Skag," he snorts, "but how did she find out?"

I answer, "Bernard Barton is on the Board of Bar Examiners."

The significance of his application to join the state bar dawns on him, and the hatred oozing from his pores toward Barton strikes me as powerfully authentic. Brice now fully understands we have a mutual enemy.

"Unethical bastard," he mutters.

True enough.

I continue, "So the bad guys know about your past, which is why we need to know everything you can tell us about whatever happened with Brittany."

He takes a deep breath.

"We met as freshmen. I was her first serious boyfriend. She was my first serious girlfriend. We loved each other crazy-like, but we fought a bunch. We broke up, got back together, broke up again. During one of these break-ups, I was following her around trying to talk to her. She called the police to get back at me, claimed I was stalking her. I was arrested. She never pursued it further, we got back together, and the prosecutor wasn't interested in the case. I mean, I was just walking around campus. That's it. It was nothing. I got it expunged. Still had to report it to the bar. That stuff is supposed to be confidential."

He leaks a bit more bitterness as I review the police report. The document is scant on details, saying only that the arrestee was following Ms. Wood around and refused her multiple requests to leave her alone, leading her to call the police. When the police arrived, Brice was still following her around, culminating in the arrest. As stalking goes, it's pretty light. I can see why the prosecutor wasn't clamoring to pursue the case.

The mug shot is the worst part. The close-up, invariably taken in unflattering light, shows unkempt hair, unbalanced eyes, and an unfriendly mouth. The visual contrast among Attorney Brice, Mountain Man Brice, and Mug Shot Brice mystifies me. Who is this guy?

I go back to Sara Barton. She was a beautiful woman. Plenty of men would've jumped at the chance to bed her, and yet she landed on Brice. Maybe after living daily with the insufferable arrogance of Bernard Barton for so long, Sara sought refuge in the neediness of weaker men like Brice and Sam. It's a theory.

Scott asks, "If we talked to her today, what would Brittany say about you?"

"Nothing. She's dead."

That gets our attention. Scott crosses his arms and stares at Brice with incredulity before saying, "Do tell."

"I thought it was your job to find things out, Mr. Detective."

And Jesus wept.

The marijuana must be wearing off, making Brice cranky. The trace of a throbbing vein in Scott's temple flares with each breath. Like a good lawyer, a good cop is part actor. But I doubt the reaction is an act. Already rattled from the snake encounter, Scott has zero tolerance for insults from some dopehead attorney living like a mountain beatnik. My eyes plead with Scott not to go nuclear on him. We need the dopehead to get Barton.

Scott says, "Listen, Mr. Smart Ass, I have a good friend at the DEA who would be quite interested in the dope house you got going over there. One call, that's all. And you know the feds. They love drug charges and aren't happy unless they throw at least twenty-five counts into an indictment. You could be looking at twenty to thirty years. Now, do you want to answer our questions in a pleasant manner or would you rather answer the DEA's questions in federal lock-up?"

Brice pouts at Scott like a defiant teenager whose only defense against authority is hostility. But Brice is also a lawyer who should know that Scott has him by the balls.

Scott demands, "Well?"

"I'll answer."

Let's call that a teaching moment.

I hope that Brittany Wood's death isn't an unsolved murder. Two murdered women in the vicinity of the same lover carries coincidence beyond its stretching point. Even if Brice were in another country at the time, Millwood would find a way to pin Brittany's killing on him.

"Brittany died in a car wreck. Somebody was texting and driving and killed her."

"When?"

"The middle of our senior year. She never even graduated. It was sad."

We all pay a respectful silence to the late Brittany Wood—another random victim of God's Cosmic Wheel of Fate. The illusive shadow of Mr. Smith teases me, as hard to catch in the forest as he is in the city. Why Amber and Cale? Why Brittany? Why anyone?

Scott brings me back to the present, "Anything else?" He is talking to me. If we leave now, we might beat the worst of afternoon traffic. The woods are quiet. Too quiet. A person living alone up here could easily lose his mind. I assess the disheveled mess of a person sitting across from me and make a plea for him to clean himself up.

"Brice, I need you to testify at trial, and I cannot put you on the stand the way you're looking now. This is not the image you want to present to the world at the moment the whole world is watching you."

"I don't care what people think about me. I don't even see why I have to testify. I don't know anything."

"That doesn't matter. Bernard Barton is on trial for murder and has already started throwing the blame your way. Why do you think Monica Haywood told us about your stalking arrest? You're their fall guy. Barton's lawyer is one of the best around. If I don't call you to the stand, he will. We need to be teammates here. You owe Sara that much. Barton beat her, and then he killed her. Because of *you*. Are you going to let him get away with it? Or are you going to avenge the woman you loved?"

The appeal to his thirst for revenge is nakedly cynical. Whatever works. I have a murder trial to win.

Brice nods.

24

My brother Ben calls with "some bad news." Mom crashed her car into a tree. The breathing in my chest catches—one of those instances in life when you wonder if everything you've ever known is about to change forever. I've already buried one parent. I'm in no hurry to bury another.

"How bad?"

"The car died. Mom didn't."

Thank goodness. But she did earn herself a stay in the hospital with a broken collarbone and soreness everywhere else. I shudder at the thought of her on pain pills. She enjoys her wine a little too much.

I ask, "Do we need to take her keys?"

"I don't know. She says a deer ran out in front of her."

"Plausible, I suppose."

"Yeah. She's asking for you, by the way, wondering if now you may actually come and visit her."

Within the hour, I head south on the interstate to my boyhood home ninety minutes away. Breaking the news to Lara fills me with anticipatory dread, even though I'll only be gone for a few days. The anxiety is stifling and suggests an unfamiliar neediness that threatens to take over my life. I loved Amber madly, but I never lost control of my own identity. Lara is different. I feel stripped of all volition with her.

I call from the road and give her the news.

She responds, "You shouldn't be alone during a time like this. I'll come down tomorrow to keep your company."

"What? You shouldn't—"

"Give me the address. I'll be there early evening."

The idea is galactically stupid, but I keep that objection to myself, opting instead to sink deeper with her into the quicksand.

The rest of the drive down gives me time to contemplate the relationship. The trepidation I felt earlier about leaving Lara for a few days yields to a rising foreboding that her eagerness to join me portends something darker—that the cure of being together is worse than the disease of being apart. But why? Forget the actress stuff. The fame is a nuisance, full of sound and fury but signifying nothing. Lara is just like any other woman, filled with the same hopes, needs, and frailties. Perhaps the problem lies there. She is too real. Contrasted with Amber's perfection—a myth that only grows over time—Lara's imperfection sets my instincts on edge. She remains to me a mystery.

Or maybe the trouble is closer to home. Attachment frightens me because it portends the possibility of more loss. The monastic quality of my life these past couple of years shielded me from the risk of experiencing another heartbreak—something Ella knows all too well. But the monastery doors didn't hold, and the monk sinned. The woman isn't the problem; it's the man. I need only look in the mirror to confirm the diagnosis. Lara didn't repair the destruction unleashed by Mr. Smith. She only provided a distraction. The broken man is still broken. The possibility that Lara is a mere diversion leads the broken man to a sobering thought. Is it the sex? Has it always been just about the sex?

The car ride resolves nothing. Amber is dead. Lara is alive. But what am I? I am still the broken man.

I arrive too late to visit Mom tonight. I sit in her living room, the place all to myself for one of the few times in my life. The chirp of crickets carries me back to a time long ago. I learned in high school that the average lifespan of a cricket is three months. What's the point? The meaninglessness of it all strikes me as profoundly sad. Some purpose exists in God's grand plan, I'm sure. But the cricket will never know. It lives only to die.

Lara will arrive tomorrow, and I'll make love to her in the same house where I lost my virginity. That strikes me as meaningless, too.

***

"Why do I almost have to die before you will come down and visit me?"

"I love you, too, Mom."

Guilt comes in many forms, but a mother's guilt has its own special flavor. The guilt here packs a little extra punch because it is well earned. I haven't been a good son. Seeing Mom in this condition hammers home that truth. I can blame the murders, but losing Amber and her grandson delivered its own searing emotional trauma to Mom. No man is an island. I forget that I'm not the only survivor.

To compensate, I put on my Good Son hat for the day. I buy some tabloid magazines to catch her up on the latest gossip, watch gawd awful morning talk shows with her, and sneak her some Chick-Fil-A to spare her from the hospital food. Her request for wine meets a firm denial. When her friends stop by, I shed the cynicism of the city and adopt the manners of the country, performing with perfection my role in the Southern ritual of "visiting." Eventually, as inevitable as death and taxes, she gets around to talking about the case.

"When's the trial?"

"Three weeks."

"On TV?"

"Yep."

Mom smiles. Genuine excitement fills her face only to dissolve into a kind of wistfulness as she turns to look out the window. A single tear travels a path from her left eye down her cheek, puzzling me. I consider asking her about it but decide to give her space. Mom will tell me in her good time.

"It'll be just like watching your father again. I used to go into town and watch his trials. My husband—the star of the courthouse. It made be so proud, made me feel so special. He'd be so proud of you, you know. So proud." She pauses before asking, "Are you as good as they say?"

"Probably not."

"Never took you to be the modest one. That's more Ben's line."

We laugh and return to a comfortable silence. She'll be asleep soon.

She's fighting it, but her body will demand it of her directly. I already promised to come back tomorrow, so I'm free to leave when she drifts into unconsciousness. Ben has been doing a funeral all day and will visit her tonight. Lara is due to leave Atlanta soon, giving me a few hours to stock up on supplies. She can't exactly be seen around town.

Mom asks, "Do you ever see Lara Landrum?"

"Sometimes."

"She seems nice."

"I told her about your accident. She's thinking about stopping by to see how you're doing."

"Stop it."

Sarcasm always infects our dialogue. That's just how the two of us communicate with each other. The habit is so ingrained that neither one of us even takes notice. It's part of the fabric of our relationship—something unique that belongs to us and no one else. Ben marvels at our interactions and worries so much about it that he prays for Mom and me to get along better. The prayers must've worked. The Prodigal Son has returned home.

"Ella is doing the direct examination of Lara Landrum at trial."

"What! It should be you. That's the biggest moment. It should be you."

"We have our reasons. Ella is real good at relating to female witnesses. It's a pivotal moment and needs a woman's touch."

"Nuts."

That's her pet phrase when she desires to express vehement disagreement with whatever you just said. I break the news to her today to avoid having to answer questions about it later. Now she has a few weeks to adjust to her disappointment before Lara testifies. But she's not having any of it now. The heaviness of her eyes can't mask her feelings of disgust.

I assure her, "You'll still see plenty of me on your bigscreen TV."

"Nuts."

She falls asleep.

***

Evening comes. The sun is long gone, but the residual light left behind offers its last breaths to illuminate the country around me. I rock on the front porch, waiting for Lara, hoping that she doesn't get lost without cell service somewhere in middle Georgia. Every vehicle that passes dashes my expectations and turns up the volume on my worrying. The door to the detached garage stands open, ready to hide her car as quickly as possible. In a small town, gossip is the most valuable currency and even the trees have eyes. Her coming is a needless risk in an ongoing cycle of needless risks. We've already been caught once. I won't survive a second discovery.

When she pulls into the driveway, I direct her to the open garage and hurry to close it behind us. I breathe easier with the evidence out of sight. I grab the bags and shield her from the road as we make our way to the house. I show her the powder room and collapse on the couch, feeling as though I could sleep for days. I awake from a momentary nap when she asks, "So what now?"

I ask, "Hungry?"

"Not for food."

The eyes dance. Where does she get the energy? The import of her words should excite me, but the impact falls flat. The realization that I barely know this woman hammers me, like I'm playing the most dangerous game of my life without even knowing the rules. I need some answers.

"Why are you here? Be honest. Tell me."

She is dumbstruck. The dancing eyes turn sad. She sits in a chair and stares into the flameless fireplace. I wait her out. She finally fixes her attention back to me.

"I have nowhere else to go."

The tears follow. She moves to the couch to be held. I oblige. She is every bit the lonely woman I took her to be at Sara Barton's funeral. The implications of her loneliness suffocate me. Two messed up people, mutually co-dependent, carrying out a secret affair with a looming murder trial in the background—the prospect of catastrophe appears a matter of when, not if.

I embrace her for longer than I would like. The ritualistic chirping of the crickets ushers in a new evening. Last night that familiar sound of my youth supplied me with a small dose of melancholic nostalgia. Now the chirps grate on my nerves. The steady drumbeat thumps louder and louder in my head, like an Edgar Allan Poe story where the guilty man cannot run away from his beating heart. I break the silence to thwart the march of the crickets.

"Are you going to act again?"

"I've been working nonstop for fifteen years. Since Sara died, I can't do it anymore. I have nothing left to give."

I hear the words, but I'm not really listening, content that her voice drowns out the outside noise. For the sake of my sanity, I keep the conversation going.

"Don't you have friends in Hollywood?"

"No! That place is a bunch of vipers! The men want to grope you and trade parts for sex. The women are worse. They're mean, shallow, and vengeful gossips. They'd sell you out in a second if it meant a better part for them. Everything's so fake. I loathe it with all my being. I sold my house when I was out there and don't ever intend to go back."

The sneering vehemence surprises me. I've never really asked about her career before, figuring she gets that kind of talk enough. I know without probing that her disgust stems from personal experience—intensely personal experience.

She goes on, "Remember the night we first made love? I told you that you were real. Well, you *are* real. That's why I'm here. You're the only real thing in my life right now. I can't handle the fake anymore. I need real. I need you."

I don't feel very real. And a relationship that has no outside identity apart from its own cocoon doesn't ring the bell of authenticity. But I'm tired. I pushed for answers and now regret doing so. She's too heavy for me at this moment. To change the mood, I suggest some s'mores.

Dubious at first, Lara's face brightens by the light of the firepit in the backyard. I give her a stick, supplies, and instructions. Her unencumbered joy at roasting marshmallows over an open flame restores a measure of my lost hope in the universe. We laugh—the burnt marshmallow, chocolate, and graham crackers rescuing the evening.

Lara asks, "Can we make another one?"

"We need to get inside before the storm hits."

"How you can tell a storm is coming?"

"I can smell it."

One of the skills you develop growing up in the country is an innate ability to detect the gathering storm. The process defies description. You just know. We retreat back inside, and I send her off to take a quick shower before the weather arrives.

A back staircase, missed by most visitors, takes me to the attic. It's one of those old-time attics with high ceilings, a generous-sized window, and a space that spans the house from end to end. The attic could pass for a room, but calling it an attic adds an intoxicating layer of mystery to what is one of my favorite places in the entire world. Little has changed. The rest of my family never cared for the space. As a result, the attic belonged to me alone. Even today it reflects the decorating choices I made a long time ago.

I sit on the old couch and soak in the atmosphere. Dust particles from last century populate the furniture. An old weight set sits in the corner. A drum kit—like all drum kits, begging to be played—stands in front of the window. A bowling ball and bowling pins lie behind a chest, remnants of a doomed attempt to convert the site into a bowling alley. All kids should have such a place—somewhere creative, free, and unrestricted by adult norms. I miss those days but appreciate that I was lucky to have them.

The creak of the stairs previews Lara's arrival. She glances around the room with perfunctory interest before walking with purpose straight my way. She wears a short silk bathrobe about ten sizes too small. She reaches the couch, sheds her covering onto the floor, and drops to her knees on top of it. She removes my shoes, my socks, my jeans, my boxers, my inhibitions. The excitement I feel rises, and her expert handling of me generates the expected response.

She straddles me and begins gyrating up and down in tempo with the steady rain. I close my eyes, listening to the water pound the roof, recalling my days as a drummer to keep the beat with the rhythm of her movements. The melody is slow and steady. Thunder rattles the house the moment I finish, driving out the sound of the drums in my head. She lays her head on my chest for a few seconds, kisses me for the first time since entering the room, puts her bathrobe back on, and strolls out the way she came, having never said a word since coming up the stairs. I trace her path throughout the house based on the sounds of the floor underneath her feet. The rain pelts hard on the attic window.

25

After spending another morning keeping company with Mom in the hospital, I drive up to the house and see my brother's car in the driveway. My stomach drops. Maybe Lara is hiding in a closet. I park and walk in, not knowing what I'm going to find.

They sit together in the living room. Lara greets me cheerfully. My brother gives me a look of confused wonder.

I say, "Lara, Ben. Ben, Lara."

"We've met," Ben says, adding, "I came over to get my weedeater."

The weedeater. Great.

"Ben was just telling me what you were like when you were growing up. I love small towns. I wish I had a nice place like this to call home."

"I don't get back enough," I observe.

Ben says, "You're right, you don't. But I'm glad you're here now. A couple I'm going to marry next month is joining Sally, the kids, and me for dinner. We could probably fit a place for the two of you if you're interested. I know the kids would love to see you."

Lara's slight smile reflects her curiosity as to how I will respond to my brother's invitation. I am not so sanguine. Knowing that my deceit now extends to my family only makes things worse. Lara should never have come here.

"Tonight's not a good night."

"I understand. You can walk me out then. Lara, it was a pleasure meeting you. Don't be a stranger."

We exit and face each other under the oak tree in the front yard—the site of so many adventures together in decades past. This oak tree was here when our father was a little boy and will likely stand after the both of us are gone. The thought provides a strange comfort. This tree cares not a whit about my problems. Life goes on.

"Why is she in Mom's house?"

"Witness prep for the Sara Barton murder trial. A lot of paparazzi follow her in the city. It's a distraction. I figured we wouldn't be bothered too much down here."

My answer actually solicits a laugh. Was it that ridiculous? But Ben is a hard one to fool. Ministry has prepared him well to sniff out mendacity.

"Don't lie to me."

The words are not harsh. They never are. Compassion shows in his face. Ben is Jesus in the flesh—gentle, faithful, humble, grace-filled, a true servant through and through. He delivers an amazing sermon, and he's had numerous opportunities to go to bigger churches, pursue greater fame. But he always says no, content to answer God's call on his life in relative obscurity. He often explains, "A man gets into trouble when he starts thinking about his own glory."

He is the happiest person I know.

"Ben, I don't want to talk about it."

The hurt in his eyes is genuine. We've always been close, but Amber's murder has wedged us apart. He tries to bridge the gap every few months. I refuse to reciprocate. Relationship-tending requires more energy than I can spare.

And now he has met Lara. The need for secrecy is on my mind.

"Please don't tell Sally or Mom," I say.

"I won't lie, not even for you."

"I don't think either of them is going to ask you if Lara Landrum was in Mom's house." He laughs.

"Probably not."

He pats me on the back, gets in his car, and starts his engine. Before driving off, he rolls down the window and gives me one last message.

"Be careful, brother."

***

We sit together in front of the fire. Lara drinks some wine that she raided from Mom's liquor cabinet.

"Tell me about your father," she says.

We haven't talked much to each other about the past. Even in the mountains, the dialogue between us centered on the non-personal. But it's hard to avoid history in a house like this. I reflect on my father, knowing full well that he would be aghast that I was sleeping with a witness in the same house that his great-grandfather built.

"Daddy was my hero. He was a lawyer, so I wanted to be a lawyer. He was the real-life Atticus Finch, the moral conscience of the community. His office was on the courthouse square. Seems like everyone in the town congregated there. I would go and hang out, soaking it all in. The town convinced him to go to the legislature. The folks in the legislature liked him so much they made him lieutenant governor. He was going to be governor, but he walked away."

"Why?"

"He didn't want it. He was being true to himself."

"How did he die?"

"Cancer."

That awful word. Daddy faced the end with calm equanimity—the same way he approached everything. Even as the disease ravaged his body, he would sit for hours on the porch, his marked-up Bible in his lap, looking at the trees and feeling the wind. Most people in his situation ask, "Why me?" He thought, "Why not me?" He reasoned he had lived a good life, better than most. It would be untoward to let the bad at the end drown out the overwhelming good. He died a contented man.

Lara asks, "Do you think your mom would like me?"

"Mom would love you. She would take you around to all the shops in town, show you off, and claim you as her best friend."

The image amuses. Yet that meeting will have to wait. The trial dominates our relationship so thoroughly that I rarely allow myself to think about a post-trial life with Lara. Part of me worries that the clock will strike twelve once the verdict is read, and the fantasy will end.

I say, "Maybe you can meet her after the trial."

"I would like that."

Her words provide some solace, and that hope sustains for now. The trial is the thing. I just have to get through the trial.

I change the subject and ask, "What about your parents?"

She frowns and drifts away from me. I keep to myself and let her float in her memories. I've interviewed enough witnesses over the years to recognize that prolonged contemplation of this sort rarely precedes happy talk. I wait. It's her story to tell.

"What can I say about Bill and Julia?"

The pain of the topic etches lines into her face. The beauty remains, even when hardened. Her feet rest in my lap and I rub them to show solidarity as she wrestles with the past. I can't fix whatever hurt eats at her, but I can let her know that she doesn't have to travel back in time alone. She readies herself to speak behind soft tears.

"Bill touched me in ways a father shouldn't touch his daughter. He made me touch him. The first time was when I was seven. He didn't stop until I was thirteen. Julia knew the whole time and did nothing. She let that monster rape her daughter. The day they both died in a car wreck is the happiest day of my life."

I remove my hands from her feet. The action is instinctual, and I only realize I'm no longer touching her after the fact. Her sobs grow, but I fear holding her, afraid as a man to do anything that would violate her again. I belatedly go find a box of tissues. I can do that at least. Lara sits up and dries her eyes.

She goes on, "I'll give Bill credit for one thing. He made me the actress I am today. I hid the abuse from my sister, my teachers, and other relatives. I tried to deceive myself, too, but I wasn't that good."

A bitter laugh follows her words. The tears stop, and a hungry rage takes over. She grasps her wine glass with a bear claw of a grip, and I wonder if it will up and shatter in her hands, never to be put together again. I hold fierce to my silence, convinced that anything I say will strike the wrong note.

"I'll never understand one thing. He only touched me. Never Sara, only me. We look just alike. Why me instead of her?"

Man is a beast. In no other species will a parent use a child to satisfy his own perversion. The revulsion in me rises. Bill and Julia should've been sent away to prison to face the special brand of justice other inmates reserve for child abusers. Lara lays her head on my chest, and we marinate in the quiet for a spell.

I ask, "Did Sara know?"

"No."

"Maybe your father was doing the same thing to her."

"No. I knew what to look for. Sara suspected something was up from time to time, but she never knew. I hid it well. I'm good at that. Even after Bill and Julia died, I hid it well. It's not like I wanted Bill to abuse her, too. She was my best friend. I would do anything to spare her that awfulness, the terrible smells, the gross violations. I didn't wish it on her at all. I just want to know why he chose me. What did I do wrong?"

Her hostility to Barton takes on new dimensions. Barton is old enough to be Lara and Sara's father. He married Sara when she was only twenty. One need not be a psychiatrist to see how Lara could easily transfer the horror of her own father-daughter experience to Sara and Barton. By going after Barton, I stand as the man who will deliver Lara from her childhood demons. I'm prosecuting Bill for his past crimes. I don't feel much like a white knight and grimly realize that such a foundation for our relationship is doomed to crumble.

We sit in silence for a long time.

***

The phone rings and jars us out of the mournful stillness. It's Scott.

"How's your mom?"

"Tough as ever. She won't die until she wants to."

"Glad to hear it, but this is not a social call. Something's happened in the Barton case."

I joke, "Barton confessed?"

The joke doesn't go over. Lara jerks her head to me, confusion worrying her face. I shake my head and mouth, "No."

Scott continues, "Sam Wilkins is dead. Gunshot wound to the head."

The line stays silent as I process the news about my friend. The brutal world I inhabit claims another victim. I fight the good fight, but it is no use. I cannot win.

"I'm sorry," Scott says to break the quiet.

"What do we know?"

"Not much. I got a call from the FBI a few hours ago about a body found in the East Palisades area of the Chattahoochee National River Park."

I interrupt, "Is that in the city limits?"

"Barely. I got the call and made my way over there. Very secluded part of the park. I arrived and there he was, lying on the ground with the gun next to his body. He'd been there for some time. The feds think maybe a day, yesterday afternoon probably. Since it is federal property, the FBI technically has the lead. It's too dark now to do much of anything. They'll be out early tomorrow morning to see if any evidence is about, and I'll join them."

The gun next to the body throws me for a loop. I had assumed murder. "Suicide?"

Lara's eyes go wide. I try to make Sam for suicide. That night at The Varsity, he seemed more together than at any other point after Sara Barton's murder, but that was months ago now. His mood was always one that swam with the tide—up when things were good and down when things were bad. Maybe the tide turned against him again.

Scott answers, "Don't know yet. We're not ruling out homicide. The FBI stopped doing gunshot residue testing about ten years ago, and we can't tell yet if Sam fired the gun or not. The feds are letting us perform the autopsy. I'll make sure that Cecil tests for the residue. We'll have a better idea then."

"The feds going to be a problem?"

"I doubt it. I don't think they really care and would probably welcome us handling most of it. They're not murder guys. Now if he had chopped down a tree in their park, they would be all over it. Him being dead under the tree doesn't bother them as much."

I agree. The federal connection to the case is marginal. The FBI will likely defer to us. Murder or suicide, the case against Barton just got bushwhacked. All Millwood has to do is convince one juror that reasonable doubt exists. With another dead body muddying the waters, his job becomes that much easier.

I ask, "Does Liesa know?"

"The FBI told her an hour ago. I don't know how she took it. Should I go try to talk to her?"

"No. Let her grieve. She has her children to think about."

"Okay. She might better respond to you anyway. You coming up?"

"Not tonight. I'll head that way in the morning."

We hang up. I think about Liesa and our disastrous interview following Sara Barton's murder. I doubt she would respond well to me at all. The thought is short-lived. Lara pounces on me for information.

"Who killed himself? Bernard?" Something akin to hope shows in her.

"No. Sam Wilkins. And we don't know yet if it was suicide."

"Sara's lawyer? The one who found the body?"

"Yeah."

She looks confused, which matches my own feelings. Her confusion soon gives way to agitation.

She asks, "What does this mean for Bernard?"

"It complicates things."

The answer doesn't agree with her. She stands up and stews around the room. I remain numb. The bodies keep piling up around me.

"'Why does it complicate things? You still have the gun."

"The more dead bodies, the more Millwood can divert the eyes of the jurors off the core of the case—Barton's murder of your sister. That's what we want to talk about. Now Millwood gets to talk about something else."

I pretend to be Millwood.

"'Sam Wilkins is dead. That's interesting. Sam Wilkins had the opportunity to kill Sara Barton. He's the one who discovered the body. Why was he even there at that time of night? That's curious. Did he kill her and then kill himself out of guilt over his terrible deed?' Stuff like that is the problem. It complicates things. But you're right, we still have the gun. We still have a lot of things."

I try to sound confident, but doubt seeps into my voice. The threat to the case is deeper than I let on. I know something that Lara does not. Sam was sleeping with her sister. Does Millwood know? Scott never memorialized his interview of Sam on the night of the murder, which means that no written record of Sam's admission exists. Scott planned on writing it down but never had a chance in the hurried aftermath of the discovery of Sara Barton's body. By the time he circled back around to it, we had Barton in our sights and decided the less said about Sam the better. But Scott won't lie on the stand. If Millwood asks the right questions, the information may come out unless I can prevent it on hearsay grounds. That is a battle for another day.

Lara screams, "This is crazy. Just because some guy who barely knows my sister shoots himself, Bernard may walk? You promised me you would get him!"

She smashes her wine glass against the fireplace. The glass is part of my Mom's favorite set of crystal. Mom will notice it missing within five minutes of returning home. That's not an insignificant problem in my world. But the trouble before me is a more pressing concern. I dare not tell Lara about Sam and her sister. That news would push her over the edge.

While I work out the new math in my head, Lara paces like a caged tiger in heat. The back-and-forth progression is dizzying. I need her to calm down and think straight.

"Relax," I caution.

"Don't tell me to relax. Would you relax if the man who murdered your family was about to walk?"

"Barton ain't walking."

I say it with more grim determination than I feel. Millwood is going to have me dancing around that courtroom putting out more fires than Smokey the Bear. If you're explaining, you're losing—and I'm going to have a lot of explaining to do about how Sam ended up in the woods with a bullet in his head.

Lara mocks, "'Barton ain't walking.' Please! What do you know? I don't see why I should believe you. You're going to screw it up somehow."

That gets my goat, and I try to set her straight without losing my cool.

"I know you're upset—"

"Don't patronize me! Sara's dead. Do you know what that means? She's my twin. My twin! You hurt one of us, you hurt both of us. We're conjoined forever. Now she's gone. Dead! I'm torn apart here, living with half my body missing. I can barely function. And that bastard is going to get away with it—just like he has always gotten away with things his entire life. Men like him are never held to account."

The monologue complete, frenzied eyes issue a challenge, daring me to contradict her. I answer with silence, willing the storm to pass. I retrieve a broom and dust pan to clean up the shards of the broken wine glass littering the floor. The busy work fails to deliver any cathartic relief for either of us. She continues to stare at me with unnerving intensity as I go about my sweeping. The coolness under pressure I exhibit in the courtroom deserts me before this hostile audience of one. I finally snap.

"What?"

"You need to fix this."

Bloody hell. I can't raise Sam from the dead. I inspect the floor, unwilling to meet her eyes for fear of receiving another scolding. A feeling of stress wells up in my body, and I inch closer to turning myself over to the growing anger within me. I gulp a deep breath to beat back the pressure. One of us has to remain sane.

She demands, "Well?"

Another deep breath.

"There's a reason I've never lost a trial. I'm good. There's a reason I'm the chief homicide prosecutor in Atlanta. I'm good. No trial goes perfectly to script. Complications arise. When they do, I adjust and deal with them. This news is a complication. I'll adjust and deal with it. I know this situation is emotional for you. I get it, I truly do. But you've got to trust me. I'm not going to lose. Bernard Barton is not going to escape justice."

"You can't spin your way out of Sam Wilkins' death."

"Wanna bet? A wife goes to a divorce lawyer seeking a divorce. Shortly thereafter, the wife and divorce lawyer are dead. Who's the most likely suspect?"

She smiles and concedes, "The husband."

That settles her down. We finish the night in my childhood bed—seeking refuge in the violent motion of our bodies rollicking against each other. As she rocks on top of me, I stare at a small crack in the ceiling that has decorated my room for eons. I used to lie here and ponder that crack, impatiently waiting to get out of this house to kickstart my life. If someone back then could've convinced that boy that one day he would be having sex in this same room with one of the most beautiful women in the world, the boy would've been happy. But reality always falls short of the dream.

26

The next day I wake up to a woman in a bad mood. Lara scowls at me with such accusation that I might've killed Sam myself. And maybe I did. Sharing my old twin bed through the night failed both of us. We carry our tiredness around like an anchor attached to our leg. I go through the motions of the morning, keeping quiet in the hope of avoiding the brunt of it. The silence only seems to stoke her building fury. I slide the magic elixir of coffee to her across the kitchen island. She doesn't throw it in my face, but neither does the darkness lift. The innocent wonder of roasting s'mores together seems lost forever as though two different people shared that experience.

Lara barks, "What are you going to do now?"

"Visit my mother at the hospital on the way out of town. Drive back to Atlanta. See if anyone knows how Sam Wilkins died."

"That's not enough. Bernard is going to get away with it. You need to do more."

"Well, I guess I could go ahead and kill him myself, and we won't even have to worry about the trial. Would that be enough?"

"It would solve a lot of problems."

I pretend to chuckle. She doesn't. Having avoided looking at her for the last hour, I switch gears and check her face for signs of levity. My skin turns cold. She gives no hint—not even a sliver of a millimeter—that she is kidding. Her eyes stare right back at me and demand an answer. Murder? Is she insane? I start cleaning dishes to bring order out of the chaos. Lara watches me like a hawk. I am wide awake.

"Nuts," I say.

"Do you love me?"

"Not enough to do that. Pack up your things. It's time to leave."

"I'll help you do it."

"Pack!"

I continue the process of putting Mom's house back in order. A frustrated Lara lingers a bit but retreats upstairs in the face of my conscious indifference to her. I attack the cleaning with a ferociousness I've never shown to household chores before. Ten minutes later, she enters the kitchen with the bags by her side. The hateful glare she unfurls would've staggered me at any previous point in our relationship, but not now. She moves toward the back door.

"Wait!"

We face each other like two gunslingers about to drawdown. I pull first and opt for indignant calm.

"My wife and son were shot and left to die in their own blood. My 4-year old boy. A child. I loathe murder with every fiber of my being. I'm not a murderer. If you ever suggest such an idea to me again, I'll indict you myself. Do you understand?"

"I wasn't serious. You're the one who brought it up."

"Like hell."

"Open the garage."

"Do you understand?"

"More than you know."

She walks the path to the garage, leaving me stranded in the doorway. I have no choice but to follow. She slinks behind the wheel as I lift the garage door. The crispness of the morning reminds me that I'm only in my shirt sleeves. Another storm is coming. She drives off spinning gravel along the way.

***

The hospital visit is short. I tell Mom about Sam. He stayed with us one weekend at the house when a few friends and I went to see UGA play at Auburn. Mom digs for details, but I have few to offer.

"He was such a nice boy," Mom observes.

Was he? Am I? Is anyone? Maybe once upon a time, but the detours of life divert a person in a direction he never intends to go. Sam is dead, and Lara apparently wants me to kill Barton. I should get in my car and head west. Americans have always gone west to pursue a new world. I should drive west and forever forget this sordid business. The world is dirty, and I cannot make it clean.

But the current of fate is too strong. I drive north to Atlanta, back to the city that is now my home. The fatalist in me needs to see the story through. I have no attic in the city in which to slip away—no place to call all my own. I live alone, but the house belongs to a dead woman and a dead child. I have a condo, but another woman rules that space. I own much but have little. I could go to the woods as Sam did. Was he alone? I don't know what to believe anymore. A good lawyer can persuade himself of anything—that's what we are trained to do. I fear that I have convinced myself of a great many things that are not true.

I make it to my house. I should call Scott, get an update, see where things stand. But I don't. I crumble on the bed—Amber's bed—and try to outsleep the storm.

***

Scott brings pizza and beer over in the evening—the pizza for both of us, the beer for him. I feel terrible. Long naps should revitalize. With me, they debilitate. The sleep still covers me as I stagger around the house. Coffee at night is a bad idea in the long term, but the short term demands it. That's my life right now—surviving the moment, even if the tools of survival carry with them a worse future. I check for messages from Lara and find none.

"You look like hell," Scott observes.

"Great detective work there."

"Do you want to talk about it?"

"Have I ever wanted to talk about it?"

"Good point."

We devour the pizza, kicking the can of healthy eating further down the road. The coffee leads me back to the land of the living. The beer works to take Scott away. Two middle-aged white guys, no longer married, separated from their children—the picture isn't exactly a Hallmark moment. The depressing tableau falls so short of my expectations for life that I'm left questioning the entirety of my existence. What is the bloody point? The shock of Lara's suggestion that I kill Barton has worn off. The anger dissipates into carnality. I could be mounting Lara right now and losing myself inside of her. That would be something—some Epicurean reason to be. The lust rises.

I ask, "Did you learn anything useful about Sam in the light of day?"

"Don't know. Some presence of gunshot residue is indicated, more than trace amounts, less than full blown certainty he fired the gun. But remember he was out there overnight. Some of it would've degenerated, so no telling. Cecil has the body now. We're looking at three or four in the afternoon as the time of death. One interesting thing—we found a second bullet lodged in a tree in the vicinity, a little farther back from the clearing where the body was. Ballistics is running tests to see if we have a match."

"How did you find that?"

"Total miracle. One of the feds is wandering around outside the perimeter, sees something weird, takes a closer look. Voila! A second bullet. Could be nothing, could be everything. I don't know. The whole situation rubs me the wrong way."

I agree. Everything is all wrong—suicide, murder, the second bullet, the location, everything. I feel trapped in a maze devoid of exits. I don't even know whether I need it to be murder or suicide for the case. We've entered a realm where every possibility holds the potential for ruin. That my friend's cold body now lies under Cecil's bright lights is almost an afterthought. That bullet in the second tree gets me to thinking.

"Assuming a match, you think the second bullet suggests murder?"

"Uh-huh. One kill shot. One stray shot with Sam's hand around the gun."

"Barton?"

"Who knows? I don't like the guy, but … who knows? No suicide note. I think Barton would've faked a note from the dead man confessing to Sara's murder. No point otherwise for him to do it. Is this Sam thing gonna hurt our case?"

"Probably, but at least Sam won't have to testify now. He was stiff-arming me on trial prep. We were supposed to finally meet later this week. Millwood would've sliced and diced him if he caught a whiff of Sam's deceit. I'm not sad to avoid that heartache."

"Maybe you killed Sam then."

"I have an indestructible alibi—my mother."

"I'll scratch you off the list."

I reflect on Sam's widow, Liesa. Her connection to the case is buried on page three of a document listing the cars that traveled through the traffic light that night—one name on a sheet of paper with a bunch of other names. That document is buried in thousands of pages of other investigative materials we turned over to Millwood. Even a good lawyer could miss it. Liesa is certainly due a lucky break. But the hunch is that the wheel of fortune will turn against her again. No one has ever made any money betting that Millwood won't be prepared.

I ask, "Anyone seen Liesa yet?"

"I stopped by. She didn't want to talk. Asked me to leave."

"Her husband did just die."

"Sure. You gonna take a go at her?"

"Nah. No point. She's not a talker. I'll see her at the funeral, see what shakes out. Until then let her bury Sam and comfort her children. We need to avoid antagonizing her. She may be a witness at the trial."

"You think?"

"Her car was near the Barton house that night. If Millwood figures that out, all bets are off. He'll figure a way to drag Liesa in."

Scott puts the remaining beers in the fridge and heads for the door. "Two and a half weeks," he says. I nod and contemplate the work yet to be done. I'll sputter to the finish line, even as I worry about my hold on events. But I can't wash my hands of this case. I drove north today to convict Bernard Barton and stay close to Lara Landrum. And that's what I'll do.

A few weeks ago, I bought Lara and me burner phones to facilitate surreptitious communication. After Scott departs, I text her to meet me at the condo immediately.

***

The empty condo torments me, just like Lara's non-answer to the text I sent a little while ago. Midnight approaches, and temptation hangs on me. The need to possess her lodged itself into my brain earlier in the evening and refuses to disembark. I cannot shake the desire and am unsure if I even want to. I feel sick.

Will she even show?

When I was twelve, I accompanied my father on a visit to a great plantation in south Georgia where horses were bred. To the discomfort of us both, Daddy and I were treated to a front row seat of the physical joining of stud and mare. The corralled madness of the two beasts—both primed for it by the machinations of the breeders just prior to the moment of union—demonstrated the raw power of the sexual urge. I felt the same pent up stirrings with Amber as we walked the hotel halls to our wedding suite. I feel the same need to animalize Lara now.

The turning of the key in the lock halts my movement in mid-step. Like an alert hunting dog, my ears point themselves in the suspected direction of the desired prey. Before the door even closes, I cover the distance between us and swallow her with my mouth. Token resistance—more a product of surprise than disinterest—melts into mutuality. We never make it past the kitchen.

Lara slumps to the hardwoods in the aftermath. I bend over the sink, turn on the faucet, and splash cold water on my face. Naked and exposed, my mind is blank. Lara sits before me, her legs splayed randomly on the floor, the refrigerator supporting her back. Neither of us says anything for a while. What is she thinking? I have no idea. She is the foreign language I cannot decipher—an Asiatic-type dialect made up of characters, not letters, foreclosing all hope of comprehension.

Without looking at me, she says, "I almost killed myself today."

I hold my tongue, not understanding. The scene is surreal—the prolonged silence, the smell of sex still fresh in the air, the casual mention of aborted suicide. I feel like everything is happening apart from myself. I'm an observer, and the man near the sink is a hapless stranger out of step with the world around him. She finally looks at me, demanding a response to her words—the intensity in her face matching the intensity of her body just a few minutes before.

I answer, "I don't need any more dead bodies before trial."

"Bastard. I don't know if you're serious or kidding."

"I don't know, either."

Without Lara, the picture of Sara Barton's bruised back would likely never make it into evidence. No one living could authenticate it. I reach that calculation immediately on the spot—thinking like a lawyer my old professors would call it. Standing naked in that kitchen, my response to a confession of near suicide is to analyze the rules of evidence.

"You know why I didn't kill myself? I couldn't solve the problem of how. I don't own a gun and I've never fired one in my entire life. That's out. I left all my pills in Los Angeles. Can't use those. Slitting my wrists is too bloody. Watching yourself bleed out has to be excruciating. That left hanging, which seems to be the method of choice for celebrities these days. But that involved too much engineering. I'm no good at engineering. So I'm here, sitting naked on your kitchen floor, like the good little whore you think I am."

The discomfort on my face must've been evident because she bursts out laughing at me. The frankness rattles my conscience.

"Look at you," she says. "Do my words bother you? Should nice Southern girls not speak in such ways? I'm simply stating a fact. You're a lawyer. You like facts. You summoned me over here tonight like I was an obedient whore. You pounced on me like a whore. And you used me like a whore to satisfy your cravings."

"Stop."

"You want everything to be nice and clean in your little bubble. You pretend that you're some kind of respectable man. Stop and open your eyes! I'm ugly. You're ugly. We're ugly. You think your hands are clean? I almost killed myself today, and I come here tonight for you to treat me like a whore. How do you think that makes me feel? Is that what you want? A whore? Was your wife a whore?"

"Don't talk about her."

"Did you treat her like a whore, too? Is that how you like your women? Amber the whore. I bet she was good, but not as good as me, was she?"

"Stop talking about her."

"Or what? 'I'm not a murderer,' you told me. Are you going to hit me? Look at you trying to control your anger. Be a man! Get angry! Hit me! Treat me some more like the whore you want!"

I don't move or speak.

"No? You're pathetic. I knew that this morning. You lack the nerve—you and that ten-ton conscience you carry around. You castigate yourself for the enjoyment of any pleasure. You're nothing. You're the most boring man I've ever known. Here's a newsflash for you: I've been treated like a whore by men far worse than you. You wouldn't believe the things men have asked me to do—vile, depraved things, things that would sicken your precious conscience. You and your boring life with your sweet little Amber. Nah, she wasn't a whore, but I bet you wanted her to be."

The constant mentions of Amber nearly push me over the edge. But I hold on and begin the work of de-escalating my anger. Lara is a rape survivor. She is not really screaming at me, even if I deserve it. She is yelling at the father who molested her a long time ago. The shock of Sam's death masked the significance of last night's confession about her treatment at the hands of Bill and Julia. Lara doesn't have scars. Her wounds have yet to even skin over—a minefield of memories ready to detonate at the slightest touch. No telling what happened to her out there in Hollywood, either.

I offer, "I'm sorry."

"For treating me like a whore?"

"For that and everything that has happened to you."

"Don't go Freud on me. Stick to the law and something you know. Why don't you apologize instead for not seeming to give a solitary damn that I almost killed myself today?"

"I'm sorry for that, too."

Except I'm not really sure I believe her. I don't disbelieve her. I'm just not sure I believe her, either. Everything she says feels like a rehearsed line out of a movie playing only in her head. These doubts I keep to myself.

I offer, "I would be devastated if you killed yourself. Please don't."

"I should kill you instead."

"I don't like that plot twist, either. Too much talk of killing today—Barton this morning, then yourself, now me. It solves nothing. Let's just go home and get some sleep."

"Not even a courtesy cuddle after I took care of your needs? You really do think I'm a whore, don't you?"

"You didn't seem to be in a cuddling kind of mood."

"I am now."

We lay down together on the bed. I hold her, willing the demons to go away—both hers and mine. I won't sleep. The chance that I might awake with an ice pick in my heart looms too large as a possibility. I don't really believe that, but I don't disbelieve it, either. Driving down to see Mom, the gaps in my knowledge of Lara scared me. Now I know too much. I have no idea of what I have ahold of.

I ask, "Why suicide?"

"I'm tired."

The response holds dual meanings, and she is fast asleep before I can probe further. I hold her for hours while my mind runs a marathon of disparate thoughts that I soon forget. The trial is almost here. I need to get back to work. I leave her sleeping and execute a quiet getaway.

***

I arrive at the office before anyone else. The halls belong to me alone, and I try to draw inspiration from the solitude. The trial is now a chore, but the best way to manage unpleasant tasks is to break them down into bite-sized morsels and chew a little at a time. I create a comprehensive punch list that will serve as my blueprint for everything that needs to be done before the real thing goes live. Number Eight on my list is the most enigmatic: "Sam?" Well, at least I have a couple of weeks.

Hours pass, and the purposeful flow of work supplies me with a comfortable energy. The burner phone in my right pocket vibrates, and only Lara contacts me on that number. I study it for three seconds before deciding to answer. A flood of obscenities crash into my ear as Lara berates me for abandoning her. The getaway was short-lived. My plaintive response about the need for trial preparation sounds pathetically weak. More verbal abuse follows. I take it like a punching bag until she hangs up.

The energy of the morning disappears into a vortex. I'm the tired one now. I push the punch list to the side, lay my head on the desk, and wish it all to go away.

27

"What now?"

Ella's question to me later that day floats futilely in search of an answer. The topic is Sam, and talking about the problem brings me no closer to a solution.

"I'm going to the funeral tomorrow. Maybe something will shake out."

"We have to have a strategy."

The peevishness of her tone irks me. I know very well we need a strategy without her lecturing me about it. The ice between Ella and me remains unthawed, and the forecast points to a long winter. We're stuck together for Barton, but this ride will be our last one as trial partners. Every beginning has an end.

I respond, "Much depends on how Millwood plays his hand. I'm inclined to let him make the first move and react accordingly."

"You always taught me to be the action, not the reaction—to be offense, not defense."

Just like Millwood taught me. I wonder who taught him. Maybe I should write a book—*Lessons From The Great Trial Lawyers*. I could run off to some remote place by myself, far from the world, and leave Lara here to work out her own issues. The life of the scholarly monk appeals to me. But first the problem of Sam demands attention.

"Exactly. That's precisely why I want Millwood to make the first move. If you're explaining, you're losing. I can't explain Sam's death. But I don't need to. Sam's death is irrelevant to the guilt or innocence of Bernard Barton. If Millwood thinks otherwise, let him explain why. He ain't going to be able to explain it, either. What does he know about Sam's death? Nothing. Whatever he comes up with, I can swat it away, say it smacks of desperation on the part of the defense. Unless something more definitive breaks with the cause of Sam's death, we're going to have to take our lead from Millwood."

Ella is unconvinced and shows it. The cracks between us threaten to widen as doubt in me personally bleeds over to doubt in me professionally. Or maybe Sam's death has made everyone prickly as a cactus.

I ask, "How's it going with Lara in witness prep?"

"Lara? I don't call her that. Always 'Miss Landrum.' But I guess you would call her 'Lara.' I bet you called her a bunch of different things."

The challenge in her eyes begs me for a harsh response, but I sit and take it. Fighting solves nothing. She breaks eye contact with annoyance upon realizing I won't take the bait.

"*Lara* has done all that I've asked of her. She takes direction well. I think she will be a strong witness. We don't like each other, but we can fake our way through."

Ella starts to stand up but sits back down. She asks, "Do you miss her?"

Her question assumes a fact not in evidence—that Lara and I are actually apart. That fact needs to remain out of evidence. I deflect.

"I miss what you and I had."

"Then you shouldn't have thrown it away by sleeping with a witness."

"Guilty as charged."

Better that Ella focus on the relationship between the two of us than ask more questions about Lara and me. The nuclear fallout if she discovers the truth is something I don't want to contemplate. But Ella has always been a dogged questioner once she latches onto something.

"You still didn't answer my question. Do you miss her?"

Trying hard not to lie, I truthfully respond, "I think about her all the time."

Disgust spreads in a wave across Ella's beautiful face. Her previous resort to the racial issue still riles me, but I now wonder if my subconscious did reject her based on the color of her skin. The past months show that all manner of untoward things lurk beneath the veneer of my respectability. Lara's words of the previous night ring loud—"I'm ugly. You're ugly. We're ugly."

Ella demands, "Why her? I don't understand. I could've made you happy."

"Honestly, she threw herself at me, and I caught her. Showed up at my house and started taking her clothes off. Literally. I tried to resist even then. Eventually, I stopped resisting. If you would've thrown yourself at me like that, I would've caught you, too."

"So it's my fault for not showing up at your house naked?"

"Not fault. Just an explanation. You patiently waited. She didn't. Nothing ever would've happened with her if she hadn't chased me down. I wasn't looking for it."

"Poor pitiful you."

"I'm sorry."

"Yeah, sure. You going back to her after all this is over?"

"I'm less certain of the future than at any other point in my adult life."

Ella shakes her head at me, frustrated at the divergence of who I am and who she wants me to be. She gathers her things in an agitated and distracted sort of way. Perhaps she's past anger and on to bargaining in the five stages of grief—trying to make some deal with herself to make the most of what's left in this whole business. She stands and gives me a last look filled with the sad recognition that I am a lost cause.

"Let's just win the case," she says and shuts the door behind her.

***

Sam's three kids sit off to the side by themselves when I walk through the door of the church for their father's funeral. I consider offering them condolences but leave them alone to their pain. The kids need far more than platitudes from me in a time like this.

Liesa receives visitors at the front of the chapel, and I wait my turn to pay appropriate respects. She offers me her cheek to kiss. I oblige.

"I'm so sorry, Liesa."

"Are you?"

The words hurt and contain an undercurrent of accusation. I scurry away. Jeff Yarber drops next to me in the pew. I wonder if he blames me, too. It would fit the pattern.

He asks, "Did he kill himself?"

"I honestly don't know. You knew him better than I did. Talk to him lately?"

"Two weeks ago."

"Suicidal?"

"I didn't think so."

We sit quietly and ponder. The mirror doesn't lie. All of us are older now, and the life we anticipated in law school has taken turns too dark for us to have ever imagined. Another one of our classmates, Marilyn Stubbs, was gunned down by a crazy ex-husband five years ago. Trey Miles died in a car wreck. Cancer got Barbara Allen.

"Too much death," I say.

Jeff agrees.

I skip the burial. Without even intending to do so, I end up back at The Varsity—sitting in the same booth where Sam and I last saw one another. I eat angry, furiously chewing my food as if it were responsible for the dark tide. I remember Sam across from me that night, his investigative research on Barton right next to him.

That gets me to thinking. Sam only turned over what he wanted me to know about Bernard Barton and nothing else. And no Sara Barton divorce files were in Sam's home or office when the police searched. More files have to exist.

Where is the stuff Sam didn't want me to see?

"A safe place," Sam claimed when I questioned him that night. I call Scott.

"Did you impound Sam's vehicle from that park where he was killed?"

"Of course."

"Search it?"

"Why else would I impound it? Of course we searched it."

"Find Sam's file on the Barton divorce in there?"

"I probably would've told you if I had."

"How thorough a search?"

"Really? Do you take me for some hayseed from where you grew up? I didn't *French Connection* it, but it was thorough enough."

The classic film *The French Connection* contains a scene where Detective Popeye Doyle and his fellow police officers take apart an entire car in search of heroin only to put it back together again as part of a sting operation. Scott has always wanted to *French Connection* a suspect vehicle, but this case doesn't justify it. If Sam hid the file in his car, Scott would've found the documents. Where on earth are they?

I text Liesa to ask her about the file. The dwindling options leave me no choice. The galling insensitivity is not lost on me. Yet I ask all the same.

Two hours or so later, the phone beeps its distinctive notification of an incoming text. I grab at the device and see Liesa's name. The response reads:

"Don't know anything about your damn file. At least you waited until after the funeral. Barely. If you're looking for another place of ours to turn inside and out, there's our cabin in Young Harris. 125 Bear Creek Drive. The code to the house is 0527. Sam warned me about you. He had no idea."

I stare at the screen for a good two minutes. The shame is real. But the compulsion of the case propels me forward—an unruly bulldozer clearcutting every obstacle that darts into his path. The cabin strikes me as the longest of long shots, and part of me wonders if Liesa wants to send me on a wild goose chase just for spite. If so, I'm a willing victim.

Young Harris is two hours away. A sober-minded person would wait until morning before hitting the road. But that file has invaded my thoughts, and I'm on the hunt.

I make the cabin and enter the 0527 code. The significance dawns on me. Sam and Liesa got married on May 27. Amber and I attended the wedding—a radiant picture of us together at the reception remains a favorite. The memory of the beaming faces of the bride and groom punishes me. Shakespeare wrote, "What's past is prologue." The happy past of that Saturday in late May was the prologue to the bleak future of the present. Will the epilogue be as desolate? I remind myself that Shakespeare's best works were tragedies.

28

The cabin is cold and uninviting, reflecting months of disuse. The idea to come up here sounded smart in Atlanta. Now the likely futility of the search seems foreordained. I don't even know what I expect to discover—nothing usable as evidence for sure. Searching the place all alone destroys any hope of establishing a legitimate chain of custody. Probably should've thought of that before, I chide myself. But that's not right. I know the score. I'm chasing something Sam didn't want me to find. Nothing hidden up here is going to help my case.

I start in the kitchen because it's right next to the front door. The high places are populated by dead bugs and little else. The adjacent living area comes next, but the effort is cursory. Sam wouldn't hide anything in such a high-traffic space. The used board games in the cabinet paint a nice tableau of a loving family enjoying one another's company. The story warms the heart until you learn that dad was sexing up his client on the side. But that's the thing about fairy tales—they were always dark until Disney got ahold of them.

The master bedroom is the last room on the main level. Sam wouldn't be brave enough to hide something sensitive in the same room as Liesa sleeps. No matter. Searching a house means being systematic in checking off one area at a time. Sifting through their clothes drawers strikes me as profoundly intimate and unseemly. I feel like a thief.

I go through the children's rooms upstairs without much enthusiasm. A walk-in attic holds some promise, but the pickings are sparse. I give the insulation panels a good hard look for any sign of disturbance, but come up with nothing. The false note in the otherwise perfect harmony of the house eludes me. I curse myself for the whole foolish enterprise and contemplate the drive home.

Thoroughness compels me to check the back deck. The full moon provides a partial glimpse of what must be a beautiful view in the glory of full light. I glance to the right and see an outbuilding adjacent to the house. The decent-sized shed sets off the alarm bells in my head. Sometimes you just know. The answer I seek lies in there one way or another. If it's not there, it ain't anywhere. I just wasted an hour searching the cabin. The shed is the thing.

***

The shed door is locked. I remember a set of keys on a hook in the kitchen and retrace my steps. One key fits. I pray the shed has electricity. I flip the only switch I can find, and the white light from the long, overhead fluorescent tubes flickers before catching. The surroundings before me lack the order of the main dwelling. The cabin is Liesa. The shed is Sam. I sit down on a small stool in the middle of things and scan the mess for the secret spot. I study the high places and see an unreachable shelf above the window from which Sam's workbench looks out upon the valley below. That's an odd place to put a shelf. A box on the shelf advertises itself as being a carton of motor oil. I'm dubious.

I move the stool next to the workbench and use the former to climb upon the latter. The built-in bench is made of stern stuff and easily holds my weight. I stand on my toes and grab a box far too light to be full of motor oil. I come down the way I went, sit back again on the stool, and dive into the box to see if my unplanned trip to the mountains was all for naught.

The file sits under a few layers of crumbled newspapers. I take it out and hold it with the same delicacy as if I were holding a newborn. I lay the newspapers down and put the file on top of them to protect it from the grime that covers the floor. File is actually a misnomer. Before me instead is a two-inch wide, expandable redwell file holder with the case name of *Barton v. Barton* plastered on the outside. Various smaller folders with different labels fill the redwell, representing the work product of the conscientious divorce lawyer—pleadings, discovery requests and responses, correspondence, orders, originals, financials, legal research, factual investigation. Since the divorce never made it to the courthouse, most of the folders are slim pickings. I locate a copy of the same investigative file Sam gave me some months back—nothing new there. I analyze everything in the redwell one page at a time, determined not to miss the needle in the haystack. And then I'm done. Nothing.

I don't panic. Sam placed the file in this unusual location for a specific reason. I stare hard at the redwell and the assorted contents of the file now scattered haphazardly on the crumbled newspapers. I inspect the motor oil carton again. Sam hid the redwell in the box under the crumpled newspapers, but other newspapers also lined the bottom of the box. I snatch them up and find a manila folder. Sam's handwritten note—DO NOT OPEN/ATTORNEY-CLIENT PRIVILEGED—graces the front. "You sneaky bastard," I mutter to myself. Why all the trouble?

Ignoring Sam's rather pointed instructions, I open the folder. Photographs. Lots of photographs. A deep breath fails to soothe my racing nerves. The first few photos show Brice Tanner entering the front door of Sara Barton's residence. Why was Sam staking out the house of his own client? That question evaporates with stunning speed when I view the next photos of Brice and Sara engaged in a decathlon of sexual olympics in the Barton bedroom. The photos are dated in ink in Sam's handwriting and cover multiple meetings between Brice and Sara. The last date noted is the day before the murder. Damn.

The photos are close up—too close. Assuming Brice and Sara didn't willingly allow Sam to stand there so he could take some great action shots, Sam must've placed a hidden camera in the room. What the hell? I should've stayed in Atlanta.

Things get even weirder when the next series of photos show Sam and Sara in the act. One shot captures an angry Sam looking directly at the camera in a pose of sneering defiance. My heart sinks as I study my dead friend to assess his state of mind. He put a camera in Sara Barton's bedroom, filmed the two of them having sex, and flashed a scowl of pure malice at the camera in flagrante delicto. He hated Sara. The bastard hated her.

I scan the remaining photos, fearful that yet another man sleeping with the victim may pop up and sink my case even further. But no. I'm spared that at least. The last few photos feature a naked Sara walking about in the bedroom. The best shots capture her coming and going, leaving nothing to the imagination, illuminating the same glorious body of her sister, the same flawless breasts. I stare at the images longer than I should, thankful for the momentary distraction from my growing doubt in Sam.

I stand up to stretch and get some fresh air. If Millwood gets his hands on those photographs, Barton walks. The story writes itself. Obsessed man kills his lover in a fit of jealous rage because she slept with another man. He finds a gun in her bedroom—a gun loaded by her husband—and shoots her with it, dumping the gun in a nearby park before pretending to find the body and calling the police. Motive. Means. Opportunity. The cherry on top is that the murderer then goes into the woods to kill himself out of a deep sense of guilt.

Millwood can't get these photos.

The mountain air refreshes after the growing claustrophobia of the shed. I kick a few pieces of gravel rock into the woods for no particular reason. My duty as a prosecutor requires me to turn any exculpatory evidence in my possession over to the defense. I don't ever intend to see a single dawn with these photos in my possession. I could burn them. No one would ever know. Probably. But destroying evidence is a serious crime and would cost me my law license if caught, maybe jail. That's more gruel than I can stomach. The other choice is to put everything back where I found it. I return to the shed, grab a rag, and try my best to wipe my prints from the pictures before returning them to the manila folder. Back at the bottom of the box, the manila folder disappears under the layering of the crumbled newspapers and the redwell. I return the erstwhile motor oil box back to its place high on the shelf. All is as it was before.

Except one thing.

I keep the two images of a nude Sara Barton. The act is as stupid as it is juvenile, and the shame leans heavy on my conscience. But the photos remind me of Lara, and the force of her gravitational pull overwhelms my will. I stash the contraband out-of-sight under the driver's seat.

***

The drive home is a tennis match between Lara and Sam as they volley fiercely for my thoughts. Did Sam kill Sara? That I have to ask the question at this late date feels like a defeat. The Barton trial will begin soon. Until tonight, all the evidence pointed to the defendant. I wipe the mental decks clean and tackle the question afresh. Nothing I saw tonight actually exonerates Barton. The evidence against him still stands. The photos in the secret box only serve to raise doubts about Sam. He stalked the victim and committed many crimes in doing so. But did he kill her?

I don't see it. I don't see him shooting her, walking down the street to ditch the gun, walking back, and then returning to the house to call the police to the scene. Sam Wilkins wasn't that composed. Kill her, grab his hidden camera on the go, and run—maybe I could see that, but not the other. I nod my head in agreement with my analysis of the case. Sam didn't kill her. Barton remains on the hook.

Reaching this conclusion is not a linear process. At times, I imagine Lara naked. I see myself in her, on her, and under her. Back and forth, the competing lines of thoughts between Sam and Lara battle for my attention. I arrive home mentally and physically exhausted, confident that Sam was not a murderer and that I would soon hold Lara again in my arms.

***

That night I wrap my legs around Lara's body as we soak together in a decadent bath.

The recent troubles between us go unmentioned—a much-appreciated détente as I try to focus my emotional energy toward the trial. The warm water and Lara's balmy body soothe the rough edges off me, infiltrating my pores to massage down deep to my soul. The effect revitalizes.

I needed a good cleansing. We'll make love later—gentle-like, I envision. Now, though, sex is unnecessary. The moment is perfect as is.

***

I wake up feeling full the next morning. When I turn over to reach for Lara, her pensive stare disarms my intended motion. The sense that she has been looking at me for a long time takes root. I offer a smile, but she's not interested.

She grumbles, "Shouldn't you be at work?"

"I'm going in."

"I'm worried you're not taking the case seriously enough. Bernard must pay for what he did to my sister."

She says the strangest things at the strangest moments. My puzzlement gives way to hurt, and I do a poor job of hiding it.

She groans, "Don't be a baby. Perhaps we shouldn't see each other until the trial is over. We can be together after that."

She sounds like a "Dear John" letter. Even worse, she pats my hand in a wretched show of sympathy—the bedside manner of Dr. Frankenstein. The tenderness of last night dissolved before I even had time to savor it. Mornings are hell on this relationship.

"Sure," I snap.

I rise up, get ready, and go into work just as she wants—the fullness in me now drained to empty.

29

The trial begins in less than a week. I always like to have a final plea conference in a case because you never know. Maybe the defendant wants to deal. So Millwood comes to my office, formerly his office. We sit across from each other, separated by a calm sea of brown—my desk. Nothing sits on it. No pictures. No telephone. Not even my laptop, which I keep on a small table to the side. The cleanliness projects a sense of order and sells the message that I have things under control. I'm not so sure.

Meeting Millwood tickles my nerves. So many times over the years we would huddle together in this same spot. I learned to be a lawyer in this room, devouring every crumb of wisdom as if it were manna from God Himself. Now our seats across the table are reversed. I sit in the big man's chair.

The recognition unsettles. I feel like an imposter, a boy wearing his father's clothes that just don't fit. I'm good at what I do. I know that. But I fear I'll never be as good a trial lawyer as my teacher, despite my best efforts. And the thought of having to face him, in the biggest case of my life no less, awakens a tremor of insecurity that I didn't even know was there. What if I don't measure up?

Maybe Barton will accept a plea and make all this unpleasantness go away. Millwood offers the first salvo.

"Dismiss all the charges, and we'll call it a day. We won't even insist on an apology."

"Wow. That's very generous. I run that up to Bobby, and he won't let you leave the building without a signed agreement."

"Bobby always had a nose for a good deal."

We each offer a little laugh, not even sure what we're laughing about. The joking aside, Millwood gives me a look that says, "Get on with it. This is your party." I've seen that look before.

"Twenty-five to life." Millwood shakes his head.

"No dice."

"It's a good deal."

"Not for an innocent man."

"You have a counter?"

"He is not going to agree to any time. He won't do it."

"He's that confident?"

"He didn't do it. You want him to confess to something he didn't do?"

Bemusement fills my face. I'm not even faking it. How many defense lawyers have sat in that chair and said those exact words to Millwood? The comparison lightens my anxiety about what I'm up against. Millwood now is just another defense lawyer with a guilty client. I can beat him.

"We have the gun, Jack."

"I'm not denying it's his gun, but more people have visited that house than attended the Hawks game last night. Anybody could've gotten their hands on that gun."

I figured that would be the way they would play it, but it is nice to get confirmation. I counted nineteen different people with potential access to the gun—Barton, Sam, Brice, and Monica most prominent among them.

I ask, "Where was he during the time of the murder?"

"You have Monica Haywood's statement."

The wording is curious. He doesn't contend that Barton was actually with Monica, only that she claimed it. I already produced to him the surveillance video from Monica's condo that showed Barton leaving before the murder. I assume Millwood knows that Monica must be lying in light of the video.

I say, "I don't believe her."

"Obviously."

We run out of words. No plea deal will be reached. The trial of Bernard Barton for the murder of Sara Barton begins Monday.

***

The home phone rings. Should I answer? Yes. She won't stop calling if I don't.

"Hi, Mom."

"One of my wine glasses is missing."

"Have you notified the police?"

"Stop it. I'm serious."

"Just kidding. I meant to tell you that I broke it when I was staying at the house. I'll buy you a new one."

A man should not lie to this mother. But for my relationship with Lara, the wine glass never would've been broken, which means I can honestly say that I broke the glass. I know how it sounds. Very lawyer-like. Nevertheless, I stand behind the statement. Mom is not satisfied.

"You don't drink wine. You never drink wine. And you never drink out of my wine glasses. You always use the plastic tumblers. Was somebody else here at the house with you?"

Lord have mercy. The woman is a better detective than Scott. She has a nose for stories that don't smell quite right, always has. I could lie about drinking wine on this one occasion, and it would be a lie that would be impossible for her to disprove. But a man shouldn't lie to his mother. I try another tack. Truthful sarcasm.

"You caught me, Mom. I brought a woman to the house. I said something that upset her, and she smashed your wine glass right against your fireplace. I was hoping you wouldn't notice."

I have total recall of the scene, the aftermath of learning about Sam's death. I think back to one of my English classes in college, where everything had a symbolic meaning that transcended the literal, and I see the broken glass as a metaphor for the relationship between Lara and me. The jagged edges promise pain if I don't handle them exactly right. Even then I may nick myself by accident. Sharp objects carry that inherent risk.

Mom snaps, "You don't have to be an ass and talk to me like that."

"I'm sorry, but you know I have the biggest trial of my life coming up, and you're giving me the third degree about a wine glass."

"Fine. How is that going anyway? Have you talked to Lara Landrum lately? My friends keep asking me. Did you decide to handle her testimony like I told you?"

Part of me wants to tell her that Lara Landrum broke her wine glass just to experience the wonder of her reaction. But no. I close my eyes and continue the conversation.

***

Staring out my office window at the fading afternoon sun, a wave of loneliness sinks my mood. The sad reality is that I have nothing to do and no place to go. I'm ready for the trial. The work I could manufacture requires conferencing with Ella, and that's a non-starter. The condo means the tempest of Lara. The thought of home fares no better. I live in a museum filled with ghosts, and I feel like a stranger to its history. I consider a hotel. Instead I just sit.

A wandering mind has no peace, and mine is no different. Trying not to think about anything leads to a torrent of random, unsequenced thoughts more fitting in a dream. I think of Otis Redding—another Georgia boy from the country. My father did legal work for him long before I was born. The possibility of leaving my home in Georgia to sit on a dock of a bay 2,000 miles from here is tempting. Otis died in a plane crash three days after recording that song. He was 26. I try to recapture all the lyrics, but lose the thread somewhere before thinking about the next thing—the Battle of Antietam. Over twenty-two thousand Yankee and Rebel casualties of war in a single day. For what? The world is mad.

The mind eventually settles on Erin Riggs—the first girl I ever kissed. Friday night. The football game. Underneath the bleachers. A cool fall night. Awkward. Clumsy. Amazing. She moved away the following spring, and I moped around town for a full two weeks. Never saw her again. I swivel toward my computer and search her out for a good thirty minutes, happy to have something to do. The hunt grows cold. She probably got married, changed her name. Would I even recognize her? Maybe she was on one of my juries along the way. Whatever she looks like now, the vision of her that night materializes before me as if she were in the room right now. Erin Riggs.

Then I think of Sydney.

I pick up the phone and call Chad Dallas. We go to the same church, except I don't go anymore. As soon as he answers, regret at my impulsive action descends like a paratrooper. What am I doing?

"Haven't seen you in awhile," he says. Chad is one of the most rock-solid Christians I know, and this comment is his gentle way of chiding me for abandoning church.

"I know. Been busy."

"Uh-huh."

"I'm sorry to bother you at home, but I was wondering if I could see Sydney."

"Right now?"

"If that works for you."

"I don't see why not."

I look at the phone accusingly as if it tricked me into making the call. The mind's leap from Otis Redding to Erin Riggs to Sydney to reaching out to Chad happened with astounding swiftness. I head to my car questioning my every action. Work has been my crutch for so long that in its absence I've become unreliable in how I fill the void. Maybe that's how Lara ended up in my lap. Having reached the limits of my physical endurance by working non-stop, I longed for another distraction. Now I've had my fill of her. Tonight it's Sydney's turn to aid and abet my war against emptiness.

***

The drive over changes the feeling of uncertainty into one of anticipation. I haven't seen Sydney in over two years. Will she even recognize me? As I park on the street, the thought that she might not remember freezes me in place. Experiencing that rejection would hurt. I get out of the car, put on a mask of happiness, and head to the house with slow steps. Chad greets me at the door, offers a hug, and says, "How are you, brother? We miss you at church."

"Been busy. Murder never sleeps."

"They'll still be dead Monday morning, you know."

Chad's gift is an ability to say seemingly innocuous things that nevertheless convey hard truths. The dead will still be dead no matter what I do, and using my job to avoid every other part of my life is a poor excuse for living.

Chad's wife, Olivia, joins us in the entryway. More small talk follows, and I fake friendly patience. At last, Chad calls out for Sydney. On cue, the sound of footsteps coming from the basement answers in obedience. Sydney enters the room and stops for a second before bounding toward me with unleashed enthusiasm. She remembers. Her meaty paws jump up at me, and I bend down to let her lick my face. When I kneel to get more on her level, she knocks me down in her excitement.

Amber and I adopted Sydney as a rescue border collie and boxer mix shortly after we got married. We had just returned from our two-week honeymoon in Australia and named her after our new favorite city in the world. The trip was incredible—experiencing New Year's Eve at the Opera House with a million other people, climbing to the top of Sydney Harbour Bridge, the revealing bikini Amber wore on Bondi Beach. On the flight back to the States, I looked at my sleeping wife and knew that God had given me a woman I did not deserve. Then we got a puppy.

Sydney's excitement at seeing me has yet to abate. I can't help smiling in effortless joy at the spastic display of her devotion. I've watched touching videos of soldiers returning from war to reunite with their ever-loyal canine friends. Now I'm living out my own heart-tugging moment. The pureness of Sydney's love humbles me.

I gave her away after the murders because the pain was too much. She invoked too many memories—memories that I was too mentally weak to handle. Every time I looked at Sydney, I saw Amber and Cale. So I turned the page and found Sydney a happy home, convinced that I was doing the right thing.

Chad, Olivia, and I make some obligatory small talk as required by the customs of the South. Chad brings up the trial next week, and

I respond, "I pray that justice is done." Olivia asks if I've met Lara Landrum. Et tu, Brutus? I never took her for the starstruck type. Yes, Olivia, I've met Lara Landrum, and I could tell you some things that would burn your ears off.

I leave that last part out.

Not wanting to overstay my welcome, I say my good-byes and give my ex-dog a parting hug. Chad encourages me not to be a stranger and even means it. But I am a stranger to everyone, most of all myself. The joy I felt moments ago gives way to deep sadness, and the night air judges me as I walk to the car. Reaching my door, I turn back toward the house and see Sydney staring at me through the window. I wave farewell to her and slump down in the driver's seat.

Giving away that dog is the single worst thing I've ever done in my life. I worried coming over here that she wouldn't remember me. But her unbridled happiness at seeing me again hurts much more. Sydney doesn't care that I gave her away. She doesn't care that I haven't visited her in two years. She doesn't care about any of my faults. She loves me just as I am. And during the one time I needed unconditional love more than at any other moment of my existence, I gave it away. The buoyant man who held Amber under the December summer sky of Australia would never have exiled Sydney from his life.

I hate myself.

I turn again to the house, hoping to see Sydney still manning her post. But she is gone, and I am alone. The tears burst forth like a pent-up tsunami, sending me into convulsive heaves. I never cried when Amber and Cale died. I got the shakes and the chills. I vomited. I suffered in silent anguish. But I never cried. I couldn't. The tears just wouldn't come. Now I sit in a car on a street bawling over a dog. The release doesn't make me feel better, only worse. I still hate myself.

The phone rings. Scott. I gather myself and hit the necessary button.

"Where are you?"

"Visiting Sydney."

"The dog?"

"Yes—the dog."

"Big trial next week, you know, and you're visiting a dog?"

"What do you want?"

"I don't think Sam killed himself."

"Why not?"

"Remember that second bullet we found in the tree? It matches the bullet that killed Sam. Two shots were fired that day. Does that suggest suicide to you? It's murder. One is the kill shot. That's first. The second shot you wrap around Sam's hand and fire it yourself to give him gunpowder residue. Murder. I know it in my bones."

"But who?"

30

Scott's update on Sam occupies my mind during the drive home. The breakdown from seeing Sydney over, I'm back on the case. But the disquiet from what just happened still sits as a thorn in my flesh. Trying to consider all the angles Sam's death might have on the trial, the image of Sydney looking out at me from the window intermittently tortures me. Anger replaces sadness. I can't believe I gave away the family dog. What was I thinking? I gave Sydney away to escape from the past, yet I wallow in the past every single day of my life.

I park the car in the garage, no closer to solving the Sam puzzle. Fear seizes me that I might very well lose the trial. My mind's all over the place; Ella and I barely coordinate trial plans; and Sam's death just threw a giant monkey wrench into everything. That's not even considering the Millwood factor and the probability that I hopelessly compromised the case by sleeping with the star witness. The weird thing is that I'm not sure I even care anymore. I just want it to be over. My ordered life ceased to exist the moment Scott brought me out in the middle of the night to the unhappy home of Bernard and Sara Barton.

The house is silent, but I'm not alone. I think about the old ghosts that still live here and the haunting they exert over me. If I were a better man, Sydney would be running up to greet me right now. But Sydney, too, is a ghost. I enter the living room, unsure of how I will ever pass the hours until another dawn.

"Where the hell have you been?"

The question takes a wrecking ball to the silence and causes me to jump out of my skin. I can tell from Lara's mood that she has been here for a while and that she didn't like waiting. I should've checked into that hotel.

I ask, "How did you get here? Your car wasn't on the street."

"I took Uber."

"Uber? To here? Are you insane?"

The instinct of self-preservation runs strong. An unfolding dread numbs my body and sends a flash of heat to my flush face. Her recklessness astounds. She cannot be here.

She answers, "Don't be an idiot. I had him drop me off a couple of blocks away."

"He's still going to know it's you, though. You're leaving a credit card trail."

"I have aliases. All stars do. Stop being a pussy."

The slur boils me inside. I once saw a knock-down, drag-out fight between two rednecks at a Panama City Beach McDonald's over that very accusation. It may be primitive, but the insult is an affront to one's manhood. "Fighting words" is what we call it in the law—the kind of thing they used to duel about in the old days. I can't shoot Lara, and I won't take my hand to her, but I can get her out of my house.

"You need to leave."

"Do you think you can ignore me? I've been calling you all night. Where the hell have you been?"

On the way to visit Sydney I put the burner phone in the car's glove box and haven't looked at it since. Resentment of her controlling attitude spawns within me, but her bargaining power over me is immense. She can ruin my career, my reputation, my relationship with my best friend. I feel like a puppet in her play.

"I was visiting a dog."

"What the hell does that mean?"

I explain myself—the whole backstory of Sydney and my reunion with her earlier tonight. I avoid looking at Lara during the retelling and instead burn a hole into the floor with my eyes. Her reaction when I finish doesn't make me feel any better. She smiles with enthusiastic mocking.

"That's damn cute," she says.

I don't take it as a compliment.

Pouring salt into the wound, she adds, "And you just gave her away? That's cold."

I can't disagree and feel as if the night has turned into death by a thousand cuts. I miss Amber.

Hearing about Sydney changes her mood. She looks around the room, finds a picture of Sydney, and inspects it with a close eye. Then she smiles.

"She's so cute. Maybe I can meet her one day."

Noticing my disbelief, she moves toward me with the silky smoothness of a sleek sex kitten on the prowl. I fortify myself against the incoming attack. Not tonight. She deploys the smile that has made men all over the world fall in love with her. But I've seen the empress with no clothes, and I'm not so easily moved anymore. It's all an act. I pray that the entire relationship hasn't been a giant put-on, but what's happening now is pure performance.

She purrs, "You've had a hard day, and you're under a lot of stress. Let me make you feel better. I'll do anything you want tonight. *Anything*."

I don't even know what that means. My resolve holds.

"Get out."

She smirks as if she has seen this movie before. Undeterred, she attempts another approach, rubbing me with her hand, pressing her breasts against my chest. "You know you want to," she whispers. Not tonight. If I give in to this seduction, I'll never respect myself again. The absolute clarity of the moment solidifies any breaches in my resistance. I remove her hand and back away.

"Leave."

She folds her arms and laughs in disbelief. I think I prefer crazy Lara to mocking Lara. Yell at a man, he'll get over it soon enough. Laugh at him, and he'll hate you forever. The refusal to take me seriously continues to stir my blood. Oblivious to my growing ire, she removes her shirt with the speed and efficiency of a sneaky panther. Those perfect breasts again shine before me in all their welcoming glory. I consider looking away from the temptation, but my anger gives me a strength I didn't know I had. She comes to me again, the panther on the hunt. When she takes my head in her hands to kiss me, I grab and twist her wrists with more force than necessary to make my point. She backs away, finally realizing her misread of the situation. Half-naked, rubbing her sore wrists, a mixture of surprise and fear on her face—Lara Landrum doesn't look so menacing.

I bark, "Get out or I swear that I will call the press myself right now and confess everything."

"You don't mean that."

"Like hell."

Threats are worthless if one is not willing to follow through. The spontaneous declaration that I would go to the media was not planned out, but I latch onto its wisdom with great speed. I'm at the end of my rope, and the absolution of confession would feel like welcomed relief. The present is faltering. I could quit the case and live the rest of my life in the woods. I've always liked Maine.

Lara's sexual aggression takes a timeout. There are no more laughs or smirks. Her shirt goes back on, and she studies me with a reappraising eye. Tonight's skirmish is over, and I won. The only vibe I get from her now is wariness. That's fine by me. I'm tired of being taken for granted. There's no profit in it. Lara picks up her purse and moves to the door. I have no idea how she's going to get home, and frankly I don't give a damn.

Her hand ready on the handle, she gives me a last hard look with eyes filled with the hostility of a disturbed hornet's nest. My resolute exterior beats back a rebellion from my weakening nerves on the inside. I show nothing. She opens the door—her stare still firmly affixed on me like a meat clever. The chill of the fresh air washes over me.

She says, "You watch yourself. I don't care how upset you are about your little dog—no one treats me like that. You get your act together or I'll ruin you in a way you'll never see coming. And you better not blow Bernard's case next week or I'll damn sure end you!"

I allow her the parting shot. A big sigh of relief escapes from me with the slamming of the door. After a discreet time passes, I sneak to the side of the front window to take a furtive inventory of Lara's movements. She's walking down the street with her phone out, a baseball cap on her head. Crisis averted. I patrol the house, checking all the locks and latches twice. Another look out the window reveals nothing. The boring night I expected a few hours ago turned into something quite different. Life comes at you fast.

Tomorrow's Thursday. Four days before the start of the trial.

31

The next day my brother is in town and we meet for lunch. I have little appetite. Last night's disaster with Lara sits undigested in my belly, and the lingering nausea is all too real. Ella will meet with Lara tomorrow to rehearse their direct examination, but I'm barred from that meeting per Ella's earlier ultimatum. I'm glad to be spared the hassle.

Ben and I embrace. He's five years older than me and looks five years younger. I idolized him growing up. I envy him now. He represents everything I lost—the wife, the kids, even the moral goodness. I hate the growing distance between us but feel powerless to do anything about it. I look at his life and see little apart from my own pain.

We talk about Mom, his family, college football, the usual. He makes the typical routine inquiries about the trial. I give the typical routine answers. He doesn't ask about Lara. I admire his restraint. Last time he saw me Lara Landrum sat in our mother's living room. Surely that merits a follow-up. Yet Ben has never circled back to me about Lara in the weeks since. We order our food and look at each other, seemingly both thinking the same thing—what now?

He asks, "How are you doing?"

"I'm fine."

He studies me with great thoughtfulness, and I recognize the signs of what's in his heart. Ben wants to minister to me. I'm not in the mood.

He goes on, "Come on. I know better. I want to know what's really going on with you. We don't talk anymore. I miss you."

"What do you want to know? Amber's still dead. Cale's still dead. I still get up in the morning every day and go to work in the D.A.'s office. That's about it."

"Cut the bull. I want to know how you feel on the inside. That kind of thing. How's your walk with God?"

My response is immediate: "There is no God, and I hate him."

The words come out of left field. Their vehemence surprises me. Such a sentiment is not the kind of thing one says to a preacher in the South, even if he is your brother. But Ben's reaction is full of sweet syrup. No dismay, no shock, no disappointment. Instead, he smiles.

"Why are you smiling?"

"Because that may be the first honest thing you've said to me since Amber and Cale were murdered. That's progress."

Fair enough. He thinks we just made a big spiritual breakthrough. I don't. Honesty. Dishonesty. God. No God. None of it matters. Everything important to me was taken away by two small pieces of lead. Nothing will change that.

Ben continues, "You say you hate God. That's good. Hostility I can work with, denial not so much. It would be the rare person in your shoes who wouldn't be angry with God after what happened. Trust me, though, God is big enough—"

I interrupt, "Listen, Ben, I'm glad you're here. It is good to see you. I mean that. I appreciate what you're trying to do, but I don't want to have this conversation now. Or ever. Let's just enjoy lunch."

Ben takes the rebuke in stride. He is a preacher. He has heard worse. I'm sure he took classes in seminary about how to reach recalcitrant people. His empathy and gift for public speaking would've made him a great trial lawyer. I could see him representing accident victims before country juries and generating headline after headline with million-dollar verdicts. But he wanted to be a preacher since he was a little boy and chose Jesus instead. I didn't understand the decision, thought he was crazy. Why choose that life? Amber changed my perspective for a time, gave me a new appreciation for things eternal. Now I'm not sure that any of it matters. Meaningless, meaningless—everything is meaningless.

"Okay. I'll keep giving you room. But if you keep stiff-arming God, you're going to stay stuck in the ditch. You'll never find peace on your own."

"Easy for you to say. Your wife and child weren't murdered."

Silence follows. I shouldn't have said that. Ben was withdrawing from the topic like I requested, and I threw the dead bodies of Amber and Cale right back in his face. The look of pain on his face is real. The murders now hang over this conversation just like they hang over the rest of my life. Everything I do is wrong. Ben speaks first.

"What about Job? He lost his family, too. Yet he said about God: 'Though he slay me, I will trust in Him.' There's life still to be lived, Chance. God's not done with you."

"Job? Really? I love you, man, but you're talking to me about things you can't possibly understand."

"That's not true."

I have no idea what he's talking about, and the suggestion that he somehow understands the experience of my anguish angers me. I tell him as much. Tears well up in his eyes. My brother is not a crier, not one to use cheap emotionalism to manipulate people to win a point. Whatever's motivating this display is real. The weirdness of the moment makes me uncomfortable. At a loss for words, I sit like a statue waiting for him to make the next move. At that moment, the food is served. Neither of us picks up our fork.

Ben finally asks, "You remember Jenny Baker?"

"Sure. Your girlfriend in college. I thought the two of you would get married."

"Yeah, so did I. We dated for a long time, and I let lust get the better of me. She got pregnant."

The disclosure floors me. The story is human enough but shocks all the same. Now the two of us sit across from each other joined together in the revelation of a long-kept secret—me surprised by what he told me, him surprised that he told me at all. But Ben is only half-finished. Part of me senses where this is going. I keep quiet to allow him to finish telling it in his own time. After a spell, he shares the rest of it.

"Jenny told me the news, and of course, I wanted to do the right thing, get married, and have the baby. I asked her on the spot. She said no. She was going to get an abortion. I couldn't believe it. Tried to talk her out of it. Begged her not to do it. Broke down crying in front of her more than once. But she wouldn't budge. She was going to get an abortion. Her heart was set on law school."

He looks at me with a slight accusation that I'm somewhat responsible for every person who ever decided to go to law school. His confession tracks what I figured. I digest the information, chaos swirling around my skull. Nothing is as it seems. The foundations of my life crumble one by one. Maybe they all are already gone, and I'm no longer even standing, like the cartoon coyote who doesn't realize the bottom has already fallen out from under him.

Ben says, "Abortion. Can you believe it? 'For you created my inmost being; you knit me together in my mother's womb.' Psalms. My child. Aborted. 'And the wages of sin is death.'"

"I'm sorry."

"I know. Sorry to dump all of this on you now. You were in high school at the time, too busy chasing cheerleaders."

"Caught a few of them, too."

Ben allows himself a soft chuckle. He asks, "Any of them get pregnant?"

"Not that I know of."

"Maybe you were doing it wrong."

The joke allows us to transition to eating. I do my part and send the cold food on its way to my indifferent stomach. Ben pays less attention to his plate, nibbling here and there. The preoccupation on his face tells me he has more to say, but isn't sure how to go about it. I tell him to go ahead and say it, knowing that he wants to make another pitch to save his wayward brother. Thankful for my permission, he looks at me with a level of earnestness in his eyes that would make angels weep. I wonder if I've ever felt anything so pure in my entire life. He begins.

"I insisted on taking Jenny to the abortion clinic. The punishment of sitting there—burning with hot rage and limitless despair—struck me as just. I wanted to hurt. I deserved it. I had pledged my life to God, but then deserted Him to satisfy my own lustful cravings. I got home that night and tried to see my future. I told myself that I couldn't go into the ministry with an aborted child on my record. I was now disqualified from His service."

Ben pauses—taking a deep breath and a sip of water. He didn't expect to travel the old road of these memories over this lunch, and he's still trying to find his way.

"But I realized then that I had nothing else. The thought of not serving Jesus broke me. I couldn't carry the weight—the dead child, losing my future wife, losing my future vocation, the anger, the self-hatred—I couldn't carry it anymore. I had to give it to God. And then I heard the still voice of God deep in my soul: 'Feed my sheep. Feed my sheep. Feed my sheep.' I saw the way forward. My condition wasn't permanent. That's when I spent that month serving in the orphanage in Haiti. Remember? I had to take the focus off of myself. God rebuilt me brick by brick, and it all started with losing the woman I loved and the death of my child."

He gives me a knowing look.

"It's not the same thing," I answer.

"It is to me."

I believe he believes that. But I cannot equate his break-up with a girlfriend and the loss of the nameless fetus he never held to the violent killing of my family. The murder of Amber and Cale is the bell that cannot be unrung.

32

The Friday before trial and my pre-trial checklist is complete. I fiddle with my opening statement just to have something to do. The door to my office opens abruptly. Bobby flies through the entrance.

He likes to visit the offices of his subordinates. I reckon it appeals to his grassroots pretensions. Odds are he read about the practice in some leadership book. He wants to discuss Barton.

He asks, "You ready?"

"We're ready."

"No surprises?"

"There are always surprises. We just don't know what they are yet."

He recognizes the truth of the answer, even though he doesn't like it. His annoyed look reflects his distrust of a universe that would throw surprises at him during an election year.

He says, "Millwood is good."

"He is that."

"You're better."

With Bobby, sincerity is always a mystery. I appreciate the words in any event. He goes on.

"You're better than him and you can beat him. Don't you walk into that courtroom thinking that Bernard Barton has the better lawyer. He does not. I know Millwood was your mentor and you look up to him. I do not care. You're better. When I became D.A., I pushed Millwood out because I wanted you to have his job. It was time. You're my man. Don't psych yourself out or any other nonsense like that. You got this. Got it?"

I wasn't expecting a pep talk. His description of Millwood's departure is a new revelation, and I hope Jack doesn't secretly blame me. But Bobby's words do inspire, even if they are just for show. I felt good about squaring off against Millwood following the plea conference. Now I feel even better. I'll give Bobby credit. Those leadership books are paying off.

He asks again, "Got it?"

"Got it."

"Now go get me a guilty verdict."

***

Ella enters my office without knocking, wearing a scowl north of annoyance but south of rage—barely. She slams a legal pad onto a side table before throwing her body into a chair. The weirdness still existing between us leads me to hold my tongue. I'll know the problem soon enough.

"Our star witness is being a diva."

"How so?"

"Uncooperative. Unpleasant. Won't answer any questions. Called me a black bitch. Demanded you conduct her examination at trial. Real peach of a gal you got there."

"I'm sorry."

"You can choke on all your sorrys."

She means it. I hoped Lara would behave during their final witness prep this morning. Their teamwork to this point has held, resting on an uneasy alliance between two adversaries united in pursuit of a common enemy. But Lara's recent antics had me worried. Now I have two angry women on my hands. A new thought emerges.

"Should we not call her to the stand?"

The fewer the variables at trial, the better. Right now, Lara is a variable. I once had pegged her as a supernova of a witness—the grieving sister pulling at the emotional heartstrings of the jury, the avenging angel pointing the finger straight at the defendant, the living embodiment of the victim in the courtroom right down to the last freckle. But the defining characteristic of a supernova is that it explodes.

Ella chews on the merits of the Lara gambit for some time. One frustrated shake of the head later, she concludes, "I think we need her."

I shake my own head in response.

"We have the gun. The 911 call. The money. Motive because of Brice and the gambling. The video of Barton leaving Monica Haywood's apartment before the murder. Haywood's lie about his alibi. We have enough."

"No. This isn't some open-and-shut case where everything will go by the book. We need to nail everything down backwards and forwards. We can't give Jack Millwood even a crack or he will exploit it. Lara Landrum is a dream witness. You always tell me that trials aren't just about facts but also about emotions. She's the heartbeat of our case and can lead the jury to hate Barton. We need her. She has been fantastic in preparing for her testimony until today. We just need to knock her off her high horse a little bit and get her back on track. We also need her to get the photo of Sara Barton's bruised back into evidence. Lara took that picture."

I sigh. Something else is at play here. Ella's big moment of the trial is Lara's direct examination. The whole country will be watching. Take that away, and Ella becomes a bit player. The glory would be all mine. Knowing what she knows about me, that would be one bitter pill too many.

"I'll have to talk to her. Alone."

Ella's skeptical eyes search my soul, wondering if she can trust me. She can't, and she knows it. She gives me a reluctant nod anyway, realizing that I'm a necessary means to an end. She wants to win the Barton trial as much as I do. That's one of the reasons we've always made such a good team.

I ask, "Is she still here?"

"I don't think so. She stormed out and didn't look back."

"Expect that your preparation of the witness will resume at three this afternoon. Let me know how it goes. If she doesn't show, we'll figure it out from there."

"What are you going to say to her?"

I offer a long look and ask, "Do you really want to know?"

"Never mind."

***

Ella leaves, and I retrieve the burner phone from its hiding place. Burner phones are tools of the criminals this office prosecutes. And yet here I sit—a man with two phones leading a double life, trying unsuccessfully to keep the two lives from colliding into each other.

I turn the device on and watch it reverberate with spastic convulsions on my desk as a long series of new messages download in machine gun style. The chain of text messages runs the gamut. Expletives. Threats. Distress. Demands. Name-calling. Urgency. Ultimatums. Even another suggestion of suicide.

I text her back and instruct her to meet me in the condo immediately. I turn the phone back off, not even waiting for a response. I consider chucking it out the window, but put it back in its secret spot instead. My legs don't want to move, but I will them to stand up. I drag myself slowly along the corridor, using prodding steps to delay the moment of reckoning—just like a condemned man walking to his own execution.

I am so tired, and I have no one to blame but myself.

***

She is already there, bracing for a fight. The drive over fortified my nerve. The plan is simple. Go in, tell it to her straight, and get out. Don't give her an opportunity to play games.

She tries to take control first and bellows, "I warned you about ignoring me."

"Shut up."

"Don't you—"

"Shut up! Listen closely. You don't start behaving, we're not going to let you testify. Do you understand? Barton may walk because of it, but I don't care. You won't be a witness. But I'm not going to take you off the witness list. I'll subpoena you and have a sheriff's deputy babysit your ass in a windowless room for the entire trial. Your choice. If you decide to behave, meet with Ella again at 3 p.m. to finish your trial prep. If you're not there, then we'll have your answer."

I hold my intensity for as long as I dare before turning around to hightail it out of there. The terms set, further negotiations are superfluous. A quick exit is best. Before I can escape, a drinking glass shatters on the floor, but only after flying through the air and ramming into the base of my skull. I find a bar chair for balance, feel around for blood, and turn back toward the woman standing on the other side of the room. I have prosecuted scores of murderers, yet no eyes have ever assaulted me with such hatred. I can't comprehend how we reached this point.

Moments pass in the ensuing staredown. I stand straighter to reveal my full size to make her think twice about another attack. I wonder if she has a gun. I imagine a murder-suicide that would cover a month's worth of headlines. But notoriety is fleeting. Memories of a disgraced and murdered lawyer would fade over time, as if I had never lived.

Collecting myself, I retreat to the original script.

"Three o'clock sharp. If you're not there, we'll have your answer."

"You're going to let me down just like you did your wife and son."

I could kill her. The fresh physical and emotional wounds transform me from the hunted to the hunter. Lara recognizes the change. When I take a step toward her, she takes a different glass and hurls it in another go at my head. I snatch it out of the air with one hand—residual instinct from my days as a high school receiver—and send it back to its source at a much greater velocity than which it arrived. I miss Lara but find the wall behind her, resulting in a thunderous smash and scattering more landmines of glass all across the floor.

The surprise noise sobers both of us for a moment, and I know with as much certainty as I've ever known anything that I need to get out of this condo as quickly as possible. Another minute and she may be dead.

"Don't you walk away from me!"

Too late. I'm gone.

33

I take to the street. Possibly concussed, driving seems inadvisable. I could hail a taxi home, but Lara might show up with an ax and chop me into little pieces. Or maybe the ax would be in my hands. All scenarios are in play at this point, and I can't take the chance. The office is out, too. If Lara does show for her meeting with Ella, I want to be far away.

A hotel a few blocks down the street attracts me. I need to be alone. I check in, tell the front desk that I am not to be disturbed, and find my room. The window actually looks out toward the condo, but the distance is too great to make anything out. I draw the curtain closed. I remove all my clothes, hang up my suit, and fold everything else neatly on the table—a small dash of order in an otherwise sea of tumult. I turn the air conditioning down to its lowest setting to chase away the hot rage. The lights are off. My head still stings, but a wet towel to the injury tells me that the blood is minimal. I'll live.

I silence my phone and lie down on the bed without bothering to get under the covers. The exposure to the cooling air refreshes my naked skin. Goosebumps rise and fall in tempo with the beating of my chest. Thinking comes hard, and I swat away any stray attempts to do the requisite heavy lifting. The darkness comforts me in the knowledge that I'm unseen in a place where no one can find me. I've finally landed on an oasis of peace.

***

I bolt upright in bed, full of fear, unsure of where I am. The disorientation is immense. The darkness doesn't help. I stumble to find a light to make sense of my surroundings. A lamp does the trick, and I sit in an adjacent chair to gather myself. The ache in my head persists, and I recall the earlier scene that brought me to this room.

I check my phone.

A bunch of routine matters litter my messages and Scott wonders why I'm not in the office the Friday before trial, but word from Ella is what interests me the most. I find it. The text reads: "Whatever you did worked. She showed up and did everything asked of her. We're ready for trial."

I read the text four times to be sure. My first thought is that I have a bump on my head for no good reason. But that's applying rational motives to an irrational actor. More likely, the bump on my head was the price of admission to get Lara back on the team.

The phone rings as I continue to get my bearings. I grimace at the ID. Liesa.

She says, "Can you come over? I want to talk."

"Now? About what?"

"Sam."

"I'm not sure that's the best idea."

"Please."

I sigh before replying, "Give me an hour."

I shower and get dressed. I'll grab fast food on the way. I study the man in the mirror. He looks normal, but his head still hurts. At least the glass didn't hit me in the face. The anonymity afforded by the hotel room provided a nice respite, but come Monday I can't escape the searing publicity. Confidence in the case remains strong. It's the lawyer in charge of the case that worries me.

I check out of the hotel and walk back to the parking garage in the condo. The fresh air should do me good—if only it were fresh. The smog and smells of Friday afternoon traffic put to bed any notion concerning the rejuvenating power of being outdoors. The city is dirty. The stale air of my car tastes sweet as watermelon in comparison.

***

I drive over to Liesa's house. Before Scott's call two nights ago about the second bullet, I had all but landed on suicide as the safest explanation for Sam's death. But now murder is squarely on the table. Barton, Brice, and Liesa are all leading candidates. I am unsure what Liesa wants to discuss, but I will record our conversation. Anything Liesa says can and will be used against her in a court of law.

We sit in the same places as our first awkward meeting about the Barton case. That day seems like a long time ago. It was three months. Liesa's steel resolve, worn so defiantly then, is vanished, replaced by red and weary eyes.

"Where are the kids?"

"At my mom's."

Tears stream down her face. She grabs a box of tissues from another room and reclaims her place. The possibility of another revelation about Sam makes me antsy. I hope like heck that box in the mountains is where I left it.

"What do you want to talk about?"

"I cannot believe Sam is dead."

"Me either."

"Why did he have to die?"

I study her. Sam was probably murdered, and Liesa is a suspect. Last time we met, she played me for information while I got precious little out of her. That won't happen again. Grieving widow or not, I will hold my cards close.

"I don't know, Liesa. I really don't know."

"Was he murdered?"

"I don't know. Did you kill him?"

"Really? I can't believe you would ask me that."

She moans, takes a deep breath, and cries some more. The tissue box is empty. She throws it to the side in frustration.

"I loved that man. Loved him since the first time I saw him in the law library. He could drive me mad, could hurt me, could make me question my self-worth, but I would never kill him. I loved him too much. I gave up my life for him, and now he's gone. I need a drink."

Liesa leaves for the kitchen, returns with a bottle of wine, and fills herself a generous glass. She doesn't offer me any. She knows I don't drink. Haven't for a long time. Because of Amber. I got drunk one night, acted like an ass toward her, woke up sick and hung over. She didn't speak to me for two days. I promised her I would never drink again, and I haven't. Maybe I should. Maybe it would help me sleep, dull the pain.

I ask, "Would Sam kill himself?"

"Did he kill that woman?"

"That's the second time you asked me that. Is there something you know that I don't?"

The image of Sam's angry face as he penetrated Sara Barton infiltrates my brain. Liesa shakes her head in denial.

I respond, "Good. Because Bernard Barton killed that woman."

"Then Sam didn't kill himself."

I see the reasoning. Murdering Sara Barton would be too far out of character for the Sam I knew. But if he had killed her for some impulsive reason, then I could see him killing himself out of guilt. The nervousness of living with that burden would've eaten him alive. He may have been weak and stupid, but he was not evil.

Liesa asks, "Did you find what you were looking for in the mountains?"

"It wasn't important."

"It was important enough for you to harass me on the day I buried my husband. How could you be so cruel? You of all people should know better."

She's not wrong. I sit there appropriately chastened. She sips more wine. But the tug of the case is a hard drug to resist. I ask, "What are you going to do now? Is there any life insurance to help you get through?"

Liesa laughs. She spots my fake concern a mile off.

"You still trying to pin Sam's death on me?"

"Look, I got $2 million when Amber died. I'm not judging."

"Did you kill Amber?"

I flash her a cold, hard look.

She says, "Shoe is on the other foot. Don't like to be asked if you killed your wife, do you?"

"Amber never gave me a reason to kill her."

Point scored. Her wounded eyes wave the white flag of temporary surrender. Whatever this meeting is—old friends commiserating about shared experiences of loss, the questioning of a murder suspect, or Liesa pumping me for information—we have both brought out our switchblades to freshly puncture the spots where each of us hurts the most. I feel no bitterness toward Liesa, have no ancient score to settle. But our uneasy conversations point to some hidden antagonism. Were we ever really even friends? I reflect that all of my relationships traffic in dysfunction.

I plead, "Can you just answer a simple question?"

"You're just doing your job, right?"

"Something like that."

"Sam had a $1 million personal policy, and a $2 million dollar business policy. I get $3 million, but I didn't kill him."

"Can I ask you another question?"

"Might as well. You're going to anyway."

"Where were you on the night of Sara Barton's murder?"

Liesa does not answer. She pours herself another glass of wine. Her third? I've lost count. I need to press her for an answer before she loses her coherence to the bottle.

I say, "Can I offer you up a theory about what you were doing that night? You can tell me if I'm hot or cold. I think Sam told you he had to go out. You decided you'd had enough of whatever was going on and followed him. You see him enter the Barton residence and see him come right back out. He then sees you. Something happens between the two of you—a fight, an argument, something. The neighbors heard you. Sam tells you to get the hell away from there and gives you time to leave before calling the cops. This theory allows for the strange dichotomy that you think Sam might've killed Sara Barton and he thought you might've killed her. Thoughts?"

"I don't like that theory."

"Well, another theory is that you killed Sara Barton. Sam discovered you. Hilarity ensues."

"I don't like that theory, either."

"Me neither. I like the first theory better since I'm putting Bernard Barton on trial for murder next week."

Liesa lets the conversation stop, and I ponder my theories in the resulting silence. She avoids eye contact and stares at her wine with uneven concentration. Without looking up, she asks, "Do you think I'm pretty?"

"Sure."

"I don't. I wasn't pretty enough for Sam."

"I doubt that had anything to do with it."

I read something once. The Bible teaches David was a man after God's own heart. Yet David probably had at least 300 wives and concubines. Even that wasn't enough. He still wanted Bathsheba for himself. Or take Solomon. He was the wisest person ever, warned the multitudes against the danger of sexual sin, and then destroyed his own life chasing women. What sense does that make? Lust devours reason, no matter the man.

She says, "I don't want to date again. I'm too old to start over, too young not to. I'm stuck. Like everything else in life, it's easier for men. But I'm a single mom with three kids. Nobody will want me. Or if they do, it will be for the money. What about you? Is there someone new?"

I don't answer the question, but the reaction in my face gives the game away. There is someone. Liesa asks, "What is she like?"

I think: Lara is beautiful, insightful, twisted, passionate, crazy, fun, scared, scary, hateful, and unpredictable—wonderful at times but possessed of a negative energy that will either defeat you into passive submission or make you angry enough to kill. I think back to the earlier scene in the condo. One word crystalizes in my mind.

"Bipolar."

Saying it out loud creates in me one of those random eureka moments. Bipolar. My mind works fast. Is bipolar disorder hereditary? Ella has Sara Barton's medical files. We haven't focused on them because they lack much relevance to the case. But I will ask Ella to take a look for evidence of bipolar disorder. The diagnosis would explain a lot.

Liesa scoffs, looks closely at the wine in her glass, and decides to take another drink.

She asks, "Did you ever cheat on Amber?"

"No."

"You wouldn't. Too much of a boy scout, looking down on the rest of us in moral disapproval."

"You're drunk."

"Probably."

"Where were you the night of Sara Barton's murder?"

"I never liked her that much."

"Who?"

"Amber."

My head hurts. The memory of a concussion suffered on the football field reaches me from the past. The same signs then are present now. I ignore Liesa's provocation and wonder if I should go to the hospital.

Liesa continues, "Mind you, I didn't want Amber to get murdered or anything. She just rubbed me the wrong way. Too goody two shoes for my taste."

"Whatever you're doing, stop. You're most likely going to be a witness in my murder trial next week. We need to work together here."

"She used to lead you around by the nose, that's for sure. Everybody said so."

"I'm beginning to see why Sam cheated on you."

That shuts her up for the moment. Just like our first meeting a few months ago, my irritation with Liesa leads me to smack her in the face with Sam's adultery. Both of us are starting to boil. I felt angry enough to kill Lara this afternoon, and I'm not in the mood for a repeat performance. Liesa's drunk, and I probably have a concussion—a volatile mix. I stand up to depart.

She demands, "Who killed my husband?"

"Where were *you* when Sam died?"

"Leave. Just leave."

"You're going to have to answer these questions sometime, Liesa."

"Get out of my house."

***

The drive home is an angry one. First Lara this afternoon, then Liesa tonight. The confrontation with Liesa is the fresher event, but it is the drama earlier in the day with Lara that plays on a loop inside my sore head. I'm losing control of myself, and she is the cause. Knowing that I am dancing to her tune enrages me all the more.

The garage door closes behind me. Alone, I can begin some much-needed personal repairs. I sit in the car for a good ten minutes. My blood pressure returns to normal. I scamper into my house ready to put this sordid day to bed. I don't get far.

Lara stands before me, and part of me dies inside. She approaches without a word and slaps me with everything she has. I flinch a retaliatory punch, but stop short. No.

She is insane, and I struggle for my soul against the wave of her craziness. She kisses me hard, but I push her away. Roughly. I want to hit her. She kisses me again. Bites my lip. Draws blood. She grabs my hand and puts it on her body. I feel her desire. Emotion overwhelms logic. I flip her on her stomach over the back of the couch. Base instinct takes over.

Across the way a mirror hangs that displays the face of a wild beast—my own. She meets my crazed look in the mirror, smiling a sneer of triumph that proclaims, "I own you." My third murder trial I got a conviction of a man that strangled his ex-girlfriend. I put my hands around Lara's neck. Her eyes dare me, but I lose my nerve.

After I complete my last revenge-filled thrusts, I toss her aside. I pant heavily on the couch—the racing heart taunting me that I am no longer a young man. Sitting on the floor, she wears a self-satisfied grin that would mortify Lucifer.

Minutes pass in silence. She slithers her way back toward me and snaps my head toward her with two sweaty hands, her hot breath on my face. The loud thumps of my overtaxed heart still ring to a hurried cadence.

"You put that son of a bitch away for what he did to my sister."

Nothing else is said. The door slams shut, and I am alone. Emptiness replaces the earlier anger. I think of the loaded gun in the closet. It would solve a lot of problems. My favorite picture of Amber sits on a nearby shelf. I ask her, “What’s wrong with me?” She doesn’t answer.

Flushed with humiliation, I stagger with dizziness to the bathroom, turn on the shower, and don’t wait for the water to warm. The cold punishes, and the punishment is just. The remnants of the inferno inside me dissipate under the chill. I shiver, then sob.

I never felt so dirty.

34

The Monday morning of the trial is here, but the past weekend is all I think about. I spent Saturday alone in the woods, running from myself. Lara broke me. Two separate times—first in the condo, then the house—I teetered on the precipice of violent rage. The weight of that darkness was too much. I had to get away. I went to the woods to escape my own terror.

I covered the same ground as Sam when he walked to his death. The journey seemed fitting. Atlanta sits right on the other side of the forest, but one would never know it. I stopped at the site of Sam's shooting and shuddered. I studied the area, trying to picture the scene with fresh insight. Nothing. I left Sam and headed to the river. The walk was about me, not him.

The Chattahoochee meandered before me, taking its time, much like its native South. I sat on a bench and watched the slow flow. My mind's drift gradually acclimated itself to the rhythm of the water. Call it meditation, call it a trance, but I lost myself for quite some time. The eyes were open, but the mind was turned off. When I awoke into consciousness again, I inhaled several deep breaths. My lungs full of air, I walked back to the car, taking the long way to get there. From start to finish, I never saw another single soul.

I went to the woods to get away. But driving into work on the biggest day of my professional career, I remain lost in the forest. I think about Adam who hid in the trees to get away from God and Jesus who went to the wilderness to get closer to God—the same action spurred by opposite motivations. I try to diagnose my own motives but fail. I still don't know who I am.

***

Alone in my office, I playact my part in today's script, desperately seeking a reservoir of motivation. The lack of nervousness worries me.

Nerves focus attention and keep a lawyer sharp. I don't suffer from overconfidence. The malaise is more personal. I hope the adrenaline will activate when the gavel sounds, out of habit if nothing else. In the courtroom, I can just be a lawyer and forget the rest of it.

Ella pops her head in and asks me if I'm ready. I lie. I ask her the same, but the fierceness she exudes makes her answer unnecessary. She is overqualified to be a second chair at this point. Even if I hadn't sabotaged our working relationship, she stood ready to emerge out from my shadow.

Her intensity softens as she lingers in the doorway and takes inventory of the man who has disappointed her on so many levels. She offers, "Things are obviously different between us now, but I hope we can be like we've always been in the courtroom, at least."

"That would make me happy."

"One other thing. I looked closer at the medical records like you suggested. You were right. Sara Barton was bipolar. Does it mean anything?"

It means everything, but nothing in terms of the trial. I did my own medical research over the weekend. Bipolar disorder is hereditary, and Lara's behavior displays the symptoms. Not only did I sleep with a witness, I slept with a bona fide mental case. I kick myself in the ass for the thousandth time. Lara at least has an excuse.

I answer, "I don't know. I just had the thought. It would explain some of her reckless conduct with men."

Ella gives me a perceptive look and leaves me to wallow in more self-condemnation.

***

I stand outside the prosecutors' side entrance to the courtroom and straighten my tie. On the other side of this door, the show goes live. The air around the courthouse already buzzes, the excitement pulsating from the walls. The atmosphere feels different from any other trial of my life—hordes of reporters doing remotes from the street, lines to get into the building, a hundred small differences that highlight something special is afoot. Realizing the stakes, the familiar nervousness of the past finally makes an appearance. Good sign. I'm going to be all right.

I feel Lara's presence before I see her. She offers her hand, and I reciprocate—by all appearances a professional handshake between casual acquaintances. What interested observers overlook is the small tickle she gives my palm with her index finger. The slight touch shocks me with its electricity. Lara's eyes remain on me a fraction too long, but only by a hair. Ella watches us like a hawk and misses everything. Lara approaches her, and they exchange strained greetings.

I take my seat and stare ahead. No words pass between us, and yet she snares me back into her web with the ease of a smooth criminal. As a dog returns to its vomit, so a fool repeats his folly. I tell myself harshly, "Focus."

The bailiff announces, "Please rise."

***

Jury selection is more art than science, more luck than skill, a brew of serendipity mixed with a dash of instinct. You make your most reasonable estimate and hope for the best, recognizing the foolishness of judging individuals on the scant information provided on a jury form.

The first twelve names on the jury list march to the front of the room, and the tango begins. Judge Mary Woodcomb takes the first crack at them and asks the basic questions. Have you formed an opinion as to the guilt or innocence of the accused? Have you any prejudice or bias for or against the accused? Is there any reason you cannot weigh the evidence with an impartial mind? The potential jurors answer "no" to the judge's questions because that is what good citizens are expected to say.

I rise to take my turn and ooze friendliness as I approach the jury box. Introductions are made, and I take my first steps to building a rapport with the men and women I'm going to ask to convict Bernard Barton of murder. First impressions matter. The tone is conversational, and I make good eye contact with each of them to personalize the formation of our relationship. Better to make all of them feel comfortable before throwing them into the fire.

Only then do I ask my questions. The process proceeds through the rest of the day.

Being back in the arena feels good. The emotional drama of the past few weeks melts away in the gritty detail of picking a jury. Hours pass. The game of musical chairs in the jury box reaches its denouement. By day's end, twelve individuals—seven African-Americans, five whites, six women, six men—survive the meat grinder of voir dire. Their divergent identities now merge into a singular collective known as the jury—*e pluribus unum*; out of many, one. The last actors in the drama now set, the prosecution of Bernard Barton begins tomorrow in earnest.

35

I don't believe in long opening statements. Too many lawyers place too much faith in their rhetorical skills, in their ability to convince anyone of anything if only given enough time. Conceit of this sort kills self-analysis—the ability to edit. Start strong, say your piece, sit down. The ability to maintain focus is a lost skill in the digital age, and the attorney who bores his jurors ensures that their minds will wander to other things.

Judge Woodcomb turns the floor over to me. I remain seated for a few seconds to let the silence settle. I stand up, walk to the center of the room, face the jury, and prepare my courtroom voice.

"'He's going to kill me!'"

A lot of lawyers start with sweet introductions. Not me. Man is an emotional animal. Grab the jury's attention and tell a story. Stories move people. I muster up all the pathos I can and relay the tragedy of Sara Barton.

"'He's going to kill me!' Sara Barton spoke those words. Seventy-nine days later, Sara's prophecy came true. Bernard Barton—the defendant, that man over there—pointed his gun at his wife and squeezed the trigger. A shot straight into Sara's heart."

I pause to allow the jurors to create their own mental pictures of the scene in their heads. What the mind can see, the mind will believe. I next take the jury on a tour of what the State's evidence will show—Barton's desperate need for money; the trips to Las Vegas; the gambling losses; the $5 million of life insurance on Sara's life; Barton's affair with a much younger woman; the murder weapon with Barton's fingerprints on the unused bullets; the lack of an alibi at the time of the murder; the video of Sara and Brice and the 911 call that followed; Sara's bruised back after her husband beat her.

Thirteen minutes after starting the story, I approach the finish line. I move closer to the jurors to foster greater intimacy. The connection is strategic. I seek to enlist them as my partners in the quest for justice.

"Ladies and gentlemen of the jury, on behalf of the State of Georgia, I'm going to ask you to hold Bernard Barton accountable for the death of his wife. I'm going to ask you to listen to the evidence and follow the bread crumbs right to Bernard Barton's door. I'm going to ask you to listen ... to Sara herself."

* * *

Millwood looms large over the courtroom. Judges sit behind raised pedestals to enhance their authority over the lesser men and women who appear before them. The visual effect usually works, but not with Millwood. His presence cuts too formidable a figure to be dwarfed by such pretensions. His oak-tree frame coupled with his oak-tree integrity drew me to him the first time we met. Working at his side for years only enhanced my regard. And now we sit at opposite tables.

He begins his opening statement:

"How do I stand before you and prove that Bernard Barton did not kill his wife? I don't. That's not my job. It's the State's job to prove beyond a reasonable doubt that he did. And that they cannot do. Sure enough, the State spins a compelling story, if only it were true. Let's start with what the evidence will not show."

Millwood starts away from the jury but walks slowly to a perch right in front of them, leaking gravitas all the way.

"The evidence will not show that Bernard ever fired that gun. His fingerprints were not found anywhere on the gun, no prints on the barrel, on the trigger, or anywhere. But his prints were on the unfired bullets in the gun, says the State. So what?"

He roars the "so what?" as if to dare anyone to answer the question.

"The gun belonged to the Bartons—Bernard and Sara. He bought it for her protection for when he was away traveling on business. His prints are on the bullets because he loaded the gun himself."

I'm floored. That evidence can only come in through Barton's own testimony, and it is foolish to commit to that course of action this early. Millwood would never agree to such nonsense unless pushed into it by his client. The idea that Barton is paying Millwood a boatload of money only to ignore his advice fills me with sardonic glee. I also smell weakness. They *have* to deal with the gun, and I take comfort that they feel risking Barton on the stand is the only way to do so. Knowing I will get a crack at Barton on cross-examination already feels like a monumental win. He won't wear well.

Millwood goes on, "The truth is that anyone who visited the Barton residence had access to that gun. Brice Tanner, one of Sara Barton's lovers, will testify that he was there the night before the murder. Sam Wilkins, Sara Barton's lawyer, was there the night of the murder. He discovered the body at 10 p.m. that night. What lawyer visits his client at her house that late?"

The question is argumentative, and I could move to have it stricken, but I don't dare put a spotlight on that particular issue. Millwood stands silent for a moment and allows the unstated gossip of the question to brew into something stronger.

"Sam Wilkins won't testify at this trial, so I won't get to ask him why he visited Sara Barton so late at night. Sam is dead from a bullet hole in the head. The State forgot to mention that in their opening statement. The only person we know for sure who was at the murder scene at the time of the murder is shot shortly thereafter. That's strange, and the State has no explanation for it."

Crafty. I've been spinning my wheels for weeks trying to discern how Millwood would approach Sam's death, and he just shifted the responsibility to me. If I don't explain it, Millwood will pound the table in incredulity. I have no choice but to take the bait. When your actions as a lawyer tell the jury that you're uncertain about your case, you shouldn't be surprised if the jury reaches the same conclusion.

I immediately rule Sam's death a suicide. Murder raises too many unanswerable questions: who killed Sam, why did that person kill Sam, and how does Sam's murder relate to Sara Barton's case? That's a quagmire I intend to avoid.

"Sam Wilkins has another connection to the murder scene. Sam's wife, Liesa Wilkins, was also in the vicinity of the Barton home at the time of Sara Barton's murder. Traffic cameras caught her driving away. Do I know if Brice Tanner, Sam Wilkins, or Liesa Wilkins killed Sara Barton? No. I do not. But red flags are everywhere."

He knows about Liesa and fully intends to use her. Great.

Millwood continues the process of laying out detonation devices to tripwire my case. He doesn't share my aversion to long openings. He considers himself a builder, and building takes time. The difference in our styles—he's the tortoise, I'm the hare—grew starker over the years. And while I'm well aware of the outcome of that particular fable, the hare's downfall was one of hubris, not strategy. He took the tortoise for granted. I won't make that mistake with Millwood.

Forty-five minutes in, I steal a glance at the jurors. Because it's their first day on the job, they figure to be at their attentive, nervous best. But a few of them struggle to maintain focus. Likely sensing the growing complacency of his audience, Millwood makes his final approach for landing.

"I'm going to tell you something I've never told a jury before, and I've tried a bunch of cases in my life. You won't like my client. He's abrasive and arrogant. He cheated on his wife throughout the course of their marriage. He gambles too much, and he acts like a little boy who has never grown up. But you are not jurors in a popularity contest. You're not charged with deciding whether Bernard Barton is a good person. He's not. You're charged with deciding whether the evidence shows beyond a reasonable doubt that he murdered his wife. The evidence presented will not meet that standard."

***

The first thing I do back in my office is call Liesa. The news that she is now front and center in the Barton trial has already landed on her. I smell the alcohol on her breath over the phone.

"We need to talk about how to handle your testimony," I say.

"No we don't. I don't care about your stupid case. I care about my children. I'm not talking to you. I'm not talking to that other lawyer."

"Do you care about being accused of murder on national television?"

Heavy breathing is the only thing I hear on her end. She needs to sober up. Any erratic behavior now becomes fodder for Millwood to keep dropping hints that Liesa may be a murderer. I expect the worst. Liesa has played this thing wrong from the beginning. Little reason exists to think she'll change now.

Trying to illicit some response, I say, "Millwood's going to subpoena you, Liesa. You can't run from this."

She hangs up.

Did Liesa kill Sam? I credited her denial when I asked her the same question at her house. I'm not so sure now. Sam gave her plenty of reason. Liesa gave up everything for him only to be betrayed in favor of another woman. The insurance money is also a nice pot of gold at the end of the rainbow. Three million dollars is three million dollars. The location of Sam's murder—if it was murder—further suggests that someone close to Sam killed him. He didn't walk into the woods with a stranger.

36

Ella calls Cecil Magnus to the stand. The old coroner strides up to the witness box with the royal bearing of a king. He takes his seat with an Old World dignity that teeters on extinction. The gentlemanly nod he offers to the jurors melts their hearts. After a ho-hum series of witnesses establishing the preliminaries with some of the first officers on the scene, Cecil will kick the case into high gear.

Law enforcement witnesses require special handling in a city with a majority black population. African-American jurors carry with them a well-earned distrust of the police—a wariness foreign to most whites. Mindful of this baggage, Ella questions most of our witnesses who serve in some law enforcement capacity. The subliminal message behind this strategy is that if Ella trusts the witness, then African-Americans on the jury can, too. The exception to this typical work division is Scott. I always question him—the two of us seemingly born on the same page.

With Cecil, an additional reason makes Ella the obvious choice to handle his direct examination. I think Cecil likes me, probably could even tell you my name. I *know* Cecil likes Ella. I could say that Ella is the daughter Cecil never had, except that Cecil has two other daughters and his affection toward Ella isn't all together fatherly. She is beautiful, and I'm not the only man to notice.

Ella starts with the basics, allowing Cecil to tell the story of his long-ago journey to becoming Fulton County Coroner. I've heard the routine more times than I can count, but the telling always sounds as fresh as the morning dew. The effect in the courtroom is captivating, and the jury now has no doubts about the expertise of the witness. Whatever Cecil says going forward will be written in stone as the rock-solid truth. Millwood knows as much. He won't dare challenge Cecil, but only highlight what the coroner doesn't say.

The meat of the testimony follows. To prevail on a murder count, the State bears the burden of proving beyond a reasonable doubt that Bernard Barton intentionally killed his wife with malice aforethought. The most elemental part of this showing requires proof that Sara Barton is, in fact, dead. Cecil testifies that he confirmed the victim's identity through driving license records and a personal identification of the body by the next of kin.

"And who identified the body of Sara Barton?"

"Her husband—the defendant."

"How would you describe his demeanor when he identified his wife's body?"

"Cold. Distant. Matter of fact. In a hurry to get out of there."

Ella walks back to the prosecution table and picks up a folder. The admission of autopsy photos—like the crime scene photographs I'll later introduce through Scott—is a ritual in every murder case. A dead body demands justice. But unlike the photos of DeShawn Carter's exposed brain matter in the Corey Miller case, the pictures of a dead Sara Barton lack much gruesomeness. Instead, the ghostly pallor on the victim's face will have to do.

Establishing the cause of death is the last piece that Cecil brings to the puzzle. Some coroners get stuck in the web of medical jargon and render conclusions confusing to lay people. But Cecil avoids the weeds of too much detail and tells it to the jury straight—Sara Barton died because of a gunshot wound to the chest.

"And were you able to make any determination about the type of gun used to kill Mrs. Barton?"

"Yes. Based on the entry wound and the ammunition recovered from the victim's body, I concluded that the murder weapon was a .22 revolver."

***

Millwood strides up to the front and turns to face the jurors as he begins his questioning of Cecil. The point of this tactic—a tool used by all skilled cross-examiners—is to focus the attention of the jury on the lawyer as if it is the lawyer who's doing the testifying. When done well, the witness is reduced to a prop. Millwood's dominating stage presence only adds to the effectiveness of this technique. He commands attention naturally.

"You're the coroner of Fulton County?"

"For longer than I care to remember."

Some laughter floats about the courtroom. Millwood laughs, too, to show that he's a good sport. He is building a camaraderie with the jurors who will decide the fate of his client.

"And the coroner doesn't determine who did the killing, only how the killing was done?"

"That's fair."

"And nothing in your testimony actually shows that the defendant murdered the victim here?"

"Correct."

"Your testimony just shows that the victim is dead?"

"Correct."

Millwood asks the basic questions of the State's witnesses that Joe failed to ask in the Corey Miller trial. Instead of attacking the finding of Cecil's autopsy, Millwood demonstrates what the autopsy does not—indeed, cannot—show. Questions such as these push the jury to keep an open mind as a counterweight to the impulse to condemn the defendant after seeing disturbing autopsy photos.

"Your autopsy also doesn't show if the murderer was short or tall?"

"It does not."

"Male or female?"

"Don't know."

"Right-handed or left-handed?"

"No idea."

"Don't know the race of the murderer?"

"No."

"The nationality?"

"Nope."

"Age?"

"Can't tell."

"The only thing you can tell us is that Sara Barton is dead and how she died?"

"Correct."

Millwood sits down. The game is afoot.

***

The next round of testimony focuses on the gun. Establishing the chain of custody of the weapon is a laborious, but necessary, process. Five witnesses in total testify, starting with the neighbor who discovered the gun in a playground down the street from the Barton residence. From the playground to the evidence locker to the fingerprint lab to the ballistics testing range, we document the gun's journey and the findings of the various experts along the way.

When the last of these witnesses steps down, I take stock of the evidence. Ballistics confirms that the gun found on the playground killed Sara Barton. Fingerprint analysis establishes that the defendant's prints were on the unused bullets in the chamber of that same gun.

Many a defendant has been convicted on less evidence than that.

37

Scott takes the stand, swears his oath, and introduces himself to the jury. The badge on the outside of his jacket conveys the authority of his position. The years of experience that wrinkle his face add gravity to his words. Plain-speaking and to the point, he makes a good witness.

The testimony begins with Scott's description of what he first saw at the Barton house—the lifeless body, the blood on the floor, no signs of forced entry. I show him pictures of the scene. He affirms their authenticity, and Judge Woodcomb admits the photographs into evidence.

I distribute the depictions of Sara Barton's dead body to the jurors one at a time. I don't hurry. Eight pictures overall pass through the hands of each juror. I assess each reaction as they contemplate Sara Barton's lifeless body. The slowness of the process allows the images to marinate and sink in. The main goal, of course, is to inflame.

But more than cynicism lies behind my efforts. Murder is serious business. What's happening in this courtroom is not some mock trial with fake facts and imaginary stakes. If the jurors have not felt the awesomeness of their responsibility up to this point, they will feel it now. Unlike the antiseptic autopsy photos, the pool of red blood around Sara's body pops visually—the stark color repulsing with guttural impact. These photographs portray the reality that Sara Barton was a living, breathing woman until someone shot her dead. Once the photos make their rounds, I continue with the examination.

"Who was Sam Wilkins?"

"Mrs. Barton's divorce lawyer. He discovered her body and called 911."

I then show Scott the divorce complaint Sam provided to the police the night of the murder. I move to introduce it into evidence.

Millwood stands up, and we both approach the bench for a sidebar with the judge.

"The defense objects to the admission of the complaint on the grounds of hearsay. The complaint is an out-of-court statement that makes factual allegations that cannot be substantiated. It is squarely inadmissible."

"Response?"

"The complaint is not offered into evidence to prove the truth or falsity of the allegations therein. Rather, the fact that the victim stood ready to make these allegations public—allegations that are very damaging to the defendant's reputation—supplies a motive for the defendant to murder his wife, regardless of whether the statements in the complaint are true or not. The existence of the allegations themselves, not their truth, is at the heart of this case."

That's only half-true. The mere existence of the allegations matters, but Millwood knows as well as I do that the jurors will be hard-pressed not to view the allegations as credible under the circumstances. The close timing of the murder and the planned filing of the complaint combine to create an inference that the two things go together. The complaint represents Sara Barton's last words to the world, and those words have great weight. They are Sara telling the jury who killed her from beyond the grave.

Woodcomb mulls it over for a few seconds and says, "I'll allow it, but I'm going to give a limiting instruction." Millwood and I return to our places. The judge addresses the jurors:

"Ladies and gentlemen of the jury, you are going to hear allegations contained in a draft of a divorce complaint that the State contends Sara Barton intended to file. The allegations assert certain facts, but they are just allegations. You are not to consider a fact true simply because an allegation in the complaint says so. You may draw other inferences from the existence of the allegations, but you cannot assume the truth of the allegations based solely on the allegations themselves."

The judge can say it, but the jurors don't have to follow it. I resume the questioning and ask Scott, "Were these divorce papers ever filed?"

"No. The victim was murdered before they could be."

"Objection. The witness lacks knowledge as to whether the complaint could've been filed prior to the murder."

"Sustained. The jury will disregard that last answer."

"Is the divorce complaint dated, Detective Moore?"

"Yes. It is dated the day after the murder."

"What does that suggest to you?"

"That Sara Barton intended the complaint to be filed on that date."

Millwood holds his powder this time. Scott's answer is still speculation, but at least it's informed speculation. Besides, everyone knows what the date on the complaint means. Someone murdered Sara Barton the day before she intended to seek a divorce from the defendant.

"Detective Moore, will you please read paragraph 21 of the complaint?"

"'In a jealous rage, Defendant Bernard Barton beat his wife, Plaintiff Sara Barton, and left large bruises on her back. Plaintiff Sara Barton escaped to the couple's bedroom and locked the door.'"

To Sam's credit, he wrote the complaint for maximum impact—"rage," "beat," "escaped." The inflammatory language read by Scott is just a taste of the overall flavor. The reading of the paragraph provides the perfect transition to get the 911 call in front of the jury.

"Did your investigation uncover the existence of such an incident?"

"Yes. The victim made a 911 call."

I then play the recording for the jury:

"Fulton County 911. May I have your name and the nature of emergency, please?"

"Sara Barton. My husband is trying to kill me!"

[Loud banging on a door.]

"Where is your husband now?"

"I'm locked in my bedroom! He's trying to get in!"

[More banging on the door. Muffled voices, yelling. Crying.]

"He has already hit me! Please hurry!"

Sara gives her address, and the call from her end abruptly stops. The 911 dispatcher asks, "Hello? Hello? Are you still there?" I wait along with the jurors for an answer that never comes, all of us caught up in the intensity of the moment. Receiving no response, the 911 dispatcher hangs up, a resounding "click" that resonates like a gunshot in the stillness of the courtroom. The finality of it all feels like a funeral. I feel happy inside.

One female juror shoots a disgusted side glance at a sullen-looking Barton. He shrivels in his chair, looking suddenly small, obviously guilty. I turn my attention back to Scott.

"What role did this recording play in your investigation?"

"It certainly got my attention. A husband beats his wife, and the wife turns up murdered shortly thereafter—the husband is going to be a suspect. But I kept an open mind and went about the process of working the case, making sure to give all possibilities a hard look."

We then take a deep dive into Barton's financial history. As of the date of Sara's murder, Bernard Barton owed three different casinos a total of nearly $800,000. Testimony about the $5 million insurance policy on Sara's life follows thereafter. I don't need a billboard to advertise the obvious inference. That kind of money covers a lot of gambling debts.

Scott walks the jury through the rest of it—Barton's phone conveniently left at his house on the day of the murder, the lack of a credible alibi, Barton's arrival home in the dead of the night hours after the murder, the failure of Barton to ask who murdered his wife during that initial interview, the coldness of his manner when he identified the body, Sara's affair with Brice Tanner, the text from Barton to Sara calling her a "whore" when he learned about her sex video with Brice, and, lastly, the gun and the fingerprints. The culmination of all the evidence led to the arrest of Bernard Barton for the murder of his wife.

Now I have to deal with Sam's dead body in the Atlanta woods. Millwood cast this burden on me during opening statements, and I've felt the weight ever since. Scott notes the death and explains the circumstances in their simplest terms. Sam Wilkins was found dead of a gunshot wound to the head in a remote park, the gun that fired the shot lying by his side. Gunshot residue was discovered on Sam's hand, leading to the tentative conclusion that the death was the result of suicide. The passive-voice riddled description is clinical and soulless, boring by design, with an air of "nothing to see here," hopefully to be soon forgotten.

"Is there any evidence that you discovered that links Sam Wilkins' death to Sara Barton's murder?"

"None whatsoever."

"Did you search for such evidence?"

"Yes. We always cover all our bases. Since his wife and her divorce lawyer were both shot, we looked into Bernard Barton's possible involvement in Wilkins' death. Because the defendant was not wearing a tracking device while on bail, we weren't able to ascertain his whereabouts during the time Wilkins died."

Scott and I worked on the wording to this answer in great detail.

"Objection," bellows Millwood. He doesn't state the grounds. He taught me that, too. Even when you cannot think of a basis for an objection, object anytime you feel something is off about the question or answer. Maybe the judge won't notice.

"Response?"

"Mr. Millwood is the one who brought up Sam Wilkins' death in his opening statement. He obviously intends to throw wild accusations in Mr. Wilkins' direction, and the State is allowed to correct any false innuendo spread by the defense."

"Overruled."

"It's speculative and lacks foundation, Your Honor," Millwood adds, taking the rare step of continuing to argue an objection already rejected by the person wearing the robe.

I waste no time: "No. Detective Moore is truthfully testifying about his investigation into a death first raised by the defense in its opening."

"My ruling stands."

Millwood's negative reaction to the questioning gives the exchange more importance than it deserves. I had more questions about Sam's death planned but drop them on the fly. The moment feels like a win, and I don't want to jeopardize it. The hour is late anyway. I run out the clock with a few more inquiries, pushing Millwood's cross-examination of Scott to the next morning, allowing us to send the jury home on a strong note.

***

Scott, Ella, and I strategize in my office over a dinner of pizza and messy buffalo wings. Hot sauce splattered on Scott's tie takes the shape of a half-eaten piece of broccoli—the only vegetable in sight. Even though my waist remains trim, my heart suffers the brunt of the unhealthy habits that mar my life. Stairs I used to bound up with little effort now require a rapid-heartbeat level of exertion. The copious doses of caffeine with which I self-medicate don't help. I feel old.

Ella begs off to go to a funeral visitation for a great aunt. Scott and I bear down to prepare for Millwood's cross-examination of him. The main concern relates to Sam. His affair with Sara Barton luckily never made it into the first round of any police files. Once we later zeroed in on Barton as our guy, Scott and I decided to make our own luck and keep Sam's admission that he was sleeping with the victim to ourselves. We didn't even tell Ella, and she remains unaware even now. One of the chief challenges of the trial was going to be preparing Sam for Millwood's inevitable onslaught. But then Sam went and died on me.

But Scott is not dead, and killing him before his cross-examination would result in a mistrial. He'll have to battle Millwood on his own. Scott won't perjure himself, but his only obligation is to truthfully answer the questions put to him. Will Millwood ask the magic question? The bet is no. Millwood's trial rules include never asking a question you don't already know the answer to. Cross-examination is not a time for fishing expeditions. Millwood knows, too, that Scott is a talented witness, and a trial lawyer should never get too cute with someone who knows the secrets of the trade. The way to win a war is to pick the right battles.

On paper, all that sounds fine and dandy. But a day in the courtroom rarely goes completely according to script. Things happen. I won't feel at ease until Scott steps down from the witness box. The risk we're taking is huge. The jury will resent the hell out of me for trying to pull a fast one on them if our gamble fails. Lost trust may be impossible to regain. I don't even want to think about Ella's reaction.

I'm only willing to stomach this much danger because the combination of Sam's affair with the victim and his mysterious death would make convicting Barton a Herculean task. A lawyer who slept with his client, discovered her murdered body, and later killed himself—a kindergartner could create a Picasso out of that raw material.

If Sam were alive, the jury could measure his true nature and see for itself that this man was no killer. But dead men tell no tales, leaving Millwood instead to fill in all the blanks. The truth that Sam was weak and seduced by a beautiful woman wouldn't matter.

The result is that I take a chance that Millwood won't ask Scott a question that requires Scott to tell the truth about Sara and Sam. I pepper Scott with an aggressive volley of mock questions that Millwood may throw at him. Together we craft answers to the stickier inquiries, responses that are both technically true and purposefully deceptive. We go at it for a good couple of hours before degenerating into frivolity.

In my best Millwood voice, I boom, "Detective Moore, do you still beat your wife?"

"We're divorced."

"Do you still beat your ex-wife?"

"No. I only beat suspects."

"Isn't it a fact that you troll around local high schools and prey on young girls?"

"I haven't prayed in years."

"Isn't it true that you once slept with the chief of police's wife—a woman thirty years your senior?"

"It was more than once."

"The defense rests."

The air goes quickly out of the balloon after that. The exchange is the type that's only funny when the participants are either roaring drunk or profoundly tired. Time to get some sleep. As we start to heave our aging bodies to a cacophony of creaks and groans, Ella startles us by opening the door without warning. We slump right back down. Looking over us with a stern look of disapproval, she asserts, "You two are about the saddest looking white boys I've ever seen."

"That's racist," Scott retorts.

Ella drops herself into a chair, kicks off her shoes, and lets her hair down, figuratively and literally. I ask, "How's your family?"

"We're okay. Aunt Maddie was 96 and lived a long old life. I blamed you as my excuse to hightail it out of there. I hate dead bodies. Now I need a drink."

She looks at Scott, knowing that I'm dry as a source. Answering her inquiry, Scott offers, "I don't have anything on me, but if you come over to my place, I have a minibar in my bedroom."

"No thanks. I've sworn off white guys forever."

She looks at me, but a trace of a smile assures me that the words don't come from a place of active anger. The three of us go on like this for a while, giving each other a hard time, enjoying a break from the pressures of the trial, delaying the moment when we will trod home alone once more. The criminal justice system is a nightmare on relationships, and the people in this room have the scars to prove it. But none of that matters tonight. The gang being back together again fills me with a warm glow. Scott even purloins some contraband from Bobby's liquor cabinet, allowing Ella to enjoy that drink. Sleep is the only casualty.

38

Millwood approaches Scott with the careful manner of a lion tamer. He holds a whip in his hand to keep the lion at bay but recognizes the inherent danger posed by the beast in front of him. He will give Scott the respect he deserves. I take a weird comfort in that. A lesser, undisciplined lawyer is apt to ask Scott anything. But Millwood will steer clear of asking a question that gives Scott the opportunity to refute the innuendo that Sam and Sara were sleeping together. At least I hope.

"Detective Moore, you have no physical evidence that Bernard Barton ever fired that gun, do you?"

"No."

"No evidence of gun powder residue on his hands the night of the murder?"

"We didn't test for that."

"Indeed, you didn't ask Mr. Barton to submit to such a test, did you?"

"He wasn't a suspect at that time."

Millwood sagely nods. He'll argue in closing that had the police administered such a test, Barton would've been exonerated. Now that's a bunch of nonsense. Gunpowder residue can be washed off just like anything else. Its absence proves nothing. But the jury doesn't know that.

"And you have no witnesses who place Mr. Barton in the vicinity of his house around the time of the murder?"

"No."

"No traffic cam footage showing him near his home?"

"We barely have any traffic cameras in that area, so no."

"Yet the ones you do have failed to show Mr. Barton, didn't they?"

"That's correct. They also failed to show the defendant returning to his house that night at 2:30 a.m. in the morning, so I don't put too much stock in the traffic cams."

Millwood allows himself a tight smile in response to Scott's successful parlay in adding a counterpoint to his answer without appearing defensive or overly hostile. Scott makes a strong witness because Millwood trained him years ago how to best answer the questions of defense lawyers. Millwood's strained grin suggests the recognition that he did his job too well.

"But to be clear, Detective Moore, no evidence—witnesses, traffic cams, credit card receipts—actually shows Mr. Barton in the area that night?"

"That's correct—no witnesses, no traffic cams, no credit card receipts for anywhere that night, and no cell phone tracking since the defendant left his phone at home that day."

The obvious implication scores a point, and the lion tamer looks like he has lost his whip. Cross-examination at its finest requires possession of a club to smack the witness should he get out of line. Millwood lacks such a weapon, and Scott is too disciplined. A few more exchanges like the last two, and Millwood's going to bail. He doesn't need Scott to verify what evidence the police don't have. He can argue those points himself to the jury when the time comes.

"Let's talk about Sam Wilkins, Detective Moore. You mentioned yesterday that you investigated Mr. Barton in connection with Wilkins' death. You haven't arrested Mr. Barton for Wilkins' murder, have you?"

"No."

"Haven't taken it to a grand jury?"

"No."

"You don't believe that Mr. Barton murdered Wilkins, do you?"

Scott pauses. He testified yesterday the police think Sam committed suicide. Now is not the time to get too clever.

"No. As I said yesterday, the tentative signs point to suicide as things stand."

"And this suicide was just months after the murder of Sara Barton?"

"Yes."

"And Wilkins discovered Mrs. Barton's body?"

"Yes."

I start to hold my breath. If it's going to happen, it'll happen soon. Scott appears as nonplussed as a man waiting in a deli line to order a sandwich—no nerves at all. I want to throw up. Thinking of those pictures in the storage shed in north Georgia doesn't help. I'm playing fast and loose on more fronts than I can defend. But I promised Lara I would get justice for her sister, and I intend to honor my word.

"He was her lawyer?"

"Divorce lawyer, yes."

"And he visited his client at her home at ten o'clock the night that she died?"

"He did."

"Didn't meet her in his office that night?"

"Apparently not."

"Came over personally?"

"Yes. Brought the divorce papers over himself. I collected them from him that night."

"Didn't Wilkins' visiting late seem strange to you?"

"Most things that lawyers do seem strange to me."

The courtroom snickers in suppressed laughter. Woodcomb gives a soft tap with her gavel to restore order.

Scott continues, "Sorry for the little joke, Your Honor. I asked Mr. Wilkins about that very thing. The divorce promised to be a lucrative one for him, and the victim asked him if he would bring the papers over to her house. So he did."

"And he told you that the night of the murder?"

"Yes."

"And that's not in the police report?"

"No. Police reports are summaries, not transcriptions."

"And you don't have a separate witness statement for Wilkins that night?"

"No."

"Isn't your usual practice to obtain such statements?"

"Sometimes."

My nerves stand on high alert. Millwood focuses like a hungry wolf on the weak spot in the investigation. He knows how Scott goes about his business and recognizes the irregularity in not formalizing the interview of such a key player.

"But not from Sam Wilkins?"

"No."

"Didn't take a witness statement from the person who discovered the murder victim?"

"Beyond what's in the police report, no."

"This was an important case, right?"

"All murder cases are important."

"And because all murder cases are important, you try your best to be thorough?"

"Always."

"But being thorough here didn't require taking a witness statement from Sam Wilkins?"

"Beyond what's in the police report, no."

Millwood doesn't like it. I can tell from the tautness of his muscles that his Spidey senses are going haywire. I feel him look at me to get a read on the situation, but I ignore him with all the nonchalance I can muster. I then confer with Ella on some trivial point just to have something to do.

"You took a statement from Brice Tanner?"

"I did."

"From Monica Haywood?"

"Yes."

"But not Sam Wilkins?"

"No."

Millwood is burning his britches to ask why not but knows that he can't because he has no idea what's on the other side of that door. In a brazen act of reverse psychology, Scott unleashes a look of challenge, all but daring his questioner to give in to temptation and ask the question. Millwood trains his sights on Liesa instead.

"Sam Wilkins' wife was in the vicinity of the murder scene at the time of the murder?"

"A traffic cam caught a minivan registered to the Wilkins family over a mile away from the Barton residence around the time of the murder."

"Traveling away from the direction of the Barton home?"

"Yes."

"And it wasn't Sam Wilkins driving that vehicle?"

"No. He drove his Volkswagen Passat to the Barton residence."

"Did Liesa Wilkins admit driving the minivan through the intersection that night?"

"She didn't want to talk to the police."

"Refused to talk to you?"

"Yes."

Millwood gives the jury a look pregnant with meaning and cashes in on his gains by moving to other topics. The remaining time of the cross-examination barely registers in my consciousness, except that I intuitively know that Millwood did us no great harm—only nibbling here and there at the periphery. Even the Liesa stuff is a big bag of nothing at the end of the day. When Millwood finishes his turn, I announce, "No further questions for this witness, Your Honor." The judge excuses Scott from the stand, and I give him a slight smile of thankfulness and solidarity.

We survived.

39

Brice Tanner walks to the witness box when I call his name. He wears an appropriate gray suit. With a haircut and a clean shave, he presents like the Brice of old. I met with him extensively in the past few weeks to prepare him for his testimony. He held better than I would have thought, but the real thing is a different animal. The goal today is to introduce Brice to the jury on my own terms and safely defuse some of the land mines he presents to the case. Toward that end, the first thing is to establish that Brice and Sara had an affair. No need to beat around the bush, either.

"What was your relationship with Sara Barton?"

"We were lovers."

The next questions delve into the beginning of the relationship. He and Sara had met and flirted, but nothing more, at a series of law firm functions. That changed when Sara showed up unannounced at Brice's door one early evening. An intimate romance commenced. When Brice and Sara later found themselves alone at another Marsh & McCabe firm party, one thing led to another. They had sex on the floor of the High Museum.

We talk a little bit about the video—how he learned about it and his reaction in the aftermath. Despite the public revelation of their affair, the two continued to see each other. Sara confessed that she was scared of her husband. She told Brice to watch his own back, too.

"How did you respond?"

"I pledged to protect her, but she assured me that she could protect herself."

Brice delivers the line with appropriate gravity. His guilt-ridden eyes stare a hole in the courtroom floor. Sensing that the moment is right, I play the jury the unedited video of Sara and Brice. The proximity of the video to the 911 call necessitates a public airing of what triggered Bernard Barton's rage.

The video is high quality and shows a naked Sara in full frontal glory, sitting on top of Brice, rocking up and down. She faces the camera, and I marvel again at the sexual beauty of the Landrum twins. The female jurors look away in disgust. The male jurors absorb the evidence with complete concentration. I relive the past—kissing Lara that first time in my house, watching her remove the purple tank top, seeing those breasts in full technicolor.

I take a deep breath.

The playing of his sex tape further chastens Brice. His face bears the brunt of it. After the video runs its course, I force Brice to authenticate its accuracy, which he does with monosyllabic reluctance. His visual suffering the past few minutes pays strategic dividends—his weakness making it harder for Millwood to credibly paint him as a murderer. Barton, in contrast, has looked like a coiled ball of anger every single day of the trial.

"When was the last time you ever saw Sara?"

"The night before her murder."

"Tell the jury about that night."

"I walked over to her house, and she cooked me dinner. Spaghetti. Bernard was working late. After dinner, we went to her bedroom and made love. Afterwards, we talked about the future. She was getting a divorce. Her lawyer was delivering her divorce paperwork the next night, and she was going to tell Bernard. I wanted to be there for her, but she made me promise to stay away that night. I should've gone over there. Things might have turned out differently. When I learned that she was dead, I was devastated. We were going to run off together until Bernard killed her."

"Objection!"

"Sustained. The jury will disregard that last remark."

My blank face hides the joy I feel inside. Brice slid the shiv in Barton's gut with remarkable swiftness. I decide to wrap up by asking Brice why he left Marsh & McCabe.

He answers, "I was disgusted that the firm didn't fire the defendant after he was indicted for murder. I couldn't work there any anymore. It felt like a hostile work environment."

I nod in sympathy and relinquish the witness. Judge Woodcomb announces a 15-minute recess.

***

Millwood eyes Brice from his chair—more lion hunter than lion tamer now. The witness is nervous. Me, too. One thing we don't have to worry about is Brice's arrest for stalking Brittany Wood. Ella filed a pre-trial motion in limine to exclude any mention of the event on the grounds that the arrest never led to a conviction. Mary Woodcomb agreed, meaning we've sidestepped a rather large landmine already.

I've toughened Brice up as best I could, but Millwood will draw blood. The only uncertainty is how much. I hope for nothing worse than a flesh wound, expect something of a deeper cut, and dread a kill shot. Still sitting, Millwood asks his first question.

"What did you do when you quit Marsh & McCabe?"

"I took a break and spent some time in the mountains. Sara's death was quite a shock."

"What did you do in the mountains?"

Two odd, open-ended questions to start the cross-examination. Not good. Millwood knows something. The alarm bells in my head threaten to burst my eardrums. The imagination runs wild. Anything would seem to be on the table at this point.

"Nothing really. I hiked a little. Read some books."

"Did you do drugs?"

I remember the heavy stench of residual weed when Scott and I paid Brice a visit. May the damage stop there. I can deal with drugs, as long as Brice—who actually looks at me now—honestly answers the question. My face exhibits nothingness in response to Brice's glance. But telepathically I send him a single message. Tell the truth. Tell the truth. Tell the truth.

Millwood wouldn't ask that question unless he had the goods to smash Brice into broken pieces for a lie. Smoking weed is a little deal.

Perjury is a big deal. The biggest sin a witness can commit is to lie. The jurors figure that if you deceive them about one thing, you will deceive them about everything.

Brice answers, "Sure, I smoked some dope."

Good boy.

"Did you ever smoke dope with Sara before she died?"

"A few times."

How would Millwood know *that*? I feel outflanked. I never even thought to ask Brice such a thing. Even though I doubt the legal relevance of the question, objecting would give Millwood a free monologue to spin the drug use in whatever ways he wants in answer to the objection. That fight is not worth having.

Millwood, who remains seated still, reaches for a manila folder on the defense table. His deliberate movements ramp up the suspense. Four questions in, he has already maneuvered Brice into admitting to a crime and implicating the victim in a crime. Anticipation for the next bombshell builds. Millwood pulls something out of his folder. He stands up, ready to take the action to a new phase. Brice looks halfway on the road to being shaken.

Millwood strides toward me and hands over some photographs that he intends to present to the witness. The pictures capture a crazed-looking Brice in his mountain man phase. To call the pictures unflattering undershoots the reality by a country mile. They're terrible. The worst of the bunch features Brice shirtless with demonic red eyes that could only come from Satan himself. The image screams murder. Millwood has been busy.

He undoubtedly picked the worst of the litter, but these pictures are so bad I wonder if they have been edited. Technology can do a lot these days. It's a long shot, but I have to attempt to keep these photos out.

I say to the judge, "May we approach, Your Honor?"

I smile to keep the jury off the scent that I want to keep evidence from them. Millwood already has them eating out of his hand. I make a small joke to him as we walk up and follow it with an animated laugh disproportionate to the joke's merits—anything to distract attention from whatever Millwood showed me from the manila folder. When we reach the bench, I make my argument.

"Your Honor, it appears Mr. Millwood intends to introduce into evidence photographs taken of the witness months after the murder of Sara Barton. First, the evidence is irrelevant to the issue of the guilt or innocence of the defendant. Rather, the point of the photos is nothing more than to paint the witness in a bad light during a private, unguarded moment. Their prejudicial effect outweighs any probative value.

"Second, the photos were apparently taken without the witness' knowledge. Besides possible issues of trespassing and invasion of privacy, the witness cannot know whether these images were edited or not, making authentication impossible with this witness."

"Response?"

"This Court has my personal assurance that the photographs haven't been edited, and the witness can certainly authenticate whether he is in the picture or not. The photos are relevant because the witness is a suspect in the victim's murder and the photos show his apparent mental breakdown in the aftermath of the murder. The defendant has a right for the jury to see this evidence as part of his defense so that the jury can make its own judgments."

Judge Woodcomb sifts through the photographs from her perch. She moves at her own pace, taking time to carefully review each of the pictures. If nothing else, the delay breaks the easy momentum of Millwood's cross-examination. A murmur spreads across the courtroom as people talk among themselves, which means they aren't paying attention to us at the front. I maintain an easy casualness.

The judge addresses me, "Mr. Millwood has vouched that the photographs are unedited. Do you accept his word on that issue?"

"Your Honor, Mr. Millwood is the finest and most ethical lawyer I know, but I still get to talk to his photographer before these pictures can be admitted into evidence."

Woodcomb mulls over my words without revealing what she is thinking. She gives a second expeditious look through the potential evidence. She then hands all of the pictures back to Millwood.

The judge rules, "I'll allow the witness to be questioned about the evidence to confirm that he is the person in the photographs. It is up to the witness to tell us if he thinks the pictures have been doctored in some way and do not accurately depict reality."

I smile in defeat and head back to my seat, praying that Brice will keep it together over the embarrassments coming his way. Millwood now towers a few feet away from him. This technique is one of his favorites—using his size to convey his authority and make the witness feel small. I can't assess Brice's reaction because Millwood purposely blocks my line of sight, just as I blocked Corey Miller from seeing Tasha Favors. I slide toward Ella's side of the table to grab a partial view. Millwood hands the first picture to Brice, who stares at it with no expression.

"Do you recognize the person in this photograph?"

"It's me."

"When was the picture taken?"

"I don't know. It was taken without my knowledge."

Good answer. Emphasize the shady circumstances surrounding the taking of the picture and punish Millwood for asking an imprecise question.

Millwood says, "Fair enough. Do you know approximately when the photo was taken?"

"Objection to the word 'approximately.' It's vague."

"Sustained."

"Isn't it true that the picture was taken some time after Sara Barton's murder?"

"Yes."

Millwood focuses on Brice's days of living off the grid in the mountains. He establishes that Brice fled the city following the murder, grew long hair, grew a beard, and lived alone. Through his evocative questions, Millwood depicts a depressing mosaic of Brice's living conditions—the seldom-used dirt road leading up to the place deep in the woods, the dilapidated exterior of the house, the disheveled interior piled high with trash. Like a good cross-examiner, Millwood essentially does the testifying, reducing Brice's role to merely affirming everything his questioner asks.

To this point, Millwood has refrained from showing the jury a photo of Brice in the woods. I think I know why. Right now, the jurors have created in their individual minds an image of the witness with long hair and a beard in the woods. Based on the man testifying before them, they have probably constructed a tame, albeit slightly hairy, person in their heads. If Millwood can shatter this comfortable mental construction to pieces, the shock value of the real images of Brice soars. The move requires patient discipline to execute. Most lawyers rush to get good evidence in front of the jury. But Millwood plays the long game.

Millwood returns to the photos at the defense table. He leafs through his stack as if deciding on the perfect one, an exercise in theatrics. At last, he picks out the most damning photo—the one featuring a shirtless Brice and his red, demon eyes. He meanders back toward the witness stand and says, "I want to show you another picture, Mr. Tanner. Can you confirm again that you are the person in this photograph?"

Millwood hands over the photo with all the solemnity due to a critical, trial-turning piece of evidence. This moment represents the culmination of his work for the past forty-five minutes. Brice looks at what is handed to him and reacts in a way that startles everyone present, but especially Millwood.

Brice bursts out laughing. Hard.

No one knows quite how to react to this display. The jurors look taken aback. Spectators sit confused. Barton flashes anger. Mary Woodcomb seems mildly amused. Millwood appears stunned, something I've never seen. He doesn't take it well.

He demands, "Do you find something funny, Mr. Tanner?"

Brice answers, "I mean, this photograph is perfectly ridiculous. Look at my eyes! What did you do? Sit in a tree all day and wait to catch me at my worst moment? Getting me without my shirt on was a nice touch. The whole thing is a joke."

Mockery! Perfect. The unexpected grit in him astounds. Ella writes something on a legal pad and slides it over to me: "Wow!" Our eyes meet, and I throw her a sly smile.

Trying to recover, Millwood notes for the record that the witness did confirm his identity in the picture. He further asks that the photographs be admitted into evidence and shown to the jury. I answer with a hearty: "No objection!"

Millwood hands the photos over to the jurors, and many of them actually laugh. They look at Brice, and he laughs right back at them. The whole scene must be painful for Millwood, who waits patiently to collect the photos before giving them to the court reporter. Mental cartwheels of joy roll along inside my head.

Brice skates through the rest of Millwood's cross relatively unscathed. Millwood tries to jab him here and there—no alibi, walking distance to the murder scene, the intensity of his feelings toward Sara—but nothing comes of it. The jury grows bored, and Millwood gives up the chase. The first rule of getting out of a hole is to stop digging. Millwood had high hopes for Brice as a witness, but one unexpected response changed the whole dynamic.

Trials are like that. Good witnesses lose it in the moment and come across terribly. Bad witnesses exceed all expectations and become a strength, not a hindrance. As a lawyer, you can't take such sudden shifts personally. You have to roll with it. Otherwise, you'll become an alcoholic.

We won this round. I consider allowing Brice to leave the stand with no further questions. The easy choice would be to go ahead and claim victory. But I don't want the jurors' last impression of Brice to be one of boredom. Millwood will still try to smear Brice in closing argument as an alternative suspect to Barton. I need a different lasting note. I stand for re-direct.

"Mr. Tanner, Mr. Millwood was beating around the bush, but I will ask you flat-out. Did you kill Sara Barton?"

"Absolutely not."

I pick up the infamous picture of Brice's bare chest and his demonic eyes. I then turn the picture around and show it from afar to Brice and the jury at the same time. A few chuckles emerge.

"And you don't really have red eyes, do you?"

The question is improperly leading. I chance that Millwood won't object, but figure even if he does, he looks the worse for it. He is the one that tried to sucker-punch the witness with an unfair photograph. I suppose he makes the same calculation. He just sits there.

Brice answers, "No."

"No further questions."

I sit down, the renewed laughter of the jurors music to my ears.

40

Evening comes. Scott is off somewhere doing his day job. Tomorrow portends to be a successful climax for the prosecution. I anticipate slaughtering Monica Haywood for signing a false affidavit that Barton was with her during the time of the murder. After that, Ella closes our evidence with Lara—the star witness given the anchor leg to bring our story home.

Sitting across the table again from Ella, working deep into the night, the security of the familiar provides comfort. She no longer surveils me with that wary look of estrangement. For this moment at least, we are how we used to be—comfortable with one another, reading each other's thoughts, joined together in unity of mind and purpose. I stare at her stupidly, slightly smiling in appreciation of the growing progress toward a renewed friendship. Ella catches my stare and puzzles at its meaning.

"What?"

"Nothing. Just daydreaming."

"Well, get back to work."

I do as commanded. She eyes me to ensure compliance. Then both of our heads are back down, busy preparing for what's ahead. I grin at her again before imagining Monica Haywood in my crosshairs.

***

In a pre-trial order, Judge Woodcomb granted our motion to treat Monica Haywood as a hostile witness. Because Haywood is no friend of the prosecution, I'm allowed to cross-examine her as the other side's witness, giving me the leverage of using leading questions to shape her testimony any way I like. After Haywood takes the oath to tell the truth, the whole truth, and nothing but the truth, I launch right into her.

"Miss Haywood, you're a lawyer with the firm of Marsh & McCabe?"

"Yes."

"The Defendant, Bernard Barton, is your boss there?"

"Yes."

"You began an affair with him?"

"Yes."

"Even though you knew he was married to Sara Barton?"

"Yes."

"And now you're the defendant's fiancée?"

"Yes."

I pause and assess. Haywood's demeanor is cold, punctuated by the same lack of remorse I witnessed in the police station when Scott interviewed her. The hunch is that Millwood realized that softening her up wouldn't play. Juries can smell a fake a few time zones away.

"You love the defendant?"

"Yes."

"And you've sworn to tell this jury the truth here today?"

"Yes."

"Even if the truth harms the defendant?"

"Yes."

She waits a touch too long before agreeing, even darting her eyes to the defense table for a quick, unsuccessful consult. But the delay is the answer. She just told the jury she's willing to lie to them to help Barton. By the looks of the jurors, they received the message.

"The defendant arrived at your condo around 4 a.m. the morning after his wife's murder?"

"Something like that."

"Did he tell you that Sara was murdered?"

"Yes."

"What was your reaction?"

She gives that one a good think, too. It's an open-ended question, but I can't conceive of any answer that could hurt me. Having to come up with a response other than "yes" apparently throws her. She sits there in silence for a good thirty seconds.

"I don't know."

I don't push her on that answer. The impression that she is evasive helps me out more than nailing down a response to an immaterial question.

"The police came to your condo later that morning?"

"Yes."

"They were looking for the defendant?"

"Yes."

"They asked you if he was there?"

"Yes."

"You told the police no?"

"Yes."

"That was a lie?"

"Yes."

I allow her admission that she lied to loiter in the room a bit. Haywood's entire body language radiates a growing discomfort. She presents as tough but possesses little tolerance for taking a punch.

"Despite what you told the police, the defendant was hiding out in your bedroom?"

"His wife had just died. He needed some time for himself."

"Despite what you told the police, the defendant was hiding out in your bedroom?"

"Yes."

"You lied with the defendant in the next room?"

"It was the right thing to do."

She should stick to one-word answers. Couching her actions in moral terms is a dog that won't hunt. If she adopts a posture of self-righteousness, today will go even worse for her than I expect.

"A few days later, you went to the police station to give a statement?"

"Yes."

"You understood as a lawyer that you had no obligation to talk to the police?"

"Yes."

"But you decided to talk to the police anyway?"

"Yes."

"And you discussed that decision with the defendant before going to the police station?"

I have no proof of such a conversation, but her answers thus far foreclose the possibility that she waltzed into the police station to talk about Barton without consulting with him first. No one will believe a denial even if she gives one. She again considers the question for too long before agreeing that she and Barton talked.

"And the defendant wanted you to talk to the police?"

"He wasn't opposed to it."

"He wasn't opposed to it?"

"Yes."

"Wasn't opposed to whatever you had to say to the police?"

"Yes."

"And you told the police that the defendant was with you at your condo when Sara Barton was murdered?"

"Yes."

"You signed an affidavit under oath to that effect?"

"Yes."

"Giving the defendant an alibi that, if believed, would exonerate him from murder?"

"Yes."

"And that alibi was a lie?"

"No. It's the truth. Bernard was with me the entire evening."

While I receive the lie with clinical detachment, the little mice in my brain furiously spin their wheels to figure out what's going on. Millwood knows that the alibi is trash. He also knows that I know the alibi is trash. Yet Monica Haywood just perjured herself on the heap of that trash. I cannot fathom why. Whatever the weird motivations at work, duty now obliges me to call her on it.

The cross-examination slows to a crawl. The logistics of exposing Haywood's deceit requires maneuvering a video screen in place, playing the surveillance footage capturing the hallway of her condo, forcing her to acknowledge the digital time and date of the footage, and then playing the clipped footage that shows Barton's exit at 7:38 p.m. and his return at 3:59 a.m. the next morning. This slog eventually reaches its inevitable destination—Monica Haywood confesses that she lied about being with Barton at the time of the murder.

She remains unhumbled by the admission—not quite defiant, but decidedly unaffected by her public unmasking as a perjurer. Maybe she is just bored, which would match the rising mood in the room. Having finally proved the alibi false through the magic of video, I pick up the pace.

"You lied about the alibi in your police interview?"

"Yes."

"Signed a false affidavit about the alibi as part of that interview?"

"Yes."

"And the defendant wasn't opposed to you talking to the police?"

"Yes."

"The two and you discussed it beforehand?"

"Yes."

The conclusion draws itself. Other lawyers would no doubt try to get Haywood to concede that Barton instructed her to lie. But that's tilting at windmills. She'll deny it, then what? You're reduced to arguing with a witness. If you can't prove it, don't ask it.

"And you repeated the lie this morning before these jurors?"

"Yes."

"After you took an oath to tell the truth?"

"Yes."

"Lied anyway?"

"Yes."

"As a lawyer, you understand the seriousness of perjury?"

"Yes."

"Lied anyway?"

"Yes."

"You currently live with the defendant?"

"Yes."

"The two of you are engaged to be married?"

"Yes."

"You won't get married if he goes to prison, will you?"

Haywood thinks about that one. The sudden silence in the room leads to a re-focusing of unwanted attention on the witness, much to the witness' distaste. She takes a drink of water with hundreds of eyeballs on her movements.

"We can still get married."

"You would marry him even if he went to prison for murder?"

"Yes."

"Are you worried about going to jail for perjury?"

"I haven't thought about it."

"Is the defendant going to marry you if you're the one in jail?"

That leaves a mark. I half-expect Millwood to object, but he sits there with an air of disinterest. He hasn't objected once this morning, seemingly ignoring the entirety of Haywood's testimony. The witness looks at Barton before answering, "He loves me." If she believes that, she's the only one in the vicinity who does. After a few more questions, I sit down, and the judge dismisses everyone for the morning break.

***

Millwood stands to begin his examination. We wondered over the recess whether he would even ask anything of Haywood. Sometimes the best cross is "No questions, Your Honor." The damage she caused is done, compounded by her reckless insistence on repeating a lie easily exposed. Millwood figures only to make things worse if he engages Haywood too long. As a reclamation project, she's a poor investment.

He begins, "You love the defendant, don't you?"

"Very much."

"You want to be his wife?"

"Yes."

"And you wanted to be his wife even before Sara Barton was murdered, didn't you?"

"I did."

"And now you're free to marry Bernard?"

"I am."

Weird. Millwood is making my case for me by reinforcing that Haywood would willfully lie for Barton to help him cover up a murder. But Millwood is not stupid. Some ulterior motive lurks. I can't figure it out, and that scares me.

"And you lied this morning when you testified that you and Bernard were together at the time of the murder?"

"I did."

"You two weren't together?"

"No."

"Bernard left your apartment at around seven-thirty that night?"

"He did."

"What did you do after he left?"

That's the first non-leading question, and my insides groan. Monica Haywood's movements on the night of the murder are a mystery to me—a black hole that mocks me as incompetent. As I process the implications of this mistake, the witness wears the appearance of a frightened turtle wanting to retreat back into the safety of her shell. When Millwood asks her if she would like him to repeat the question, she meekly nods.

"What did you do after Bernard left your apartment the night of the murder?"

"I … I don't remember."

"You don't remember?"

"No."

"Did you leave your apartment that night?"

"I don't remember."

Millwood emits disbelief. I wonder how many times he and Haywood rehearsed this entire routine. When Millwood deploys the same video screen I used earlier in the morning, the thought of an unchecked box early in the investigation slaps me across the face. I turn to Scott.

"Did your guy ever check the video to see if Monica left after Bernard that night?"

"I don't think so," he says ruefully.

We all dropped the ball. Scott should've followed up with his guy. I should've followed up with Scott. Someone on our side should have at some point in the last few months thought to nail down Haywood's movements for the time in question. It will be a busy lunch.

Millwood's uncharacteristic behavior the entire morning clarifies into something else entirely: rope-a-dope—with me as the dope. My instinct told me things were not as they seemed, but I ignored the danger signs in a sea of overconfidence. The direction Millwood wants to travel now is clear. The ultimate destination is not. How far is Monica Haywood going to take this charade?

Millwood plays the same surveillance footage I peacocked before the jurors a little while ago. Except now the date and timestamp on the video herald a later time in the evening—8:26 p.m. Sure enough, Monica Haywood exits the condo hallway at that moment to go forth into the night. Millwood stops the recording and faces the witness again. Unmoved, Haywood sits there with practiced nonchalance.

"Ms. Haywood, would you agree that the video we just watched shows you leaving your condo at eight twenty-six on the night of the murder?"

"Yes."

"Do you have any reason to doubt the accuracy of this footage?"

"No."

"Does the video refresh your recollection as to your whereabouts at the time of the murder?"

"I wasn't at home."

"Where did you go?"

"I don't know."

Haywood shifts her eyes down and away from the jury, using body language to evoke evasiveness. No one in the room credits her professed ignorance. I know she's lying to protect Barton, but maybe the jurors believe she's lying to protect herself. I study their reaction to the farce on display and don't like what I see. Too many of them appear interested in what Millwood is peddling.

"You don't know where you went?"

"No."

"Any idea?"

"No."

"You know the location of the Barton residence?"

"Of course."

"Been there many times?"

"Yes."

"Your condo was close to the murder scene?"

"Four and a half minutes away."

The answer is devastating in its ingenuity. Five minutes is a generalized rule of thumb—the kind of estimation each of us calculates daily. "Four and a half minutes" is something else entirely. Its specificness suggests studied deliberation—the kind of detail one would only know by being up to no good.

"Four and a half minutes?"

"Yes."

Her certainty about the time it takes to get to Barton's house contrasts sharply with her proclaimed ignorance as to her whereabouts at the time of the murder. A hallmark of lying is remembering small, precise details while forgetting the big, important things. That concept, though, is a hard one to explain to a jury in a digestible soundbite. Millwood knows what he is doing.

"And did you drive to the Barton house the night of the murder?"

"I don't remember."

The courtroom is deathly still. The answer is literally unbelievable. She either drove to the house that night or she didn't, but she damn well knows which one it is. Haywood's sacrificial offering of herself takes lovesick to a pathological level. But her mendacity precludes feeling any sympathy for her. She's aiding and abetting at this point.

"You don't remember if you drove to the house?"

"No."

"You might have gone over there?"

"Maybe."

"You can't rule it out?"

"I cannot."

"What time did you get home that evening?"

"I don't remember."

"Any idea?"

"No."

Back to the video monitor. Millwood plays more footage from the now well-familiar hallway. The timestamp reads 10:13 p.m., and the audience sees Haywood returning to the building. Millwood, wearing the look of a disappointed school teacher, refocuses on the witness.

"Does this video refresh your recollection as to when you returned to your home on the night Sara Barton was murdered?"

"Based on the video, shortly after ten that night."

"Does knowing that you returned home after ten help you remember what you were doing earlier in the evening?"

"No. I still don't remember."

"So to summarize—you left your condo around eight-thirty that evening, don't know where you went, you might have gone to the Barton residence, only four and a half minutes away, and you returned shortly after ten o'clock?"

"Correct."

The spectacle amazes. Millwood's assault is not a sneak attack on an unsuspecting witness. Rather, Monica Haywood is a willing victim. I can hear the drumbeat of Millwood's closing argument already in my head—maybe the girlfriend did it. Reasonable doubt. Reasonable doubt. Reasonable doubt. My eyes meet Barton's and catch the hint of a smirk.

"No further questions."

The lunch hour strikes. Millwood's timing is predictably impeccable. The jurors will have plenty of time over the break to digest the possibility that Haywood killed her lover's wife, maximizing the lasting impression of the morning's testimony. Many of the jurors watch Haywood carefully as she leaves the witness box, their doubt in my case growing with each step.

Piercing the illusion of Millwood's impressive magic trick will prove daunting. Monica Haywood will not be an easy person to cross-examine the second time around. Handling a witness who lies out of self-preservation is standard trial fare. The obvious self-interest casts an incredulous light onto everything that person says. But the witness who lies herself *into* legal jeopardy represents something else entirely. The lie gains credence merely from the assumption that no one would willingly expose herself to such a big risk. Humans tend to believe the bad stuff people tell about themselves.

Court adjourns. I instruct Scott to have someone trail Haywood the entirety of the recess. I then head straight to my office to get to work.

41

"Did you kill Sara Barton?"

My first question to Monica Haywood after the break goes straight to the big ask that Millwood specifically avoided during his examination. Right at the start, I need to know just how far Monica will take this masquerade. Will she actually admit to the murder on Barton's behalf?

"No."

Ella and I disagree over how to handle the witness. She thinks I should launch a credibility attack on Haywood's numerous lies. By showing her to be a liar, the crafted deception to protect Barton falls apart. Ella's reasoning is sound. Cross-examination, by definition, challenges the impression created during the other side's questioning.

I have something different in mind: jujitsu—the art of using an opponent's own strength against him. If Bernard Barton wants the world to think that his mistress killed his wife, so be it. He is in for a surprise. I continue.

"You've already admitted lying under oath to this jury. Are you telling the truth now?"

"I am."

"You don't know if you went to your lover's house that night, but you know that you didn't kill his wife?"

"Yes."

"How many hours did you prepare with Mr. Millwood on your testimony?"

"Objection! May we approach, Your Honor?"

Mary Woodcomb nods. I join Millwood for the huddled conference out of the jury's earshot. Millwood crouches in real tight. He doesn't want the jurors to hear what he is about to say.

"Your Honor, I object to the disclosure of any communications between the witness and myself on the grounds of attorney-client privilege. I represent Ms. Haywood in connection with this matter."

"What!"

My aggressive response draws the attention of the front half of the courtroom. The judge gives me a quick look of admonishment before focusing on Millwood with the intensity of a laser beam.

She suggests, "Mr. Millwood, isn't that a conflict of interest?"

"No, Your Honor. The interests of Mr. Barton and Ms. Haywood do not conflict here. Both are also seasoned lawyers who have knowingly agreed to my dual representation of them."

Nonsense. Consternation wrinkles around the features of Woodcomb's face. Millwood doesn't blink in the onslaught of her skepticism. The judge asks me for a response.

"Of course there's a conflict, Your Honor. He set her up as an alternative murder suspect to the defendant in his questioning this morning. There's no way ethically he can represent the two of them at the same time."

"That's not your call to make," rebuts Millwood. "My clients get to pick their own lawyer, not you. And you're not the ethical arbiter for the State Bar of Georgia."

"Yet he raises a good point, Mr. Millwood," interjects Woodcomb.

"Your Honor, all I can say is that I'm comfortable with the arrangement. Mr. Barton is comfortable with the arrangement. And Ms. Haywood is comfortable with the arrangement. We're all sophisticated lawyers."

Frustrated, the judge heaves a sigh while assessing Millwood with profound distrust. She then accepts his argument and explains to me that if Barton and Haywood want to join their fates at Millwood's hip, she is not going to stand in their way. But I'm not quite ready to give up the fight.

"Your Honor, the jury should at least be sent out of the room, and the witness questioned about this arrangement before we simply accept Mr. Millwood's description of the situation. Ms. Haywood's confirmation of the attorney-client relationship should be on the record."

The judge agrees and sends the confused jury out of the room. Their collective petulance reveals a feeling that they are somehow being punished for unknown offenses. After Woodcomb confirms with Haywood that Millwood is her lawyer despite the potential conflict of interest, the jurors trod back to their assigned seats, wondering what the rest of the world now knows that they do not. The disruption of their routine sharpens their focus and breaks them out of any post-lunch doldrums. I have their full attention if nothing else.

I resume, "Ms. Haywood, after your testimony this morning, you went to lunch with Mr. Millwood and the defendant, didn't you?"

I stare at Millwood and dare him to object. He refrains. I can ask if they ate together, as long as I don't ask what they talked about. Haywood confirms that she, Millwood, and Barton ate lunch together.

"You went to the restaurant in Mr. Millwood's car?"

"Yes."

"The three of you?"

"Yes."

"The defendant sat in the passenger seat?"

"Yes."

"You sat in the back?"

"Yes."

I pause to deliberate, imbuing great significance to these details that otherwise would appear inconsequential. Anything can be dramatic if presented in the right way. The ingenious brainstorm to follow the defense during lunch is already paying off.

"The three of you went into the restaurant together?"

"Yes."

"Sat down at the same table?"

"Yes."

"Ordered?"

"Yes."

"You got the salad?"

"Yes."

"Y'all ate the meal together?"

"Yes."

"Mr. Millwood paid for the lunch?"

"Yes."

"And you were in the restaurant together for sixty-three minutes?"

"Yes."

That's a good sign. Little chance she knows the exact length of time they were in the restaurant, but she agrees with me anyway. That I know what she ate for lunch should give her great pause about what other unexpected facts I might also have up my sleeve.

"And then the three of you got back into Mr. Millwood's car?"

"Yes."

"Drove back to the courthouse?"

"Yes."

"Entered the building together?"

"Yes."

"Now you're back on the witness stand and they're back at the defense table?"

"Yes."

The line of questioning runs its course. The jurors shoot stares of skepticism at Millwood. Any attempt by him in closing argument to paint Haywood as the real murderer now must sit side-by-side with the visuals of defense lawyer, defendant, and alternative murder suspect enjoying lunch together in the middle of the crucial testimony. But I'm not done by any stretch.

"So, Ms. Haywood, you didn't kill Sara Barton?"

"I did not."

"Didn't pull the trigger?"

"No."

"Because the defendant did?"

"No!"

"Isn't it true that you and the defendant conspired to kill Sara Barton?"

"No!"

"The two of you talked about killing her?"

"No!"

"Planned it out together?"

"No!"

"So the two of you could be together?"

"No!"

The zombie witness of the morning is gone. Haywood is fully animated, pleading even. The detour in the questioning is not to her liking. The defense anticipated that I would attack Haywood by showing how she couldn't have committed the murder. That would lead to a messy back-and-forth where the witness evades, evades, evades and makes herself look even more guilty. Instead, I'm doubling down on the defense's premise that Haywood was involved—only I'm adding Barton to the mix. More than one path can lead to a murder conviction.

"You lied to the police to give the defendant an alibi as part of that conspiracy?"

"No!"

"You didn't lie to the police?"

"I did, but—"

"You lied to the police about the alibi?"

"Yes, but—"

"Because you saw the defendant pull the trigger?"

"No!"

"Because you were with him?"

"No!"

"You were at the Barton house?"

"No!"

"You weren't at the Barton house?"

"I wasn't."

And there's the first breach in the perimeter of her fairy tale from this morning. Monica's good at memorizing lines, but bad at improvisation. The only way to get this witness to tell the truth is to make her think that the truth helps Barton. I press on.

"Being asked if you saw the defendant pull the trigger makes you now realize you weren't at the house?"

I stand between her and the defense table, purposely blocking her view. She actually cranes her head to the side to see around me. I turn my head in a slow, dramatic fashion to follow her gaze and eye Millwood and Barton with great amusement. The jurors follow my eyes just as I followed Haywood's. With so much attention focused on them, Millwood and Barton remain on their best behavior. I then face the witness again and say: "You don't need to look at them to answer. Would you like me to repeat the question?" She nods.

"Being asked if you saw the defendant pull the trigger makes you now realize you weren't at the house?"

"No. Yes. It's just that I remember now."

"Remember seeing the defendant pull the trigger or that you didn't go to the house?"

"Didn't go to the house."

"But you've already lied to the jury today?"

"Yes."

"Lied to protect the man you love?"

"He didn't do it."

"He didn't pull the trigger?"

"No."

"But you weren't there, were you?"

She slumps. The question remains unanswered. That's okay. Everyone in the room can taste her defeat. I let the moment breathe, hoping that the constant refrain of "pull the trigger" tattoos the image of Barton shooting Sara into the brains of the jurors.

"You lied to the police in your condo on the morning after the murder?"

"Yes."

"Lied to the police in the police station a week after the murder?"

"Yes."

"Lied in this courtroom this morning?"

"Yes."

"Lied in this courtroom this afternoon?"

"Yes."

"Lied about not seeing the defendant pull the trigger?"

"That's not a lie."

"You didn't drive the four and a half minutes to the Barton house to help the defendant kill Sara?"

"No."

"Isn't it true that the reason you know your condo is four and a half minutes from the murder scene is because you and the defendant timed your getaway?"

"No."

"You parked your car near the playground as part of that getaway plan, didn't you?"

"No."

Surprise registers with her. The specificness of the question catches her off guard. I doubt she helped Barton murder Sara, but the question and others like it will at least get the jury thinking about what a conspiracy between the two to kill Sara would look like.

"You tossed the gun in the playground on the way to your car?"

"No."

"You didn't do any of that?"

"No."

"Because you weren't there?"

"I wasn't there."

I decide to wrap up. Lara awaits. The damage to Haywood is fatal. I glance at the defense table and take in a sullen Millwood and a truculent Barton. I breathe a sigh of relief. The gambit worked. I approach the witness again.

"Are you going to have dinner with the defendant and Mr. Millwood tonight?"

"Objection!"

"Withdrawn. No further questions, Your Honor."

Millwood's glare accompanies me back to my seat. For him to break character and reveal his true emotions, the questioning must've been devastating to the defense. He tried to offer up young Monica as substitutionary atonement for the sins of the defendant, but the trial gods rejected the sacrifice. Still entrenched in the witness chair, Haywood sends a plaintive look toward Barton, but he is in no mood to receive it. I doubt dinner is in the cards. After some tense moments of silent contemplation, Millwood releases the witness.

42

Ella's voice announces loudly, "The state calls Lara Landrum."

Lara stands, drawing all eyes to her like an outdoor light beckons the summer bugs. Her celebrity hangs over the trial like the carcass of a dead animal. The cameras in the courtroom, the looks the jurors steal toward her, the extra buzz radiating throughout the building—the origin of all of it is Lara.

She now walks the walk of a confident beauty queen. Her blue dress is properly conservative, and she wears it well. She is gorgeous but not in a way likely to be offensive to other women. The men on the jury are impressed. Be careful what you wish for, I think.

Ella asks, "Will you please state your name for the record?"

"Lara Denise Landrum."

I dumbly realize I didn't even know her middle name. I watch her now, still mesmerized despite the razorblade slashes that mark our history.

"Did you know the victim in this case, Sara Barton?"

"Yes, she was my twin sister."

"Tell us about Sara."

"Sara was the happiest little girl. She loved to draw and give people her drawings to make them smile. She had big dreams about how she was going to change the world. I remember one time—I think we were six—she saw a news story about an orphanage in Nigeria. The next day she sold all her dolls to raise money to give to those kids. That was the kind of person Sara was."

Lara continues along these lines. Millwood could object to the testimony as improper narrative but refrains. Americans are suckers for celebrities, and the jurors sit there transfixed by Lara's presence. Interrupting her now would only bring their annoyance down on his head. As he taught me, sometimes the best objection is the one not made.

Lara finishes her answer, "But Sara married the wrong man and lost all her dreams in the process."

Millwood flinches but nothing more. The words are already out there. No need to bring even greater attention to them.

"Who did Sara marry?"

"Bernard Barton. The defendant."

Lara looks away from Ella and the jurors. She directs her attention across the courtroom to Barton, not with eyes of anger like I would expect, but with profound sadness. I've never seen a witness simultaneously convey pathos and accusation, all without saying a word. Since Ella banned me from all trial prep with Lara, now is the first time I'm seeing any of this. The performance is powerful.

"What were your observations of the marriage?"

"She got married too young. She was only 20. He was 41. I told her he was way too old for her, but she didn't listen. She loved him. It got her killed."

"Objection, Your Honor." Millwood has to object to that.

Judge Woodcomb rules, "Sustained. The jury will disregard that last sentence. The witness will avoid such editorializing in the future."

Lara addresses the judge, "I'm sorry, Your Honor."

Her apology overflows with sincerity. Woodcomb nods and falls under her spell. Millwood notices it, looks at me, and rolls his eyes slightly.

Ella stands at the end of the jury box farthest away from the witness stand. This positioning creates the feel of an intimate conversation among Lara, Ella, and the jurors. As she answers questions, Lara makes good eye contact with both her questioner and the jury. I worried beforehand, but Ella and Lara have good chemistry. One would never guess that they hate each other.

"What problems did you observe in the marriage?"

"Bernard was controlling, liked to have his own way. He treated her as a subordinate, not an equal partner. His infidelity began early on with lots of different women."

Ella draws out some more of the marriage backstory in a series of little vignettes, including the time years ago when Barton grabbed Sara's arm and pulled her away from the sisters' ten-year high school reunion. Barton wanted to leave, and Sara didn't. They left. Lara could still see the marks from Barton's grip the next day.

Through stories like this one, Lara paints an ugly picture of a man who brooks no dissent. Barton sits over there shaking his head throughout the testimony. Millwood tries various covert and overt methods to stop the head-shaking, but he has lost control over his client.

Ella moves the questioning to more recent times and asks if Lara knew of her sister's affair with Brice Tanner: "Yes, that was the first time she ever cheated despite years of Bernard's womanizing. But when she found out about Bernard and Monica Haywood, something snapped inside of her. She didn't care anymore. She wanted to do something to make herself feel good again, and Brice Tanner was the outlet. That one of their encounters was secretly taped was a cruel twist of fate."

"How did the defendant respond when he learned about Sara and Brice?"

"Rage. I've known Bernard for a long time, and he can't stand being made the fool. To see his wife cast him aside for a younger, more virile man wounded his pride. He could do whatever he wanted outside the marriage, but Sara had to remain faithful to him."

On cue, Barton's face turns blood red as he and Lara engage in a deadly staredown. Lara's words—especially the "younger, more virile man" bit—were no doubt calculated to produce this very reaction. She has great talent for getting a rise out of people. The bulging vein in Barton's neck speaks truth to everything she just said. Everyone in the room sees it. The man sitting next to Jack Millwood looks like a murderer.

"Have you heard the 911 call your sister placed?"

Lara nods, and tears cloud her eyes. She uses a tissue to blunt the impact, but the angst seeps through nevertheless. Her makeup remains perfectly in place.

"I'm sorry. Thinking about the fear in my sister's voice on the 911 call is very upsetting to me."

"Did you talk to your sister after the 911 call?"

"Yes. The next day. She told me she was scared and afraid for her life. She also had bruising on her back."

"How do you know that?"

"I took a picture of her bruises."

Ella begins the process of authenticating and introducing the photograph of Sara Barton's bruised back into evidence. Lara describes the scene when she visited her sister shortly after Barton's attack and confirms that she took the picture to later use in a possible divorce. Barton scowls like a skunk at her the entire time. The photograph is passed from juror to juror. Once the jury has had the time to absorb the evidence of the defendant's physical abuse, Ella continues.

"Why didn't Sara just leave at that moment?"

"I told her to. She wouldn't listen. She was still shaken from the attack. She told me she feared that Bernard would kill her before he allowed that to happen. A few months later, she did summon the courage to leave. And then …"

Wary of the judge's earlier admonishment not to editorialize, Lara allows the rest of us to complete the thought for her. She sheds a few more tears, the tissue in her hand riding to the rescue barely in time again. In a move of calculated thoughtfulness, Ella gives the witness some time to compose herself—the unsaid accusation still hanging above the courtroom. Barton glowers on, digging his own grave by the second.

"When was the last time you saw your sister?"

"The day before she died. We had lunch. She had decided to leave Bernard and was filing the paperwork in a few days. I was happy for her. Sara was hopeful for the first time in years and prepared to take back control of her life. The dark cloud hanging over her was gone."

More tears, then Ella announces no further questions.

***

Millwood spies Lara Landrum from across the courtroom as if he doesn't know what to do with her. After a promising morning, the defense's fortunes have suffered a hard afternoon. The heaves of Millwood's chest suggest a profound weariness with both his client and this entire affair. He stands with more effort than the movement deserves. Not much good can come from cross-examining this witness, and Millwood well recognizes the lay of the land. Lara is too sympathetic, too polished, too ready to inflict maximum hurt on one Bernard Barton. He approaches her out of professional obligation and little else. I'm looking at a man that just wants to go home and pour himself a stiff drink. Or three.

"Ms. Landrum, you weren't present when your sister was murdered?"

"No."

"You didn't see Sam Wilkins when he arrived at your sister's house that night?"

"No."

"You didn't see what he did or didn't do?"

"No."

"You have no personal knowledge whether your sister was alive or dead when he arrived?"

"No."

The focus on Sam is sound. Distract. Highlight what the witness doesn't know. Introduce elements that the witness cannot possibly speak to. Draw attention away from the angry little man sitting at the defense table. Even when his heart isn't in it, Millwood knows how to play the game.

"You don't know if Liesa Wilkins was there that night?"

"I do not."

"You don't know if Brice Tanner was there?"

"No."

"You don't know anything Tanner might have done?"

"No."

"You weren't there?"

"Correct."

Millwood pauses. He looks down at his yellow legal pad, wondering if he should call it a day. He once told me if you have to debate with yourself whether to ask any more questions, you almost certainly shouldn't ask them. Just sit down. One question too many has slain every single trial lawyer at one point or another. Millwood remains standing.

"You weren't present during the incident when your sister called 911?"

"The 'incident'? No, I wasn't present during the 'incident.'"

Lara is the wildest of mustangs, not easily bridled like the vast majority of other witnesses Millwood has wrangled over the years. Her enunciation of the word "incident" drips with honey-coated sarcasm, making her questioner look foolish in his attempt to re-frame his client's beating of her sister. A slight, yet uncharacteristic, grimace tells me that Millwood wishes he had sat down when he had the chance. But he can't end his examination on that low point. With the mare still on the loose, he gets his rope out for one more try.

"You weren't there?"

"I wasn't there. I wish I was."

"You didn't witness Bernard hit your sister?"

"No. Only the aftermath."

"And what you know about that is only what your sister told you?"

"That's not true. I've heard the 911 call just like everyone else, and I saw her bruised back with my own two eyes."

Millwood actually gives a soft chuckle. She's good, and he has seen enough witnesses to admire her skill. She bats earnest eyes at him that say she can play this game all day. Again loathe to end on a sour note, Millwood draws his bow one last time.

"But you didn't see Bernard bruise her back, you only know what your sister told you?"

"True. I only know what my dead sister told me."

Millwood sits down, giving up the fight. We have no questions on re-direct, and Lara Landrum leaves the witness box having delivered one of her greatest performances. I give her an appreciative nod as she passes. I then whisper to Ella, "Good job." She whispers back, "Damn right."

***

The mood during the nightly meeting with Scott and Ella is celebratory. The change in momentum from the low point of the lunch hour to the success of the afternoon is one of my proudest moments as a lawyer. Ella sips a red wine, and Scott gulps a beer. I drink some coffee with smug satisfaction.

A television in my office is on in the background. One of the nightly crime shows plays the 911 call. An image of Lara on the witness stand accompanies Sara's pained screams. We all stare at the screen and take in the devastating juxtaposition. The noose around Barton's neck just got tighter.

"I hope the jurors are watching," Scott says. He turns to Ella, "You handled her well today."

The response: "I hate that bitch."

Scott laughs. Ella doesn't. She drinks some more wine and avoids looking at me. The hangover from her comment dampens the mood in the room, which is just as well. The trial isn't over yet.

Scott asks, "What is Millwood's play now?"

"Plea bargain," Ella proclaims, enjoying her joke a little too much. She may be slightly drunk. But we all know that Barton won't deal. Nor would I even offer anything less than life in prison at this point. He might as well roll the dice. We're going all the way to verdict.

The both of them look at me for my assessment of the opponent's next move. I lean back in my chair and stare at the ceiling. After being blindsided by Monica Haywood this morning, I try to imagine as many outlandish possibilities as I can envision. But only one viable avenue presents itself to my mind's eye.

"Liesa. Millwood has to go after Liesa. She's the weakest link we have left. He has no other choice."

Scott responds, "Has she gotten back to you yet?"

"No. And she won't. Too stubborn and proud for her own good. But if she can survive Millwood, we should be home free."

43

The next morning, I stand before Mary Woodcomb and announce in good voice: "The prosecution rests." Millwood goes through the motions of asking for a directed verdict on the grounds that the State didn't meet its evidentiary burden. The judge denies the request and informs the defense that it may now put on its case.

"The defense calls Liesa Wilkins."

The momentum of the entire trial against him, Millwood doesn't waste any time slow-playing peripheral witnesses to begin the mounting of his counterattack. He calls Liesa right out of the box, hoping to land the haymaker that he needs. Nothing about this case even hints at a random attack. Someone chose Sara Barton for a reason, and Millwood needs a scapegoat.

Liesa maintains her icy demeanor as she passes me on the way to the witness stand. She then swears her oath with the intensity of an unplugged robot. She hasn't look at me once.

Millwood says in that deep baritone of his, "Your Honor, the defense believes that the witness' late husband, Sam Wilkins, may have been involved in the death of Sara Barton. We contend that the witness was in the vicinity of the Barton residence on the night of the murder, and we intend to aggressively question her as to her whereabouts. We ask, therefore, for permission to treat Mrs. Wilkins as a hostile witness."

Judge Woodcomb asks me for a response.

"Mr. Millwood pulled Liesa Wilkins away from her grieving children and forced her to testify today so he could conduct a fishing expedition. I would be surprised if she wasn't hostile. But Mr. Millwood cannot assume hostility. Liesa Wilkins is a licensed lawyer and a respected member of the state bar. She understands her duty as a witness, and I see no reason to depart from the typical rules of direct examination."

Millwood jumps in, "Your Honor, you allowed the State to treat Monica Hayward as a hostile witness. Turnabout is fair play."

I counter, "Not so. Monica Hayward lives in the defendant's house as his fiancée. Mrs. Wilkins is a neutral third-party witness. Apples and oranges."

A direct examination would force Millwood to ask open-ended questions that do not suggest an answer, which would increase the difficulty of pinning the witness down. Millwood, instead, wants the questioning to be treated as a cross-examination, giving him enhanced control over the direction of the testimony.

Judge Woodcomb considers the respective arguments and announces, "I'm going to hold off on a final ruling for now. Mr. Millwood can start with a direct examination, and we'll revisit the issue if we need to."

That's a bit of good news that I wasn't expecting. Millwood's dejection is perceptible if you know what to look for. He brushes the disappointment away and approaches Liesa with resolve ringing in each step.

"Mrs. Wilkins, were you married to the late Sam Wilkins?"

"I was."

"And what was your husband's relationship with the decedent in this case, Sara Barton?"

"Sam was her divorce lawyer."

"Was it your husband that discovered Sara Barton's body and called the police?"

"That's what I'm told."

"Do you have any reason to doubt that?"

"No."

Liesa's answer to the question about Sam's discovery of the body had an undertone of snippiness in it. Millwood met that peevishness head on and put her on the defensive in response. Here's hoping that Liesa internalizes that lesson. I look at her with meaning, but she still has yet to glance at me since entering the courtroom.

"Why was your husband visiting Sara Barton at ten o'clock in the evening?"

"To get her to sign divorce papers to be filed the next day."

"Did your husband have a practice of making house calls with female clients late at night?"

The question drips with unmistakable innuendo. The jurors throw Liesa anticipatory looks, the undercurrent of sex piquing their interest. Liesa doesn't flinch and answers with cold steel resolve.

"I wouldn't call it a practice, but Sam had met with clients in their homes before, both men and women. Mrs. Barton requested that Sam bring the documents over, and he did. Sam expected to make a lot of money off this divorce, so he was willing to accommodate her."

Great answer, and I hope the jury processes the full implications of what Liesa just said. Sam wouldn't have killed Sara Barton because she represented dollar signs to him, and the divorce was going to be an expensive one for Bernard Barton.

Millwood continues, "Did you consider Sara Barton a beautiful woman?"

"I didn't consider her at all. I never met her."

"Did you know that Sara Barton was Lara Landrum's twin sister?"

Liesa pauses—thinking instead of answering. I hope she says yes even if it's not true. People are gossip hounds and will assume Sam told her. They won't believe otherwise.

"I know now obviously. But I can't tell you when I learned that, whether it was before Sara Barton's murder or after. Sam didn't share many details about his clients with me. He liked to leave his work at the office."

"Or at his client's house that he visited late at night?"

Woodcomb looks at me, ready to sustain the objection she anticipates. I let it pass. Liesa is holding her own, and if Millwood wants to go sarcastic on a young widow, I'll graciously keep out of the way. Instinct tells me it doesn't play well.

Liesa answers, "That, his office, the courthouse, wherever—the point is that Sam didn't like to bring his work home."

"You say that your husband didn't like to talk shop with you, yet earlier you testified that you knew the Barton divorce was going to be lucrative?"

"Oh, we talked about money. Definitely that. I was interested in that—the other details not so much."

A few jurors laugh and nod their heads. Married couples talk about money. They usually argue about money. Disagreements over finances are the number one cause of divorce. Liesa's words ring true, and she just bought herself some extra credibility.

"How much life insurance are you due to receive on account of your husband's death?"

And boom goes the dynamite. The somewhat jovial moment of a second ago transforms with astonishing swiftness into something decidedly somber. Millwood's gut—honed through decades of trials in this very courthouse—just hit pay dirt. The dramatic shift in the tone and content of his questioning maximizes the attention of everyone in the room.

"Three million dollars."

The answer sounds like a confession of murder, and Liesa's resolve weakens a touch with the admission. No shame should follow having generous life insurance. But at a murder trial, the imagination of the jurors can do a lot with the thought of $3 million dancing in their heads. Millwood just landed a body blow. I would be more worried if Barton himself didn't stand to collect $5 million.

Millwood continues, "Where were you on the night of Sara Barton's murder?"

"I have no idea."

"Really?"

"Really."

Millwood's look of skepticism prowls throughout the courtroom. He senses that momentum is now on his side, and the renewed vigor flowing from this belief creates the feel of kinetic energy in the air. He grabs a file, studies it, takes out a document, hands me a copy, and approaches Liesa with the resolve of an assassin.

"Mrs. Wilkins, I hand you a document listing all the vehicles that traveled through an intersection close to the Barton—"

"Object to the word 'close,' Your Honor. Mr. Millwood is going outside the document to describe the document, which is an improper characterization. The intersection is over a mile away from the Barton home. Whether that counts as close in a compacted place like Midtown Atlanta is up to the jury to decide."

"Sustained. Mr. Millwood, you can ask about the closeness in your questions if you like but not when explaining the contents of the document to the witness."

Millwood's annoyance is mild, but there all the same. His frustrations with the judge add up. If the jury comes back with a guilty verdict, Millwood gets to appeal all the rulings he disagrees with to the Georgia Supreme Court. I hope he gets the chance.

"Mrs. Wilkins, will you please turn to page three of the document I handed you. In the middle of the page, an entry exists for a Chrysler Minivan owned by Sam Wilkins. Do you see that?"

"Yes."

"What time did this Chrysler Minivan cross the intersection according to this printout?"

"9:51 p.m."

"Detective Scott Moore has already testified that your husband drove a Volkswagen Passat to the Barton home that night. Do you have reason to doubt that testimony?"

"No."

"Would anyone besides yourself have been driving your family's minivan on the night of the murder at 9:51 p.m.?"

"No."

"What were you doing out at that time of night?"

An open-ended question to an adverse witness typically begs for trouble, but Liesa is on record saying she doesn't remember what she was doing that night. Any departure from that testimony will allow Millwood to hammer her credibility.

"I imagine I was going home. We live three miles from the intersection. I'm on that road all the time."

"And where were you coming home from?"

"I have no idea. I couldn't possibly tell you where I was on a particular night that many months ago. I was running some errand probably. I'm a mom. I'm always running errands somewhere."

Millwood looks at her contemplatively. He wants to push here but lacks any kind of stick to force her to play nice. He continues to tread a line between the right amount of aggressiveness and going that one step too far.

"So to summarize your testimony up to this point—on the night of the murder, at around the same time your husband was calling the police, you were in your car close to the murder scene, and yet you have no idea what you were doing out that late. Is that correct?"

I should object, but don't—playing a hunch.

"That wasn't my testimony. I have no idea how close I was to the murder scene because I have no idea where Sara Barton lived—still don't know to this day. Sam said he was going to a house in Virginia Highlands. That's all. I have no idea what I was doing the night before or after the murder, either, except to say I almost certainly drove on that same road those days, too. I resent your veiled hints making me or my husband out to be some kind of murderer. I have children, Mr. Millwood."

Powerful. Wrapping herself in the mantle of motherhood, Liesa delivers a dignified response filled with righteous indignation. This Liesa is the one I remember from law school. She should've made Sam stay at home with the kids. Unfazed, Millwood doesn't miss a beat.

"Permission to treat Mrs. Wilkins as a hostile witness now, Your Honor?"

Woodcomb chews on it a brief moment before acquiescing, "Granted." A spring forms in Millwood's step.

"You have three young children?"

"Yes."

"Ages 11, 8, and 5?"

"Yes."

"They have bedtimes?"

"Yes."

"They weren't in the car with you at 9:51 p.m. on the night of the murder, were they?"

If my earlier figuring is correct, Liesa followed Sam to the Barton residence, no doubt leaving her kids at home as she did so. Sam discovered Sara's dead body, exited the house, and found Liesa there. Because they saw one another at the scene, each of them suspected the other might be the murderer, which explains their strange conduct throughout the investigation. But even if my figuring is wrong about some of the precise details, Liesa was there that night for sure. Now she must lie herself of her predicament.

"As I said before, I have no specific memory of driving that night. I cannot tell you if my children were in the car or not."

"But it's possible that your kids were not in the car?"

"It's possible."

"Possible that you left them home all alone?"

"It's possible."

"Your children—ages 11, 8, and 5—left all alone late at night?"

"I wouldn't have been gone long. The oldest is very responsible."

"You know you wouldn't have been gone long, but you have no idea where you were?"

This sequence demonstrates the power of momentum and leading questions. Millwood is in the zone now, and Liesa borders on looking criminally negligent as a parent.

"You're twisting my words. They may very well have been in the car with me. They probably were that late. If they weren't, it means I was running a quick errand."

I grimace. The problem with lying is the lies. Liesa is getting pretzeled by Millwood because failing to tell the truth creates a whole bunch of other plot holes in the narrative. Liesa the Good Mother would never leave her kids alone that late. Liesa the Mad Wife would.

Millwood pounces, "You just said that you didn't know if they were in the car with you. Now you say they probably were in the car with you?"

"I just don't remember."

"You don't know?"

"No."

"You don't know anything about your actions that night?"

"No."

"The night your husband discovered a beautiful woman murdered in her home?"

"No."

"And he discovered her around the same time you were just down the street?"

"If you say so."

"And now your husband is dead, isn't he?"

"Yes."

Millwood pauses to let the audience catch its breath. The "if you say so" answer is just what he wants to hear. A beaten down person who agrees with whatever the questioner asks is the holy grail of witnesses—like a suspect being grilled by the police for hours who eventually confesses to everything just to hasten the end of the ordeal.

"Your husband died of a gunshot wound?"

"Yes."

"In a secluded area of the woods?"

"Yes."

"The gun that killed him right by his side?"

"Yes."

"The gunshot wound was to his temple?"

"Yes."

"And this was after the murder of Sara Barton?"

"Yes."

A toddler still in diapers would have no trouble connecting those dots. Liesa makes eye contact with me for the first time. I slowly make a fist with my hand as it hangs near my face to indicate that she should stay strong. Millwood has scored some points, but Liesa hasn't admitted a single damaging thing yet. The questioning is more sizzle than steak at this point.

"Your husband died only three weeks ago?"

"Yes."

"And he was due to testify at this trial, wasn't he?"

"Yes"—a pause—"that's what killed him."

The answer comes of out nowhere—a sudden break from the monotony of Liesa meekly saying "yes" to whatever Millwood puts in front of her. Worry seizes my insides. I have no idea what she is talking about. I swallow my concern and nearly choke on it. My entire trial strategy hangs in the balance. Millwood shares my shock. Confused, he actually blurts out, "What?"

His disorientation leads him to make a mistake. He asks a witness on cross-examination an open-ended question to which he doesn't already know the answer. With rare exceptions, cross-examination questions should almost always elicit a yes or no response. Giving the witness a free platform to answer an open-ended question in a way that can hurt your case is a cardinal sin. Millwood just sinned.

"Sam wasn't a strong man mentally. He knew clever lawyers would accuse him of something bad just because he was in the wrong place at—"

Millwood yammers, "Move to strike as non-responsive, Your Honor."

I blast out of my seat and assert, "No, Your Honor. Mr. Millwood posed a question. He asked, 'What?' The witness is allowed to finish the answer to that question without Mr. Millwood interrupting her."

Judge Woodcomb agrees and tells Liesa that she may proceed with her answer. Millwood stands there numbly, fearing the worse. The slow-moving pitch to Liesa sits right over the middle of home plate waiting for her to knock it out of the park.

Liesa takes her swing, "As I was saying, Sam was a nervous sort. He was worried about testifying because he knew that finding the body automatically made him a suspect. He knew what the lawyers would do to him, drag his name through the mud. You're doing it to him now, even after he's dead. It was too much for him. He wasn't built for that kind of pressure. If he had just left that house instead of doing the right thing and calling the police when he discovered the body, he would still be alive today."

Grand slam. Millwood must regroup and fast. He asks, "But your husband was a divorce lawyer, right?"

"Yes."

"And he was a good divorce lawyer?"

"Yes."

"He was used to battling out contentious divorces?"

"He was a good divorce lawyer because he was full of empathy for hurting people going through a difficult time in their lives. He could never do what you do, Mr. Millwood."

The Ice Queen just sliced off pieces of Millwood's body onto the floor. Millwood again moves to strike the answer as non-responsive. This time the judge agrees with him, but no matter. The wound is real, and it is gaping. A few female jurors throw looks of disgust Millwood's way.

Liesa starts crying.

I grab a box of tissues and lift them up toward Millwood. He burns a hole through me with the intensity of his stare, but with the jury watching him like a hawk, he knows what he must do. He takes the tissue box like a dutiful child and makes the slow march to the witness box. I wonder if he remembers pulling the same stunt on opposing counsel years ago. That's where I learned the trick—the spontaneous remembrance of that incident paying huge dividends in the present.

"Here you go, Mrs. Wilkins," Millwood says, offering her the box of tissues before walking back to his corner of the courtroom. I know he loathes ending his examination at this point, but any further questions would invite an encore performance from the witness. He sits down.

Judge Woodcomb asks me, "Should we take a short break now or wait fifteen minutes?"

"I'm ready to go now, Your Honor."

***

I won't take fifteen minutes. The examination of Liesa ricocheted with swift blowback against the defense, and I don't intend to give Millwood another crack at reversing that negative momentum.

"Mrs. Wilkins, did you kill Sara Barton?"

"No."

"Didn't drive your car to her house on the night of her murder for some nefarious purpose?"

"No."

"You don't even know where the house is, do you?"

"No."

The ease with which she lies is a spectacle to behold. Remarkable. I take the measure of the jury. Liesa has won them over. Millwood's gamble backfired. I mentally prepare the finishing touches.

"Mrs. Wilkins, you're a grieving widow with three small children?"

"I am."

"And you were forced to come down here to testify?"

"Yes."

"Mr. Millwood subpoenaed you?"

"He did."

I stand near Millwood and give him a stern look of reproach. Liesa dishes up a disapproving look of her own. With twelve pairs of eyes from the jury studying him closely, Millwood has no choice but to say nothing and take his medicine. He's no match for the grieving widow with three small children.

Still looking at him, I ask, "And you have no idea who killed Sara Barton?"

"I do not."

"And you don't even know anything relevant to this case?"

The question demands an objection. Relevance is an issue of law beyond the competency of any witness. I'm daring Millwood to object. A lesser lawyer would, but Millwood sits there stony-faced still. He knows the witness is lost. Protesting too much now only lowers the jurors' estimation of him. The flipside of cashing in your gains is limiting your losses when the hand doesn't go your way.

Liesa answers, "No."

"Mrs. Wilkins, I'm very sorry for your loss. And I'm sorry you had to come down to the courthouse today. You're a brave woman. No further questions, Your Honor."

44

Millwood calls police officer J.D. Hendrix to the stand. Hendrix responded to Sara's 911 call and made the decision not to arrest Barton. He is Millwood's witness, but our guy. We prepped his testimony many times, emphasizing that at no point whatsoever should he get clever or cute in his answers to Millwood. Listen to the questions, let Millwood score his points, don't argue, don't evade, be polite. Scott sat in on these prep sessions to put an exclamation point on the seriousness of these instructions as if from God Himself. Hendrix got the message. He's a good kid.

Millwood's mission is no mystery. In the hands of an angry jury, the 911 call is enough to convict Barton itself. One need not possess an active imagination to believe that a man who hits a woman has it in him to kill her, too. Millwood will use Hendrix to show that nothing at the scene indicated domestic violence. Anything Barton says on that score will be instantly disbelieved. To dilute the impact of the 911 call, Hendrix is the only game in town for the defense. How Millwood deals with the photo of Sara Barton's blackened back remains to be seen.

Following a few background questions, Millwood asks Hendrix, "Describe the demeanor of Mrs. Barton when you arrived at the house."

Millwood doesn't fear the answer to this question because he holds Hendrix's incident report in his hands. Contemporaneous with the event, the document describes Sara Barton as being calm, composed, and apologetic for involving the police in a private matter between husband and wife. By Hendrix's telling, Sara confessed that she overreacted to her husband's yelling in calling 911. And just like we trained him to do, Hendrix hews the line established by his report. Sara Barton was calm, composed, and apologetic when Officer Hendrix showed up at her door.

"Where was Mrs. Barton when you arrived at the house?"

"In the living room."

"Did you have any indication that Mrs. Barton had been physically assaulted?"

"No."

"How long did you talk to her?"

"Fifteen minutes."

Millwood draws out the details of this conversation. Sara denied to Hendrix that she had been hit and emphasized that she had overreacted to an otherwise unexceptional domestic quarrel. Barton, also, presented a picture of absolute calm, denying that anything was amiss. The questioning is effective, transforming a scene of violence into an innocent misunderstanding.

"And after visiting the scene and talking to Sara Barton, you decided not to arrest Bernard Barton?"

"That's correct."

"No further questions."

***

My cross-examination is short and to the point. I start by showing Hendrix the photo of Sara Barton's injuries at the hand of her husband.

"Did you see these bruises?"

"No."

"Sara Barton was wearing a shirt?"

"Yes."

"And you couldn't see her back?"

"Correct."

"If you had seen these bruises, would you have arrested the defendant, Bernard Barton, for punching his wife?"

"In a heartbeat," Hendrix responds.

I then play the 911 call, using the opportunity to get the frightened words of Sara Barton before the jury again. I establish that Hendrix didn't hear the 911 call prior to arriving at the Barton house. Rather, the dispatcher only told him that a domestic disturbance was in progress.

I ask, "If you had heard the 911 call prior to arriving at the residence, would you have arrested the defendant, Bernard Barton?"

"Absolutely."

"Why?"

"I put more credibility in what's said in the heat of the moment to 911 than what's said to the police once they arrive at the scene. Many women are coached by their abusers to stay silent for their own good."

Millwood jumps out of his chair, "Objection! No evidence indicates that my client coached anyone to do anything. That is just rank speculation."

"Sustained. The jury shall disregard any suggestion that Mrs. Barton was coached to stay silent."

I expected that. No matter. The seed has been planted. I move behind the jury box, forcing Hendrix to look right at the jurors as he answers. The connection between witness and jurors needs to be tight for my big finish—because I know something that Millwood doesn't.

"Did you ever see Sara Barton again?"

"Yes."

"When?"

"She was dead on the floor of her kitchen. I was one of the first officers to secure the scene."

"What did you think when you saw Sara Barton dead on the floor of her kitchen?"

"I wished I had arrested her husband."

45

Roy Winston approaches the witness box for the defense. Winston is Marsh & McCabe's managing partner and figures to testify about the money Barton makes, with a dash of character reference on the side. Winston refused to talk to me when I called him up after seeing his name on the witness list. He's a mergers and acquisitions lawyer by trade, and a meaningful possibility exists that today is the first time he has ever set foot in a courtroom.

Corporate law has treated him well. In the witness box, Winston wears a $3,000 suit and a look of profound unease. My guess is that he makes north of $3 million a year, all without ever having to dirty himself in the trenches of real law. But his money does him no good here. I have plans for him that won't be to his liking.

Winston's discomfort doesn't abate as Millwood introduces him to the jury through a series of background questions. The witness sits erect, considers every word from Millwood with the utmost of care, and only answers when he is good and ready. With the end of the day nearing, Winston's measured detachment tests the patience of the room—those who are awake at least. Millwood conceals his irritation with Winston's extreme deliberateness, but hurries through the basics all the same to get to the point.

"In your capacity as managing partner, do you know how much money Bernard Barton earns each year?"

Pause. "Yes."

They next go to the particulars. The testimony establishes that Barton's share of partner profits totals approximately $1 million a year. Additionally, Barton's interest in the firm retirement plan is $3.3 million in total. The numbers aren't new. Millwood referenced them in his opening statement. The jury looks interested but uncommitted. Rich men kill people, too.

The financial evidence established, the questioning takes a turn into the personal.

"Mr. Winston, how long have you known Bernard Barton?"

Pause. "Twenty-five years."

Millwood next solicits Winston's observations that the Barton marriage was over, and neither wife nor husband exhibited much discernable regard for the other. Winston offered to terminate Brice Tanner for the offense of sleeping with a partner's wife, but Barton laughed off the sex tape and wanted no retribution taken on his account. The general knowledge within the firm was that Barton had moved on to Monica Haywood. Winston gave Barton the name of the lawyer who handled Winston's own divorce, and that was that. The testimony concludes with the witness describing Barton's extensive work in fundraising for domestic violence shelters.

I stifle a yawn. I have a text of Barton calling his wife a whore, a 911 call of him yelling at her on the same day he learned about the sex tape, and a color photo of Sara Barton's bruised back. The documentary evidence doesn't lie. I don't care how much money Barton gives to good causes. Millwood turns the witness over to me.

***

Winston eyes me with the wariness of a house cat that still possesses a healthy dose of tiger DNA in its blood. He is obviously a competent lawyer, but corporate law has domesticated him. Now he finds himself in the wild on unfamiliar ground and doesn't like it. I approach friendly-like, more for the jury's benefit than Winston's. Jeff Yarber told me the day after Sara Barton's murder that Marsh & McCabe has had to settle numerous sexual harassment lawsuits on Barton's behalf. I doubt Winston knows I know. That is about to change.

"Mr. Winston, you're managing partner of Marsh & McCabe?"

Pause. "Yes."

"One of the largest law firms in Atlanta?"

Pause. "Yes."

"And your firm employs a great number of women?"

Pause. “Yes.”

“And some of these women have accused Bernard Barton of sexual harassment?”

Winston reacts as if punched in the face. He calculates the awful equation in an instant. His firm now has bigger problems than one of its partners on trial for murder. The #MeToo movement just showed up on its doorstep on national television. An unresponsive Winston looks to Millwood for rescue.

Millwood objects, “Objection, Your Honor. Beyond the scope of direct examination.”

I answer, “Your Honor, the question goes to witness credibility. If the witness has covered up for the defendant in the past, then the jury may infer that he is covering up for the defendant now and thereby disregard the entirety of his testimony.”

“I’ll allow it.”

Millwood appears over all of it. No doubt he specifically asked Barton about other potential grenades out there. No doubt Barton lied to him. Difficult clients keep lawyers up late at night, and Millwood wears the look of a man that can no longer stomach Bernard Barton.

I watch Winston expectantly. He still sits there on mute. I slowly restate the question in a louder voice: “Have some female employees of your law firm accused the defendant of sexual harassment in the past?”

The attention of every spectator in the courtroom oppresses him as his silence grows louder by the second. Finally, he offers, “Pursuant to confidentiality agreements, I’m unable to testify about such matters.”

“Agreements. Plural?”

“I’m not allowed to testify on such things.”

“This is a murder trial, Mr. Winston. It trumps the secrecy of your hush money payoffs. Answer the question.”

Millwood jumps in, “Move to strike, Your Honor!”

“Granted. The jury will disregard counsel’s last remark.”

Millwood continues, “I also object to this whole line of questioning as being unduly prejudicial and lacking relevance to the present charges. Mr. Barton is on trial in connection with his relationship with Sara Barton, not irrelevant relationships with other women."

I respond, "Your Honor, the questioning still goes to Mr. Winston's credibility or lack thereof. Also, how the defendant acts towards women who reject him is at the heart of this trial."

The judge rules, "I'll allow it. Mr. Winston, you have to answer the questions asked of you."

Winston slouches in disappointment before resuming the edifice of his erect posture. The cracks are showing. The earlier wariness now reads as a foreboding of impending doom. The king of the boardroom is no match for the courtroom. I relaunch the ambush.

"Have some female employees of your law firm accused the defendant of sexual harassment in the past?"

"Yes." He doesn't pause. He has finally let his guard down when it should be at its highest. He made Millwood run around the mulberry bush and back to extract the answer to the simplest questions. Now he figures to give me what I want without much fuss. Cross-examination has that effect on people.

"This harassment consisted of unwanted comments?"

"Yes."

"Unwanted touching?"

"Yes."

"Of women who were his subordinates?"

"Yes."

"Who he had power over?"

"Yes."

"More than one woman?"

"Yes."

The problem is what I don't know. I don't know how many women Barton harassed, who he harassed, what he said to them, how he touched them, or how many settlements Marsh & McCabe paid out to cover for him. When I later asked Jeff Yarber for these details, he wouldn't spill them, confidentiality and all. Without the specifics, I'm forced to probe Winston around the edges to see what I can scare up.

"You found these complaints credible?"

That stops him. He can't very well throw all the women who complained about Barton under the bus on national television. But if the complaints were credible, why is Barton still a partner at the firm? I wait with all the time in the world as he makes up his mind.

"Yes."

"So credible in fact that your law firm paid out financial settlements to these women?"

"Yes."

"Sizable settlements?"

"Yes."

"Hush money, in fact?"

"Absolutely not. They were payouts on disputed legal claims."

"Did the settlements have provisions that prohibited these women from talking about what the defendant did to them?"

"Yes. Confidentiality clauses are standard contract language in settlement agreements."

"The firm bought the silence of the defendant's victims?"

"I wouldn't characterize it like that."

But everyone else would. The disgust that the jurors feel toward Winston is evident. The feeling is likely reciprocal. The witness hasn't once looked in their direction. His focus now on me, I lounge around to let him twist in the wind a little longer. The small specks of sweat evolving at the border of his hairline speak to his distress. I give him a fake, sympathetic smile before resuming.

"Bernard Barton is still a partner with your law firm?"

"He's currently on leave."

"Paid leave?"

"Yes."

"A million dollars a year, right?"

Winston sags. Back at headquarters, I imagine the partners of Marsh & McCabe are scurrying to divorce themselves from Barton as we speak—and maybe Roy Winston, too. Clients are the currency of Big Law, and Corporate America wants no part of the negative press the law firm will soon endure. Marsh & McCabe just became toxic.

"You had multiple complaints of sexual harassment against the defendant that led to sizable settlements, yet you still allowed the defendant to work at the law firm?"

"In hindsight, that was a mistake."

"The firm covered up for a predator?"

"I reject that characterization. We settled legal claims, and we should've severed our relationship with Bernard because of it. Conduct like that is unacceptable."

"Yet you accepted it, didn't you?"

Pause. "I'm afraid so."

***

That night, Ella and I sit on opposite ends of a conference table, married to our yellow legal pads—the lawyer's perpetual best friend. Scott is off attending a school event for his daughter. The end is close. By this time in every trial, the body runs on fumes, 20-hour days exacting their due. I prepare for Barton's upcoming cross-examination. Ella toils on jury charges. We end up doing arm stretches at the same time, sending each other awkward glances in the process. Ella breaks the silence.

"Millwood seems to be struggling."

"It's not his fault. Barton hasn't been square with him. Jack had no idea about the sexual harassment settlements. He never would've put Winston on the stand if he had known. Barton is directing his own defense and it shows. Jack's fed up. I don't blame him."

"Why would you hire one of the best lawyers in Atlanta to defend you and then not listen to him?"

"Barton probably thinks he's the best lawyer in Atlanta."

"How are you going to handle him on cross?"

"Try to get under his skin."

"That shouldn't be too hard. He might kill you in open court."

"That may be his best defense at this point. Mary would have to declare a mistrial."

We get back to our work. At some point, I close my eyes. When I open them far later into the night, I see Ella asleep with her head cradled in her arms on the table—all peaceful like. I watch her rise and fall in rhythm with her breath. Look at what I threw away. I get up and gently rouse her.

With her head still on the table, she asks, "What time is it?"

"Late."

She sits up and shakes the sleep out of her eyes. A piercing yawn follows. She says, "I was in the middle of a dream. It was about you."

"A good dream?"

"I don't know. I didn't get to finish it, but I doubt it."

I offer a sage nod, reckoning she guessed right. We exit the room to go home but with the knowledge that we'll be right back here again in a few hours. Before we part, Ella stops and looks at me with studied intensity.

She asks, "Why are you the way you are?"

I thoughtfully ponder the question before answering, "I wish I knew."

46

"The defense calls Bernard Barton."

Barton walks to the stand—his legs not quite confident, not quite jelly. Only a sociopath wouldn't be nervous in his shoes, and Barton is no sociopath. He's a gambler. The huge debts he ran up in Vegas led him to take the biggest gamble of his life in murdering his wife. He now doubles down on the high-risk strategy of testifying on his own behalf—something murder defendants almost universally avoid. Barton suffers from the gambler's curse. He wagers that one more gamble can wipe away all the previous losses, that lady luck will be on his side with one more roll. He should know that the house always wins.

Millwood proceeds slowly through the background questions. The goal is both to humanize his client and to chisel off some of Barton's nerves before getting to the meat of the testimony. Even though the State contends that Barton is a cold-blooded killer, he sits there in the witness box right next to the jurors, well within striking distance before security could ever stop him. Everyone accepts the arrangement as normal. One of the benefits for Barton in testifying is to make himself one with this non-threatening normalcy. The effect would be stronger if Barton's pot hadn't been boiling over for most of the trial.

The testimony borders on boring, but that's a feature not a bug. Boring people seem incapable of murder. I myself wrestle with inattention as the story drags. Trials are exciting on television and in movies, but the reality of listening to witnesses drone on hour after hour after hour day after day after day drains the energy of every viewer. Paying attention to the small details demands a constant refocusing of the mind.

Millwood finally finishes with the fluff. He doesn't say a word, but the noticeable change in his demeanor perks up the courtroom from its recent lethargy. He stands at the far end of the jury box away from Barton, forcing his client to look into the whites of the jurors' eyes. I pick up my pen. Now the testimony begins in earnest.

"Mr. Barton, you stand accused of murdering your wife, Sara Barton. I ask you directly: did you kill your wife?"

"Absolutely not."

The burden of proof in any murder case always rests on the prosecution, but jurors still want to hear a defendant deny under oath the charge against him. Silence in the face of false accusation is unnatural. The thought persists in a juror's mind—"If I were wrongfully accused of murder, you better believe I would get up there and deny it." Barton just solved one of his problems. I wonder how many other fires Millwood will risk trying to put out.

"Do you remember the police arriving at your house in response to a 911 call by your wife?"

"Yes."

"Tell us what you remember about that day."

"That was the day I learned about the video of Sara and Brice. A colleague showed me the footage. I couldn't believe it. I texted my wife and called her a not nice name."

"What did you call your wife in that text?"

"I called her a whore."

"Why?"

"I was upset. If she wanted to have affairs, that's fine. I've had plenty, and she had her own before Brice, too. I was upset that she got caught on film and that everyone in Atlanta had apparently seen the video. I knew then the marriage was over for good. It was actually a relief. I could leave in good conscience. But I called her a whore anyway because it was the petty thing to do, and I felt like being petty."

Millwood and Barton spent quality time together choreographing that paragraph. The answer checks off a number of boxes—a backhanded swipe at Sara Barton for an untold number of previous unidentified affairs, a balancing act that acknowledges the video "upset" Barton but not too much, a relatable all-too-human confession for the intemperate "whore" remark, and the placement of responsibility for the end of the marriage on the reckless actions of his wife. Nice story.

Millwood asks, "What happened when you arrived home that night?"

"I intended to pack a suitcase and move out. I went to the bedroom to get my things, and the door was locked. From the other side of the door, Sara told me to go away. I told her I would, but I needed to pack a suitcase first. She still wouldn't open the door. We started yelling at each other through the door at that point, and that's when she called 911."

"Mr. Barton, describe what you were doing during this call."

"Just trying to get in the bedroom so I could get out of there."

Millwood then plays a snippet of the 911 recording that focuses on the sound of his client beating on the door. Barton grimaces with each loud boom.

"Describe what we just heard."

"That's me banging on the door to get Sara to open it so I could pack a suitcase and leave."

"Did you at any point strike your wife?"

"Absolutely not."

"How do you explain the fact that your wife said you hit her on the 911 call?"

"We had been unhappy for a long time and obviously heading for a separation after that video. I think the whole 911 call was a performance for her to gain leverage in the divorce. I never touched her. I've never hit a woman in my entire life. My dad hit my mom when I was growing up. I promised never to be like him. I've given over $250,000 to domestic violence shelters over the years. I've served on the Board of Directors of the Alliance Against Domestic Violence. It is an issue I'm quite passionate about. Sara knew that accusing me of spousal abuse was the cruelest thing she could do to me."

Barton wrestles with the emotion bubbling up within him. I'm unmoved. I've seen psychopaths blubber like babies on the witness stand. Everyone's emotional about something. I glance at the jurors and discern no visible reaction to Barton's display of weakness. He is a hard man to humanize. The alleged aversion to domestic violence is a non-starter. Men who batter women often feel terrible after doling out their beatings.

"What happened after your wife got off the 911 call?"

"Sara opened the bedroom door and told me the police were on the way. I was dumbfounded. The whole thing was stupid. She wasn't even afraid. I mean, why call the police from behind a locked door and then unlock the door before the police arrive. It felt like a set-up."

I give Barton's words a good hard think. Officer Hendrix testified that Sara Barton was in the living room when he arrived in response to the 911 call. Why unlock the door? But maybe Sara Barton didn't unlock the door. Just because Barton said she opened the door doesn't make it so. Maybe he kicked it down and threatened to kill her if she didn't behave for the police.

"Mr. Barton, you were in the courtroom when Officer J.D. Hendrix described visiting your house after the 911 call. What is your response to his testimony?"

"Officer Hendrix described everything accurately. Sara and I were together in the living room waiting for him to arrive. She was calm and admitted that she overreacted. Officer Hendrix talked to her for a long time to make sure that she was okay before he decided to leave. He didn't arrest me. I hadn't laid a hand on her."

"What happened after Officer Hendrix left your house?"

"Sara apologized, and we made love for the first time in months. We then went out to a late dinner."

"Did your wife have a bruise on her back at that time?"

"She did not."

Millwood then introduces a dinner receipt from that night paid with Barton's credit card. The dinner shows entrees and drinks for two. Scott interviewed the waitress that waited on Barton's table. She had no memory of Barton or his dinner companion. The only evidence, therefore, that Sara and Barton ever kissed and made up is Barton's word and a little piece of paper with numbers on it. I'm skeptical.

Even still, the business about Sara unlocking the locked door bothers me. Judge Woodcomb adjourns the trial for lunch.

***

Millwood heads straight to the night of the murder once the proceedings begin after the lunch recess.

"How did you learn about your wife's death?"

"I arrived home at around 2:30 a.m. to find the police in my house. They told me that Sara was dead. I asked what happened, and they told me she was murdered."

"What was your reaction?"

"Complete and utter shock. Numbness."

Energy in the courtroom is at a low ebb. No matter the trial, no matter the courtroom—lethargy invariably pervades the hour after the lunch break. That today is a Friday only adds to the sensation of weariness. Most juror naps happen during this time slot. Starting with the night of the murder might perk up the audience, but Millwood swerves away from that topic after a few more questions.

Instead, the next hour features a defensive Barton explaining away a lot of the evidence against him. He searched high and low for his phone the morning of the murder but could never find it. He bought a gun a few months before the murder because Sara was scared about crime in the neighborhood. He loaded the gun himself, which is why his fingerprints were on the bullets. He went to Monica Haywood's house after the murder because he often spent the night there and that made the most sense. He rejected Cecil's characterization that he had been cold and distant when identifying his wife's dead body, describing the entire experience as emotionally traumatic and the most difficult moment of his life. The gambling debts were nothing to him. He had more than enough money to cover them. He never told Monica Haywood to lie on his behalf. She thought she was helping him because she knew he was innocent.

I don't object a single time, content with allowing the monotony to proceed without interruption. Half of the jurors are checked out, no need to bring their attention back to the proceedings. Millwood makes the points that he can hammer home in closing argument. But no one is moved. Barton's success as a lawyer stems from being an attacking bulldog—the unstoppable running back who pounds through tacklers yard after yard. His skills of persuasion evaporate when he is on the defensive. Without the ability to bludgeon, he loses all his fierceness. Millwood continues.

"Mr. Barton, what time did you leave Monica Haywood's condo on the night of the murder?"

"Approximately 7:30 p.m."

"What time did you arrive at your house and discover the police there?"

"Approximately 2:30 a.m."

"What were you doing between 7:30 p.m. and 2:30 a.m.?"

"I went to dinner at The Tilted House, had a few drinks there, then drove to the house of my sister-in law, Lara Landrum."

Everyone's awake now. Judge Woodcomb bangs the gavel to quiet the murmurs. Heads in the jury box swivel from the witness to Lara, sitting behind me just to the right. A disgusted Lara gives a short shake of her head. Millwood allows the excitement to dance for a bit before resuming his questioning.

"What time did you arrive at your sister-in-law's house?"

"Around nine."

"What did you do when you arrived?"

"I let myself in and had another drink. Lara told me she was meeting with some producers and might be late. I waited for her."

"And what happened when she made it home?"

"We had sex."

I actually laugh out loud—part performance, part sincere incredulity. I assess Millwood and conclude that even he doesn't believe the product he is hawking. That's all the confirmation I need. Barton is lying.

Lara's emphatic shaking of her head draws every eye from the jury. The indignation bleeds out of her. She just testified without testifying—refuting Barton's words in real time.

The judge has to give her gavel multiple raps to control the crowd this go around. The room is on edge.

Barton adds, "She can shake her head all she likes, but she knows it's true."

He is back to being a bulldog, and the role suits him. His forceful manner gives him authority. But Lara isn't an easy one to intimidate. She returns his stare with determination of her own and continues shaking her head in denial. The two of them hate one another, making Barton's testimony all the more incredible.

Millwood announces, "No further questions, Your Honor."

The judge calls for the afternoon break, and a stampede to the exit follows. The excited media will be speaking in tongues from this shock. Ella, Scott, Lara, and I leave through the side door and congregate in a nearby conference room.

"It's not true," Lara steams.

The rest of us credit her denial. But we're not the jury. I lean against the conference table and analyze what just happened. The others nurse their own thoughts in silence. Then I start laughing.

Ella snaps, "What?"

I answer, "I mean, it's a brilliant tactic. I'll give them that. It's a bombshell, and titillating to boot, so it grabs everyone's attention. We can't disprove it. We have no record of his whereabouts during that time period. It also casts doubt on the strongest witness against them, making the whole trial come down to a 'he said, she said' contest. That the 'she' is a famous actress only adds to the explosiveness. Who knows how the jury will react to that? We've gone from a boring domestic dispute between husband and wife to a possible love triangle involving twins, one of whom is a celebrity. Drama sells. It's brilliant."

Lara moans, "But it's not true."

"Of course not. It's a Hail Mary pass. It's desperation. It's the only thing they could've done to have a chance at all. It's so unexpected and out of left field that now the jury is looking at things with fresh eyes. But at the end of the day, it's all empty calories. No proof. Nothing. Just the word of a disliked defendant trying to save his neck at the last minute. Don't worry. Just continue to play indignant. I'll handle Barton on cross."

47

Most murder defendants avoid the witness box like the Bubonic plaque. A good cross-examiner could make Mother Teresa look guilty as sin. The risk invariably outweighs the reward, and the right to remain silent consequently rules these parts. But now Barton is giving me an opportunity as rare as a unicorn sighting.

I grew up consuming Perry Mason reruns on TV and dreamed of one day forcing a confession on the stand from a witness powerless in the face of my withering verbal assault. Today won't be that day. Real life doesn't work like that, and Barton wouldn't confess even at gunpoint. Rather, the goal is to remind the members of the jury why they dislike the defendant—no knockout blows, just a series of well-placed jabs that do great cumulative damage over time.

A liveliness fills the room that was missing earlier. The trial just became interesting from a certain point of view. Barton and I measure each other across the empty space. I pick up a trial transcript and walk to my spot.

"Mr. Barton, do you remember in opening statements when your counsel said—and I'm reading from the transcript: 'You won't like my client. He's abrasive and arrogant. He cheated on his wife throughout the course of their marriage. He gambles too much, and he acts like a little boy who has never grown up.' Remember that?"

"I remember."

"Are you abrasive?"

"Can be."

"Arrogant?"

"Yes."

"Did you cheat on your wife?"

"Repeatedly."

"Gamble too much?"

"Probably."

"Act like a little boy who never grew up?"

"I guess so."

The game of getting under Barton's skin begins. Already he shows annoyance. He's dying to prove that he's smarter than me, that he won't fall into my traps. Good. I hope to use his arrogance against him.

"Do you lie?"

That's a tough one for him to answer. He sits there plotting for a critical stretch of seconds.

"Everybody lies."

"We're not talking about everybody. We're talking about *you*. Do *you* lie?"

"From time to time."

I can work with that answer. Barton gritted his teeth in giving it to me. Being on the receiving end of the harsh treatment he has doled out his entire career doesn't agree with him. Bullies don't like to be bullied.

"Speaking of lying, let's talk about Monica Haywood. Your testimony is that she lied for your benefit without your knowledge?"

"That's right."

"The morning after the murder, you were at her condo?"

"I was."

"The police were looking for you?"

"Yep."

"Haywood told them you weren't there?"

"She did."

"Yet you were hiding in the bedroom?"

Barton pauses for a second, scowls, then contends that he wasn't hiding, he was just in the bedroom when the police rang the doorbell and that Haywood decided on her own to lie to the police.

"Did you tell Monica after that to stop lying for you?"

"Didn't talk about it."

"A few days later, she went to the police station to talk to the police?"

"She did."

"She lied to give you an alibi?"

"Yep."

"You didn't know she was going to do that?"

"No idea."

He is no actor, that's for sure. Every answer comes across as curt with a helping of attitude on the side. Barton has been on the stand all day with his literal freedom hanging in the balance. He's getting tired. He's getting cranky. I smell blood.

"And you were in the courtroom when Monica admitted lying to this jury?"

"I was."

"And you didn't know she was going to lie for you then?"

"I did not."

"The two of you live together?"

"We do."

"Engaged to be married?"

"Sure."

"And you didn't know that she was again—for the third time now—going to lie on your behalf?"

"Nope."

"But as you admitted earlier, you do lie from time to time?"

"Just like you, Counselor."

He smirks, proud of himself for that one. I smile honey back at him. It's happening. He's imploding right before my eyes. Millwood, knowing that his client is a lost cause, barely tries to hide his own contempt toward Barton at this juncture.

"How many women have you sexually harassed in the workplace?"

Anger replaces the smirk. No "yeps" or "nopes" here. He's going to have to give an actual answer, and all his possible options on that score hurt him. I await patiently while he struggles to pick his poison.

"I've never intentionally harassed anyone."

"How many women have you unintentionally sexually harassed?"

"None. I don't think I've ever sexually harassed anyone. Everything was consensual, flirting on both sides."

"These women wanted it?"

"I didn't say that! It was mutual banter between friends."

"And the unwanted sexual touching was that also banter?"

"You weren't there. You're twisting things. The touching was friendly, welcomed."

"And yet all these women still reported you for sexual harassment?"

"They wanted money."

"They lied for money?"

"Pretty much."

"All of them?"

"Yeah."

We are so often in life our own worst enemy. Barton is overheating and leaking oil at the one moment that he needs to be the calmest. The females on the jury flash their disgust. The pattern is clear. Barton blames women for all his problems—Sara for the 911 call, Monica for lying about him without his knowledge, the women he sexually harassed for making stuff up.

"And Roy Winston—your own witness—was he lying when he said the claims against you were credible and that your conduct was unacceptable?"

"He was just covering his ass."

Someone in the audience gasps. The judge bangs her gavel. The top of Barton's head collects tiny pockets of perspiration. The courtroom light falls harsh on him.

"Let's talk about the gun, Mr. Barton. You bought it a few months before the murder?"

"Yeah."

"Sara wanted you to buy it?"

"She did."

"She felt unsafe?"

"That's what she said."

"She wanted the gun for her protection?"

"Yep."

"And that was the gun that killed her?"

"That's what I'm told."

"Your gun?"

"Apparently."

That bit will make it into my closing argument. The very gun that Sara wanted to protect her life took away her life. That's a nice narrative hook. But I won't stop there. The only evidence we have that Barton bought the gun for Sara comes from Barton's own mouth. But maybe he got the gun because he already planned to kill her. Remember Sara's own words: "He's going to kill me!" Based on the evidence, the only person Sara feared was Bernard Barton.

"At some point you learned about a video of Sara and another man having sex at a firm party with you in the room next door?"

"I did."

"And the man in question was a younger attorney whose office was right down the hall from yours?"

"Yeah, I guess."

"The video made you mad?"

"I didn't care that she slept around. I was mad that she got filmed doing so."

"You called her a whore in fact?"

"If the shoe fits."

Dear God. Even Judge Woodcomb—the epitome of courtroom decorum—shoots a glance of malice Barton's way after that one. The meltdown is becoming uncomfortable. Maybe he will confess on the stand after all.

"Even though you yourself repeatedly cheated on Sara throughout the marriage, you called her a whore?"

"I guess I'm a hypocrite."

"And you were hanging out with your own mistress at the same event?"

"Same answer."

"So you're angry about the video, go home, and start beating on the locked bedroom door with Sara on the other side?"

"I wanted to pack some clothes. She wouldn't let me in."

"And you contend that her call to 911 claiming you were about to kill her was some kind of set-up to help her divorce case?"

"All I wanted to do was get my suitcase. She escalated it. She was going to try to milk me in the divorce."

"Except the night before she was due to file her divorce papers she was murdered?"

He doesn't provide an answer, and I don't press him for one. Every person here can do that math. I remember the phrase: "She was going to try to milk me in the divorce." The jury will hear those words again in my closing.

"From your work on domestic violence causes, you know that battered women often lie to the police to protect their abusers?"

"They do."

"These women lie because they're afraid of more abuse if they tell the truth?"

"Women who are abused, yes. Sara was not abused."

"You never hit Sara?"

"I did not and that's exactly what she told the police."

"Let me get this straight—Sara lied on the 911 call to stick it to you in the divorce, but told the truth exonerating you when the police arrived?"

He spots the contradiction immediately and stares at me blankly. If Sara Barton had wanted to maximize her leverage in a divorce case, Barton would have left his house that day in handcuffs. He didn't.

"I guess she thought better of it."

"You don't think she was ever afraid you were going to kill her?"

"She couldn't have been."

"Yet she was murdered two months later?"

"Not by me."

"Murdered in your kitchen?"

"Not by me."

"With your gun?"

"Not by me."

"Two months after she told 911 you were going to kill her?"

"I didn't kill her!"

He screams out that answer and earns himself a stern admonition from the judge. A courtroom deputy moves closer to the witness stand just in case. The jurors closest to Barton shift their bodies in their seats to get farther away from him. Veins bulge on his thick neck as they did earlier in the trial. I keep up the attack.

"You didn't kill her?"

"No, I did not."

"Just like you've never sexually harassed any women?"

"That's right."

"Just like you never instructed Monica Haywood to lie?"

"Same answer."

My body stands parallel with the jury box as I ask these last questions. My eyes rest only on the jurors, not Barton. The audience and I are on the same skeptical page. I allow myself a second or two to enjoy the thrill of what's happening—to savor the moment. I was born to do this. Life is good.

"Let's go to the day of the murder. From approximately 7:30 p.m. to 2:30 a.m., you have no proof of your whereabouts?"

"My testimony is proof."

"You don't have a receipt from The Tilted House for that dinner?"

"I didn't keep it."

"But you did keep the one from the night of the 911 call when you claim you and Sara went out?"

"I paid with a credit card that night. I keep those."

"You paid cash at The Tilted House?"

"I did."

"You have no receipt or credit card charge that could corroborate your story?"

"Doesn't look like it."

"And your cell phone can't be used to track your movements because you left it home that day?"

"Couldn't find it."

"No phone, no receipt, no credit card purchases, no other witnesses that can back up your claim as to your movements between seven-thirty at night and two-thirty in the morning?"

"Lara could, but she won't."

"She'd lie about it, just like your wife lied during the 911 call, just like the multiple women who accused you of sexual harassment lied?"

"Pretty much."

The man is a misogynistic marvel. He wears his contempt for women like a badge of honor. Putting on my psychiatrist hat, I bet growing up seeing his father batter his mother internalized in him a hatred of women. When Sara got the better of him with Brice in such a publicly humiliating way, that hatred boiled over. I size him up for one final run.

"Let's talk about your testimony about your sister-in-law, Lara Landrum. You never told the police about this alibi, did you?"

"No. I knew she wouldn't back me up."

"You never told the District Attorney's office?"

"Same answer."

"You believed *she* would lie?"

"Yes."

"That if *you* told the truth to the police, *she* would lie to the police?"

"Yes."

"Even though, if you're telling the truth, she would know that you didn't kill her sister?"

"That's right."

"She would choose to lie, see you convicted, and her sister's real murderer go free?"

"She doesn't like me."

"She doesn't like you."

My words are a statement. The implications of Barton's answer sink in around the courtroom. If Lara doesn't like him, then she wouldn't sleep with him. Perfect. I drop my remaining questions and sit down. Millwood doesn't even bother with a re-direct. The defense rests, and court adjourns for the weekend.

48

Friday night feels heavy. I sit at home alone and assess the state of the case. Unless I put Lara back on the stand to deny Barton's last-minute alibi ploy, all the witnesses have said their piece. The rest is up to Millwood and me as we deliver dueling closing arguments. I relish the opportunity. Every closing is personal for me—the chance to act as the voice for victims everywhere.

Barton's testimony sank him. He came across as a villain, and that's enough. I wasn't expecting a confession. The attempt to make Lara his alibi, while brilliant in its way, had little chance of success. I know enough about Jack Millwood to know that he didn't draw up that play. Lara's look of revulsion and her well-timed shakes of the head delivered an instant rebuke to Barton's lies. Calling her back to the stand is unnecessary. The jury heard her loud and clear.

I sit behind my desk—my father's antique desk from his law office—and stare at the blank legal pad before me. Much of the closing is already written out, but I like to do a fresh rewrite at the end to make my words more organic and well-tuned to the twists and turns every trial takes. Neat stacks of evidence sit expectantly on the wood top—the ingredients to the great recipe I hope to cook up. Trial transcripts, photographs, the autopsy report, a printout of the 911 call, the picture of Sara Barton's blackened back, and the like—all of it awaits to be used for the greater good.

I'm worn out. I need to sprawl myself on a beach somewhere and let the sunshine carry my soul back to good health. Too much of my adult years have been spent under artificial light. I need the real thing. I have the money. I can disappear for a good long time.

Sara Barton should've left—look what staying got her. I put the autopsy photos side-by-side with the photo of her back after Barton beat her. So much pain. Why did she stay? Lara has money. She could've moved in with her. Instead, Sara stayed. The choices we make condemn us to death, and we don't even know it. We swim with the tide, thinking the current will take us wherever it wants anyway. Sara was so beautiful, but nobody looks good in an autopsy photo, the blood all drained from the face. One morning a beautiful woman woke up never to see another day. Happens to ugly people all the time. Everyone should leave when they have the chance.

I access the secret compartment in my father's desk and remove the two naked pictures of Sara Barton I removed from Sam's shed in the Georgia mountains. Visions of an inviting Lara cloud my eyes. She would meet me tonight if I said we needed to talk about the trial. This weekend figures to be the only time I will ever be able to hold her again. Once the verdict is read, she'll slip away from me forever. I stare at her dead sister's nude body some more, wrestling with the decision, wanting one more taste of the poisoned fruit.

I pass. I'm too tired to handle Lara tonight. Tomorrow maybe.

I think of Sam. Millwood could never effectively work him into the trial. Putting Liesa on the stand was a disaster for the defense, killing any chance to parlay Sam into a not guilty verdict. Sam remains an enigma, much like his death. A healthy helping of conscience reminds me that the failure to turn over that box in Sam's shed had everything to do with what happened at trial. I refuse to accept the blame. The box was never mine to turn over. Those photographs belong to someone else.

"Then why are there naked pictures of me on your desk?"

I ignore Sara Barton's question. You can't argue with a ghost.

Not much work is getting done. I consider throwing in the towel for the night and starting anew in the morning. I have the weekend. But I resist the impulse to get up. Sam still tugs at my mind. I'm missing something. An inkling chews at me but scurries away when I try to catch it. I'm missing something, and the signs point to Sam. The harder I think about the problem, the less I see.

I prod myself to focus on something else for a few minutes. Reshuffling the cards in my mind usually works wonders when I'm stuck on a mental puzzle. When I return to the problem with fresh eyes, new insights invariably emerge. Seeking a distraction, I again consume the naked pictures of Sara Barton and think of Lara's sculpted body—the marvelous mystery she first revealed to me a few paces from the spot where I now sit. Bad idea. To dampen my incipient lust, I pivot to studying the autopsy photos again. I'm running on fumes at this point. I need this trial to be over.

Back to Sam.

I go back to the night of the murder and see Sam's sad face as he tried to extricate himself from the fine mess he'd got himself into. I see him at Sara Barton's funeral, staring at Lara with a cringeworthy intensity. I wince at the memory of him storming into my office with a fake John Wayne tough guy act. I remember the uneasy peace the two of us reached at The Varsity—the last time I ever saw him alive. He gave me his research to throw my scent Barton's way. It worked. The call from Scott informing me of Sam's death punches me in the gut one more time. Lara's hysterical reaction in the aftermath started the tailspin that eventually crashed our relationship. Lastly, I return to the mountains and work over the implications of Sam's porn stash of Sara Barton and her various lovers. I even replay all my dealings with Liesa.

All these things I think about and still come up blank. What is Sam trying to tell me?

I stand up to stretch. Standing on my toes, straining my Achilles to the max, the flash of a memory breaks through the fog. I refuse to believe it and doubt the accuracy of my recollection. It would be an easy thing for me to mishear in the moment. I pace around the room wrestling mightily with my brain to squeeze out as many details as possible. What I now remember can't be, which means that I'm misremembering. I've been around enough eyewitnesses to know the vagaries of how humans process their memories. All of us carry around things we remember that never actually happened, and most of us refuse to be moved off our certainty of the invented past. I pace some more.

But once I fixate on it, the memory possesses the clarity of crystal. Yet it makes no sense. I try to work out a scenario where what I think I remember would fit some logical possibility. I fail. You're wrong, I tell myself. Either the wording wasn't exactly as you now remember, or she didn't say what you think she said—simple as that. Don't tie yourself into knots over this imagined complication. Focus on your closing. Doubt is the enemy of faith.

I walk back to the desk, now ready to work. Then I see it. The scales fall from my eyes, and everything fits into place. The evidence before me cannot be written off as a false memory. I can now see nothing else. With one exception, I work out everything in roughly a minute. The one open question requires careful thought and massaging. I can't do this alone. I need Scott.

I pick up the phone to call him, eager to get started on the weekend of work ahead of us. I then set the phone aside to mourn a little for myself. The thrill of the chase is no tonic for the pain of knowing that my lover is a murderer. All I have to do is prove it.

49

Monday morning arrives sooner than I would like. The task before me portends nothing but despair—bad medicine that no amount of drink will ever wash down. Scott and I did what needed doing over the weekend. What happens next rests in my hands alone.

Just before we enter the courtroom, I tell Ella, "I'm going to put Lara on the stand to rebut Barton, then we'll go into closing." She remains in the dark about what I know and doesn't understand my reasoning. The pushback is fierce.

"We don't need to put her on the stand. You destroyed Barton on cross."

"I'm going to put her on."

"She's my witness. If we need her to deny it, I should be the one to ask it of her."

"I'm doing it."

"You're dictating things all of a sudden? We had an agreement that I would handle her."

"I'm doing it. That's final. I have my reasons. Please trust me."

"Well it damn sure doesn't appear that you trust me."

I avoided telling Ella over the weekend to sidestep this type of conversation. I lack the emotional capacity. After today, I intend to disappear for quite a long time. Ella enters the courtroom ahead of me in a huff. I follow her as if entering a torture chamber.

***

Before the judge enters, I take Lara to the side and explain, "I'm going to call you back up to the stand first thing this morning to refute Barton's alibi. Just follow my lead and answer the questions. You'll do fine."

"I wish I had more notice."

"You'll do fine. Just follow my lead."

Lara remains uncertain but takes her seat. The judge enters and calls the room to order. Woodcomb turns the floor over to me, and I recall our star witness to the stand. As she makes her way up front, I scribble a quick note to Ella. The note says, "I'm sorry." She reads it and looks at me with austere neutrality. I stand up, knowing that my life will never be the same.

"Ms. Landrum, you were in court Friday afternoon when the defendant, Bernard Barton, testified that he was with you on the night of your sister's murder. How would you respond to that?"

"It's a lie."

"Have you ever had a sexual relationship with the defendant?"

"Absolutely not."

The answer is delivered with the perfect note of indignation—not too much, not too little. She's very good. The room eats it up.

"Is it possible that the defendant mistook your sister for you?"

The snark oozes. Millwood objects, the witness looks confused, and the courtroom snickers. I withdraw the question and begin again.

"Let me rephrase that last question. To your knowledge, has the defendant ever mistaken you for your sister?"

I give her a slight nod for assurance. The tightrope I'm walking will give way at any moment. I need her to think we're on the same team for as long as the pretense can last.

"No, he can tell us apart."

"Was your sister ever arrested?"

"Yes. For DUI. A long time ago."

The abrupt change of pace unsettles the air. I grab a sheaf of documents and show them to Millwood. He looks at them and looks at me, frowning before handing me back the papers. Barton whispers something to him, but Millwood waves him away with his hand, instead eyeing me intently. I approach the witness.

"Ms. Landrum, I'm handing you the arrest file for your sister's DUI. Have you ever seen it before?"

"No."

"And is that your sister in this mugshot?"

"Yes."

"Okay. Thank you."

I collect the documents and walk back to lay them on counsel's table. Ella pens a note on a legal pad and pushes it toward me: "What are you doing????" The composure in her face masks the uncertainty in her heart. I nod. The gesture is meaningless in the context of her question. Her eyes narrow. Silence fills the courtroom. I stumble along, content to portray an aura of incompetence. The jury is irrelevant. My performance is for a more limited audience.

"The defendant also denied ever hitting your sister. How do you respond to that?"

"He hit her. I saw the bruises on her back with my own two eyes."

The answer is comfortable, confident—the product of her being on surer ground. She glares at Barton for emphasis. I study the both of them, trying to decipher the one piece of the puzzle that still escapes me. The analysis doesn't bear any fresh insight. I shuffle along and laboriously set up two easels adjacent to each other. I leave the easels empty and redirect my attention to the witness.

"Have you ever seen the defendant hit your sister?"

She hesitates. I walk toward the wall where I retrieve two enlarged photographs. The witness follows my movements with great interest. My eyes look expectantly toward her for an answer. I then start the cumbersome task of carrying my jumbo-sized photographs back across the courtroom.

"He wouldn't have dared to hit her in front of me."

"Objection!"

"Sustained."

Millwood has been itching to get more involved. I welcome the diversion. Better the witness thinks about him than me. I place one of my giant photographs on an easel—a blow-up of an autopsy photo earlier admitted into evidence. I straighten the picture on its perch and assess the naked torso with the bullet hole adjacent to the heart, checking once more just to be sure.

"Ms. Landrum, this is an enlarged copy of an autopsy photo of your sister admitted earlier into evidence. Have you ever seen this photo before?"

"No."

"Does it upset you?"

"Objection, relevance."

"Sustained."

The other photo is a blow-up from the Sara Barton and Brice Tanner sex tape. Sara rides Brice cowgirl-style right there on the museum floor, her bare breasts flowing proudly in the figurative wind. Even though the video played earlier in the trial, the high definition quality of the photo, freezing this particular revealing moment in time, shocks in a way the video did not. The ludicrous thought that I probably just caught the television censors unaware seizes me with unseemly glee. Life is absurd, and the mind is an untamed animal.

Millwood wants to say something but realizes that I'm offending half the room while perplexing the other half. He once taught me that no duty exists to rescue in the courtroom. You're not a lifeguard. If opposing counsel is drowning, don't throw him a life preserver. Let him sink. I hope he follows his own advice now to give me the time to do what I need to do. Ella's countenance of neutrality wobbles on the brink of panic. Her stare informs me that I'm throwing away the case. She's not necessarily wrong. Judge Woodcomb looks at me askance but holds her tongue. I've built up a great deal of credit with her over the years, and she's a pro. The photos on display aren't any more offensive than the bloody crime scene pictures regularly admitted into evidence. Murder is an ugly business.

"Ms. Landrum, this is a photograph captured from the video of your sister and Brice Tanner admitted earlier into evidence. Do you recognize your sister?"

"Yes, of course."

I take a deep breath. Millwood studies me with the focus of a world-class poker player trying to get a read on his opponent. I feign impassivity, but a torrent of colliding nerves wreaks havoc on my internal equilibrium. I focus my attention on Bernard Barton and ask my question.

"Why is there a tiny scar on your sister's left breast in the autopsy photo but no scar in the picture taken at the party?"

The room is slow to react. The question floats unanswered. Millwood breaks character, his wrinkled expression betraying deep indecision as to the meaning of my words. He releases me from his sight to look at the pictures for himself. Barton squints to do the same, his reaction revealing little, except poor eyesight. I turn to the witness. Concern and confusion contort her beautiful face. My manner cajoles, imploring her to give what should be an obvious answer if only she would see it. The encouragement is a lie, designed to keep her off balance. The witness isn't the only one who can act.

She offers, "I don't understand. Can you repeat the question?"

I remove a laser pointer from my pocket. I send the thin red beam across the courtroom to the autopsy photo and land on a tiny, weathered scar adjacent to the dead body's left breast. I then move my laser to the same spot on the photo of Sara and Brice, except there's no similar mark.

"Why is there a scar on your sister's left breast in the autopsy photo but no scar in the picture taken at the party?"

"I … I don't know."

Disappointment shows in my face. Her eyes plead for help. She's trying hard to connect the dots, thinking we're still on the same team. That illusion is about to shatter. Everyone's trying to figure everyone else out. The witness looks at me. I look at Barton. Barton looks at the witness. Millwood's back to looking at me. Ella looks confused.

"Do you have a scar on your left breast?"

I know she doesn't.

Barton slowly awakes to what's happening. His emotions are an open book, and he looks punch drunk with surprise. I return my attention to the stand. The witness and I glare at each other, both of our masks now dropped to the wayside, each of us knowing that the other one knows. No one in the courtroom dares take a breath for fear of missing the witness' answer.

"I resent that question."

I grab Sara Barton's arrest report and besiege her, "Why don't the fingerprints from Sara Barton's arrest match the fingerprints of the person in this autopsy photo?"

"I have no idea."

"You're Sara Barton, aren't you?"

"No!"

Murmurs—sounds, not words—start percolating around the courtroom. The secret is out, and the implications start to accumulate. I bear down on the witness before all hell breaks loose.

"Do you have a scar on your left breast?"

"Stop it!"

I take one last measure of Barton. I have to be sure. We could've arrested the witness any time over the weekend. But double jeopardy prevents Barton from being tried for the same crime twice. The whole purpose of today's charade is to flesh out whether Barton had a role in this mess or not.

Scott and I spent hours working it every way we could and settled on two possibilities. Scenario One: Barton and his wife conspired to kill Lara Landrum, only for Sara to leave him holding the bag at the end of the day. Barton couldn't very well tell the truth under this version, forcing him to dig out of his predicament in some other way. Scenario Two: Sara killed her sister by herself, intending to frame Barton from the start. She posed as Lara and seduced Barton, knowing that he couldn't admit sleeping with his sister-in-law at the time his wife was murdered, especially if "Lara" refused to corroborate his alibi.

I demand, "Did you conspire with your husband to murder your sister?"

"No!"

A stupefied Barton jerks toward me and shakes his massive head in a helpless spasm of denial. I believe the bastard. Millwood smiles like a kid at Christmas. War stories are the stock in trade of seasoned trial lawyers, and Millwood will be telling this one for years.

"But you did kill your sister?"

"No!"

I yell, "The fingerprints don't lie, Sara. The photographs don't lie. Look at them! Insanity is your only defense. You better start telling the truth."

Mike Tyson once said, "Everyone has a plan until they get punched in the mouth." Keeping up the attack while she's dazed and confused may be the only path to get at the truth. She's too cunning for me to give her a chance to regroup and invent some escape hatch. I can prove she is Sara Barton but not that she actually squeezed the trigger on the gun that killed Lara Landrum. I need her to admit that. Throwing out the possibility of an insanity defense might be the hook that yields the catch.

"Are you bipolar? I have your medical records if you want to see them. Are you bipolar?"

"Yes … I mean no … no."

Dangling the carrot, I follow up, "Were you under the influence of any medication at the time of your sister's murder?"

"I don't know."

"Were you off your medication?"

"I don't know."

"Do you still deny that you killed your sister?"

"I didn't."

The answer lacks conviction. The fight starts to seep out of her. The crying commences. Real or pretend tears—I cannot begin to guess. She beseeches, "Can I take a break?"

"No. Isn't it true that you resented your sister's Hollywood career while you were stuck at home with a bad husband?"

"I loved my sister."

"What was your father's name?"

The tears cascade into a flood. She heaves as if struggling for breath. The last piece of the disguise crumbles. I've been chipping away at it, but her father is the sledgehammer to deliver the final blow. A real person emerges from the wreckage of everything she has endured.

"It was Bill, wasn't it?"

She doesn't answer.

"Isn't it true that Bill molested you, but not your sister, and you have hated Lara ever since?"

"Damn you! Damn you! Damn you!"

"Think back to your childhood. Your father violated you in repulsive ways, but never laid a finger on Lara. And it made you crazy and you had to kill her, right?"

"Yes! Are you happy now? Yes!"

I back away from her. Breathless. I did what I had to do, but I don't have to feel good about it. The stunned courtroom teeters on the precipice of upheaval. The tearful moans resume with more force, and a sense of discomfort from spying such raw emotion constrains the crowd to maintain proper decorum. I grab a box of tissues and place them in front of her before retreating to a safe distance. The spontaneous gesture on my part sobers her up quick. The tears dry out. Cold fury replaces pain.

I tell Judge Woodcomb, "I think that is all."

Millwood helpfully announces, "No questions from the defense, Your Honor." The judge nods. I signal Scott to do his part. He approaches the witness box, takes out his handcuffs, and tells her she's under arrest.

"You have the right to remain silent—"

"Get your hands off me!"

A scuffle ensues, and the bailiffs rush to lend Scott a hand. She makes it half way toward me before they wrestle her to the floor. As they drag her from the courtroom, she looks at me and me alone. She bellows, "I'll kill you."

I believe her.

50

"Your honor, the State moves to dismiss the indictment against Bernard Barton with prejudice."

Stunned liked everyone else in the courtroom, Judge Woodcomb takes a few moments to collect herself and asks, "Any objection, Mr. Millwood?"

"None, Your Honor."

"So ordered. Mr. Barton, you are a free man. Ladies and gentlemen of the jury, thank you for your service. Your obligation has been fulfilled. Whether you talk to anyone about the case—the lawyers, the press, whomever—is solely up to you individually. You may return to the jury room to collect your things. Court's adjourned."

The gavel strikes, and people explode from the courtroom. I want to crawl into a hole and stay there forever.

Ella asks, "When did you know?"

"Friday night."

"Why didn't you tell me?"

"A deep, abiding, unquenchable feeling of shame and ruin."

She gets up and leaves. I watch her depart and feel a piece of my heart go with her. Millwood comes over to shake hands.

He declares, "I know I taught you better than to come to court and wreck your own case."

"Well, you weren't doing much damage to it, and I figured somebody had to do something. You're no longer my boss, and I'm still having to do all your work."

"Did you tell Bobby beforehand?"

"No."

"Good luck with that." He laughs and walks off.

Barton exits the courtroom—a mixture of shock and relief carrying him out the door, the smugness gone for a moment at least. I should send him a bill. Framed for murder by his own wife, he avoided spending the rest of his life in prison by a hair's breadth. The jury was going to convict. But I still can't view him as a victim. He remains a sexual predator. The wrath of the #MeToo movement will be his just due.

I look around the courtroom one more time and head back to my office. Another trial over. My first loss.

***

Bobby bursts into my office.

"I have one question. This is the biggest murder case for the office since I became D.A. The eyes of the nation, and more importantly, the eyes of Fulton County voters are watching what happens. And what do you do? You go and drop a hydrogen bomb in open court that proves the defendant did not commit the murder that we charged him for. Do I learn about this from my trusted deputy before the fact? No! I have to find out about it on live television. Why?"

"No time."

"You make time for that!"

"I was working the case."

"I don't want to hear about working the case! You went and lost the case!"

"I know you don't want me to convict an innocent man."

"Don't make this about me! It's about you. If I lose the next election, you won't be working any cases. I need to know everything that might affect my electoral prospects."

"Sorry."

Having made his point, he is losing steam on his demonstration of righteous indignation. But I know what he will say next, how I will respond, and how poorly he will react to my response.

"Well, you get a chance to redeem yourself. The media is gonna want a press conference, and we're going to give it to them."

"I can't."

"Excuse me?"

"I'm spent. I can't do it."

The wheels of calculation spin behind his eyes. How far should he push? He wants his press conference. But he doesn't know his chief prosecutor and the murderer were having an affair. He is sitting on dynamite without realizing it. I try to give him an out.

"Look, we don't know how this thing is going to play out in the media. If it goes south, you're going to want a fall guy. Hold me back from the reporters for right now. Take the temperature of where this is headed. Make me the scapegoat if you have to. But if you put me out there right now, you become too tied to me and you might regret that later."

He thinks on that and nods his head slowly. He likes the plan. It gives him time and flexibility.

"Okay. I'll bite. But I need to know if there is anything else I don't know that could blow up in my face?"

It's a shrewd question, and frankly his asking it makes him smarter than I give him credit for.

I lie.

He says, "All right then, we'll do it your way for the time being. You stay away from the press. I will do it alone. But I need your help. They are going to ask me why we didn't immediately dismiss the charges against Bernard Barton when we finally figured this whole thing out. How do I answer that?"

I offer the following:

"Despite repeated requests from law enforcement, Bernard Barton consistently refused to provide any information to shed light on his whereabouts at the time of the murder. Last Friday in open court was the first time this office learned of Mr. Barton's account that he had spent the night of the murder at the residence of his sister-in-law. Based on this testimony, prosecutors over the weekend developed the theory that Sara Barton murdered Lara Landrum, assumed her identity, and staged the death to make it appear that Sara Barton herself was murdered. An open question remained as to whether Bernard Barton was a willing co-conspirator in this plan with his wife, or if his wife was trying to frame him for her own murder. This morning's questions focused on that point. At this time, we do not believe that Mr. Barton had any involvement or knowledge of his wife's actions. The investigation is ongoing."

Bobby reflects for a second and says, "I can work with that. Write it up."

Before leaving, he warns, "You know, you're not the only good trial lawyer in the city. You can be replaced."

"I know."

"Good."

He walks out as a man with a lot on his mind. I lean back in my chair and close my eyes.

***

A light knock on the door, and Ella lets herself in. She says, "I just got a call from Murph at the jail. She's demanding to see you. He wants to know what we want to do."

I can list a million reasons to stay far away. Yet the pull of having a real conversation with her is strong. I also have one more question I want answered.

I respond, "Only if you come, too."

"I actually insist on that."

***

Ella and I sit down across the table from her. The murderer is handcuffed to a chair. Murph, the ancient jailer who knows where all the bodies are buried, leaves us alone in a large visiting room. We have the place to ourselves. I waste no time.

"Well?"

She focuses on Ella.

"What is she doing here?"

"I wanted her to be here."

"Afraid to face me on your own?"

I stay mute. I don't know what I feel. At one time I felt myself falling in love with the illusion represented by this woman. Now she wears handcuffs and prison clothes. Maybe I should feel relief. She could've killed me, too.

Always the diligent prosecutor, Ella says, "On the night of the murder, you pretended to be your sister and slept with your husband. But why didn't Bernard know it was you and not Lara? The two of you were married. He had to know."

Ella hits on the question that vexed Scott and me all weekend. Was there any way Barton wouldn't have known that he was having sex with his own wife? Until I saw his bewildered face in the courtroom during the questioning this morning, I remained convinced of Barton's involvement in the murder for this precise reason. But he didn't know. I still don't understand it.

Sara Barton smirks. She answers Ella's question but looks only at me while doing so.

"You should know better than anyone, Chance. Men are stupid. You believe what you want to believe, and every man wants to believe that he is God's gift to women. You men live in your porn-filled fantasy world where women want nothing more than for you to rip off our clothes and dominate us. Idiots! That's not how women think!

"Bernard was easy to fool. He lusted after Lara for years. In Lara's house, he saw Lara. With the lights off, it was Lara in his arms. His ego wanted it to be true. Just like Brice believed that another man's wife would simply ring the doorbell to his apartment and throw herself at him. Just like Sam believed that a client going through a divorce would naturally seek comfort in his arms.

"And just like you, Chance. A famous actress shows up at night in your living room and starts taking her clothes off. Really? That didn't make you suspicious? Why not? Because you wanted the fantasy to be true. You're a man. You're stupid."

I certainly feel stupid.

A confused Ella asks, "You had an affair with Sam Wilkins? Did you kill him, too?"

I pretend to share her surprise. Sara laughs and rolls her eyes. She responds, "I'm done answering your questions. I want to say something to him, without you listening in. So just go over there and let the two of us have a moment. Be a good girl and run along."

Ella looks unsure. I give a nod. She hesitantly walks back against the wall, out of hearing range. Sara leans in.

"Here's what you're going to do—you're going to quit your job and be my defense lawyer. Make the best deal you can with your girlfriend over there and get me as little jail time as possible. You do that, I'll keep our little secret."

"You're crazy."

"Am I? It seems pretty sane to me. I know I have to do jail time, but I am still a young woman. You have a good career going. We can make this work. If not, I'll ruin you."

"I am prepared to accept the consequences of my actions. You should do the same."

She sneers, "Nice of you to start playing Dudley Do-Right now, but you don't want to go down this road with me. You've seen what I can do." True enough. But hers is a wild play, and she knows it. No more deals with the devil. Instead, I have a question.

"Why did you kill Sam?"

"You're not pinning that one on me."

"I know you did it. We were at my Mom's. You broke the wine glass. You knew Sam died from being shot, but I never told you that. You already knew because you shot him. Why?"

She stares at me a long time but eventually admits, "He figured me out."

Then I remember Sara Barton's funeral and finally comprehend the significance of Sam's intense staring at the woman claiming to be Lara Landrum. Barton's ego blinded him from recognizing his own wife, but Sam cracked the code, probably from memorizing his secret cache of pictures. The story from there is easy. Sam told Sara what he knew, wanted to learn the reason for her deception, and maybe even hoped to share her bed again. She has that kind of power—the same power with which she lured him to the woods to put a bullet in his brain.

Resentment lights her face. I'm just another man who has disappointed her along the way. I remember our discussions about her father—the truest words she ever spoke to me. Everything starts with the family. She grew up abused by a monster and ended up marrying a man who preys on young women. The separation between Barton and her father is one of degree, not kind. History repeats itself.

She goes into attack mode.

"You know, you were the easiest one to dupe. You were under my spell the first time you caught a whiff of it. You couldn't get your pants off fast enough. You dropped your girlfriend over there faster than a hot potato."

She looks toward Ella and snorts before turning her glare back to me.

"How dumb do you feel? You bought everything I said hook, line, and sinker."

She's not wrong, but my pride won't let me concede the point. I respond, "Says the woman handcuffed to a chair, wearing an orange jumpsuit."

She spits at me and misses before launching another broadside.

"There is more than one type of prison. You may not wear a jumpsuit, but you're no freer than I am. You're a prisoner of your own lack of imagination. You call what you do living? I gave you a chance to break out, to be different, be a man of action who chases after what he wants, consequences be damned. And you know what? It was the only time you've been free in your life. When you're on your deathbed bemoaning the end of your sad little existence, you'll be thinking about the thrill of sneaking around to thrust yourself inside me. But you couldn't handle it. Remember the last time we were together? You couldn't handle it. Instead of enjoying the moment, you hated yourself for being happy."

I think of the memory and my crazed eyes staring back at me in the mirror. I did hate myself, but not for being happy. Consumed with moral sickness, I saw for the first time the depths of my debasement that night—personal, professional, spiritual.

"Did killing your sister make you happy?"

The question scores a body blow. She refuses to answer. More insults follow. I stop listening. She cannot say anything to me that I have not already said to myself. I get up to leave, turn my back, and walk away from her forever.

As I reach Ella waiting by the door, the murderer raises her voice and says the only words in the world that could make me turn around.

"I know who killed your wife."

I turn and stare. I have no idea what she knows or how she knows it, but she is a master of surprises. She smiles at me with sadistic pleasure. I don't believe her. I'm afraid to believe her.

"Don't you want to know?"

I offer a slight nod. She smiles some more and milks the moment a little longer before the big reveal.

"You did."

I stagger as feeling returns to my body. Blood shines in my eyes. I take a step toward her mocking face, but only one step. She wants me to lose control.

"She's dead because of you. I know it. You know it. You didn't pull the trigger, but you loaded the gun. No signs of robbery. Nothing sexual. Just a random killing because the man who was supposed to be the victim was not there. Those bullets were meant for you, yet your wife and son paid the price. You live with that the rest of your life, you son of a bitch."

Ella screams at her, "What's the matter with you?"

I approach the murderer, look her dead in the eyes, and say, "Remember what I promised you? I promised you that I would bring your sister's killer to justice, and I did."

She tries to stand, but the handcuffs that keep her attached to the chair pull her back down as quickly as she rises. She kicks the table in anger, her legs flailing in every direction—up, down, east, and west. The racket she makes is terrible. Her momentum finally gets the best of her. The chair loses its balance and tips over, leaving her squirming on her side on the floor. Gravity always wins in the end.

Old Murph pops his head in, "Is everything all right?"

I point to the body on the floor, touch Ella on the arm, and lead us both out of the room. No more looking back this time. She is somebody else's problem now.

"You hear me. You killed them. You live with that—" I don't hear her anymore. I don't hear anything.

I walk back to my office brooding over her parting shot. I loathe to give her credit, but she finally spewed an insult that delivered. I fear that she speaks the truth about my dead wife and son.

51

Alone again in my office, I pick at my lunch without enthusiasm. A tired-looking Scott pushes through the closed door and crashes into a chair. The weekend was hell on both of us as we worked like rented mules to unravel our own case. Scott pursued the fingerprint evidence of Sara Barton's ancient DUI arrest that eliminated the last remaining remnant of conceivable doubt.

He says, "We searched Lara Landrum's residence."

"Yeah?"

"I'll spare you the details, but you need to see one thing."

He hands me a USB drive with my name handwritten on it.

"Some video files on there. I watched a little bit before turning it off. No one else knows about it. No one." His voice has a special emphasis as he says these last two words.

"What is it?"

"Why don't you watch it and see for yourself?"

I continue to look at the little item in my hand, as if it were some mystifying object from the far-off future. I don't like the direction of the conversation.

Scott continues, "I need you to promise me something. Like I said, I only watched part of it. I'll let you watch the whole thing. I need you to use good judgment here. If there is evidence relevant to the Lara Landrum murder case on there somewhere, I need it back. If not, as far as I'm concerned, that USB drive does not exist. Understand?"

I nod—starting to comprehend.

As he leaves, he says, "I'm cataloguing evidence the rest of the afternoon. If I need to catalogue what's in your hand, let me know. Otherwise …"

He does not finish the thought.

I lock my office door, put the USB into my computer, and hit play. The empty bedroom of a Midtown Atlanta condo fills the screen. Soon Lara Landrum and a man enter the shot and begin having sex. I put the man under the microscope to decipher his state of mind. But he is unreadable. I study the woman for signs of deception and deceit, some clue as to the massive fraud she is orchestrating. Nothing. The storage drive contains two similar scenes, the man making love to a woman who is already dead. The last video file runs out and turns to black, leaving nothing but accusation in its wake.

Ever the lawyer, I note that Georgia Code Section 16-11-62 makes filming someone with hidden video cameras a felony. Prosecution is unlikely. The perpetrator has bigger problems on her hands, and the victim does not wish to pursue charges. The recording fails to shed any light on the identity of Lara Landrum's murderer and may safely be destroyed.

I drop the USB drive on the floor and smash it with my shoe, using my heel to crush the grinds into a vanishing dust. I bag the remains and throw them in a trashcan down the hall, far from me, pushing the contents down deep, just to be safe. Do other copies exist? The murderer's earlier threats about exposing me take on a new light. Maybe I am not as prepared to accept the consequences of my actions as I let on. But maybe I won't have a choice.

The sin we think is done in secret never is.

***

Ella muses, "She has a way with men, doesn't she?" The question is rhetorical. Ella's tone does not carry judgment. She simply states a fact.

I wonder, "How could I have been so wrong about so much?"

"You're not the first man to be led astray chasing some tail."

I guess so. We sit together in my office. The afternoon winds down. Exhausted by the end of another murder trial, we say little. Ella is here as a friend, worried about my mental state, watching out for me even now, despite everything. The fading light slips past the slits in the blinds, creating a hazy halo in the room. The dust particles dance in the sun's rays.

Ella wants to know, "How did you figure it out?"

"Compare and contrast. The woman in the autopsy photos had a tiny scar on her left breast. The woman in the video with Brice did not. I've seen the video and the autopsy photos 100 times each, and the front page of the autopsy report notes the scar. The proof was right in front of my nose the whole time."

"Plus you had independent corroboration that today's witness had no such scar on her breast."

The tone is neutral, with the faintest hint of bemusement around the mouth. But yes, my intimate knowledge of the living twin's perfect breasts helped to crack the case. The mountain theft of Sam's furtive photos of a naked Sara Barton clinched it. Sam's crime, combined with my crime, solved the crime. The murderer's slip of the tongue about Sam shooting himself—her one mistake—put me on the right scent. Ella remains in the dark about these last particulars, and here darkness is a friend to both of us. I continue the story.

"From there I pulled the thread. Sara Barton dies, and Lara Landrum drops out of all her movies and avoids contact with anyone from her old life.

"The 911 call—who first told us about it? Lara Landrum the day after the murder. Why did Sara unlock the bedroom door if her husband was going to kill her? Why tell Officer Hendrix everything was a misunderstanding? Because she wanted the audio of the 911 call but still needed Barton to stay in the marriage long enough to get framed. And when Hendrix left that night? Barton says he and Sara had sex for the first time in months. She was keeping him close lest he walk out and defeat the whole plan.

"The photo of the bruised back—every single thing we know about it comes from one person.

"The gun—Barton claims Sara wanted it, and she made him load it for her. A playground near the murder scene is a stupid place to ditch a gun, unless the murderer wanted the gun to be found. But why? To allow the police to discover Barton's fingerprints on the bullets.

"The missing cell phone on the day of the murder—a wife could hide her husband's phone with ease.

"Now think back to the night of the murder. Sara told Sam to meet at ten to ensure that the body was discovered while Barton was out of pocket with her, destroying any chance Barton had at an alibi. She made Brice promise not to come over that night in case he messed up her plans. And remember Barton's testimony, 'Lara' wasn't there when he arrived at her home that night. She arrived later. She was too busy killing her sister."

Ella mulls it all over—connecting the dots as I did Friday night. She says, "Amazing. Something was always off with her. But what about the sex tape with Brice?"

"Luck is where preparation meets opportunity. I don't see how she could've arranged being filmed. Best I figure she planned to use Brice as the trigger in some way. Jeff Yarber told me that Sara and Brice were already dirty dancing in full view of everyone before sneaking off to fool around. She planned to flaunt her affair with Brice to get Barton to bite. The video just did most of the heavy lifting for her."

She chews on it some more and adds, "So she slept with Brice to give Barton a motive for murder. She slept with Sam to make sure that he came over to the house that night. Posing as Lara, she slept with Barton to steal his alibi right from under him. She slept with you—why?"

"Because I was an easy mark."

The truth hurts. We both ponder it awhile in mournful silence.

Barton survived a close call. The certainty of his guilt never wavered in my mind. The evidence demanded it. Now every conviction I've ever secured screams at me about injustice. Have I always been so wrong?

The remembrance of murder trials past breaks when Ella sizes me up with a deadly earnestness. She doesn't want to talk about the case anymore. Something else is on her mind.

She asks, "Do you love her?"

"I love you."

The spontaneous response is pure, unfiltered, unscripted. That it escaped from my heart reveals again how little I understand myself.

The old gold prospectors in north Georgia would pan for treasure by allowing rushing waters to clear the clutter of distraction and debris, leaving behind the one true thing. The river of life does the same for us by sifting the wheat from the chaff. What remains are the people who love us the most. But whether the discovery is one of gold or identifying the individuals who matter above all others, a trail of tears follows us like a cloud in the sky you can never escape.

In a loud whisper, Ella Kemp—the woman I love—says, "You can't have me."

"I know."

A good woman is hard to find and easy to lose. The pain behind Ella's words is evident. The deep freeze of the recent past melts away, but she will never let me get close to her again. The broken trust can never be welded together without the fault line of that original crack showing.

Ella asks, "What are we going to do?"

I stare into the abyss of an uncertain future. I miss my wife and son desperately. Still.

I answer, "I'll resign. You should have my job. I'll talk to Bobby."

"I don't want that. This job is your life."

"How's that working out for me?"

We laugh together—the moment providing a needed dose of shared humor. But time is ephemeral. Ella waits for a moment before becoming serious.

"For the past few months, I've been looking for a new job. A business litigation firm in town needs someone with significant trial experience. They've made me an offer. It's triple the money. I think I'm going to take it."

We try not to look at each other. Life is a product of our choices. This exquisite creature stood ready to love me forever—the promising foundation to rebuild the man that once was. I chose a different path.

"Ella, you don't—"

Scott bursts in. The tension between Ella and me releases. The interruption does us good. Scott wears a death mask.

Ella asks, "Who died?"

Her attempt to lighten the mood combusts before taking flight. Scott's face jumps from misery to horror. Somebody did die.

Ella and I study him, fearing the worst, without even knowing what the worst could be. I see it at once. Sara Barton killed herself. She figured out the engineering and hung herself in a county jail cell. The certainty that I am right provides a cold, remorseless comfort that her death cleanses me from my sins—like a murderer who breathes a sigh of relief when another man is executed for his crimes.

Failed by his typical strong voice, Scott hoarsely delivers the news.

"Just got a call. Tasha Favors was shot and killed in Clayton County a little while ago. Execution-style. A piece of duct tape covering her mouth. No witnesses to report yet."

The words don't register at first. I remain stuck on the blond woman. But Ella's scream forces me to confront the truth. A flush of heat burns me from head to toe and strips me of all physical feeling. Scott sits down, unable to support his weight. I stagger up, trying to navigate the task of standing with no mental awareness of my legs. My mind howls, "Tasha!" Dizzy. I have to get out of this toxic place. I smash my phone against the wall, wanting no more connection to this brutal awful world. That beautiful, brave little girl. Dead. Corey Miller's smug face flashes through my mind. Q-Bone's parting words to me ring out: "That little girl is going to get got." May both suffer the eternal tortures of the damned. I make for the door.

Down the hallway, Bobby steps out of his office and temporarily stops my escape.

"Did you hear about the Favors girl?"

Tasha, her name is Tasha.

Bobby looks at me and knows the answer.

"There could be some bad press on that, but I'm hoping the news of the Barton trial will drown it out. We need to change the strategy we talked about earlier. I need you. Are you ready to do a press conference on Barton yet? And we need to make clear that the Favors girl was not killed in Fulton County, but in another jurisdiction. Let Clayton County take the heat."

The utter vulgarity. I need fresh air. I walk away with no intention of ever coming back. That beautiful, brave little girl. Dead. And the politicians want to cover it up.

"Hey! Where are you going? I need you on this."

I reach the street. I start to breathe again in the smog-infested freshness of the air. I walk toward the parking garage. A reporter sees me and shouts my name. She and her cameraman launch a mad sprint. I hurry into traffic to get away. Near misses. Horns blow. I'm across and still alive. I see the street sign out of the corner of my eye—Martin Luther King Jr. Blvd. The realization stabs me in the face. Another person gunned down by the hateful and dark rage of the human heart. Amber. Cale. Lara Landrum. Sam. Tasha. Every murder case I've ever tried. Dr. King. Too much death.

That beautiful, brave little girl. Dead.

I drive off into the abyss.

EPILOGUE

Tasha's murder drove me to the end of myself. I now sit before the graves of my wife and son. Dried mud cakes my dress pants, and my black, well-heeled shoes are soaked with the wetness of a recent rain. I came to this spot because it was the only place I could think to go. Running from death brought me to a graveyard.

Anguished hours pass. I feel deader than the corpses that surround me. Memories of Amber and Cale flood forward from the past. The journey from the white wedding dress to the red blood on the living room floor is a story of joy and pain. For the first time since the murders, I long to remember the good. Sara Barton is another matter. I wallow in a ravaging self-disappointment, unsure of whether it was love, lust, or loneliness that made me so blind. The parents of Sara Barton murdered an innocent girl, and the wreckage from their long-ago crimes keeps collecting fresh victims. But abuse only explains. It cannot excuse. The human toll remains. My friend Sam is still dead, and Sara killed him.

The tears come in torrents when I think of Tasha. I picture her scared little eyes at the end, distraught over humanity's casual cruelty. The duct tape over her mouth sickens me. The senseless violence that defines my adult life shows no sign of abating. The blood-dimmed tide is everywhere, the ceremony of innocence drowned—and I am too small to stop the evil.

Things fall apart. The center cannot hold. My heart cries out, "O God, O God, O God." I am broken.

I stay through the night, mired in the mud, nowhere else to go. In the midst of my sinking depression, a voice among the trees whispers, "Come to me, all you who are weary and burdened, and I will give you rest. For my yoke is easy, and my burden is light." Looking at the headstones of my wife and son, the promise is a hard one to trust. I played my part faithfully before, only to receive unimaginable suffering in return. Why should I believe again? But the tug of repentance pushes me to an unavoidable decision point.

Change or die.

A deep tiredness permeates me in a way that goes far beyond the physical. My soul seeks respite, and dying feels easier than change. Two roads diverge—the good and the bad. A deep breath grabs hold of my lungs. I wrestle with God in the early hours and lose. The language of salvation calls to me. You are a new creation in Christ. I want to believe.

I stand and stretch, eager to tread the road less traveled, praying that God's forgiveness will allow me to forgive myself. The moment is short-lived. The sense of closure that brought me to my feet seconds before evaporates into the mist. The same small, still voice speaks in a soft undertone, "You're not finished."

The confusing words return me to the sacred ground. The mystery eludes my grasp. Frustration that I am missing something obvious takes root. The harder I strain, the more I flail. The voice commands: "Be still." I obey. The stirring, at first faint, graduates from a simmer into a boil. The clear instructions despair me because I want no taste of the bitter cup being offered.

"I can't."

"You must."

Dawn beckons, but one last step remains. I open my heart to Corey Miller, Q-Bone, and even Mr. Smith. To each of them, I whisper, "I forgive you." The words are few, but the healing power behind them restores a measure of myself lost over these past two years. Whether they heard my grant of absolution doesn't matter. Forgiveness isn't for them. It is for me. The wisdom of Dr. King rings out across the generations: "Hate is too great a burden to bear."

Amen.

Nature's morning rituals signal the start of the fresh day—the hummingbird nourishing itself off the moist wildflowers, a rooster crowing two times in the distance, the perspiring dew. The brightness of the growing sun slips through the cracks among the trees to reach the graveyard's edge. Footsteps beat a tentative path in my direction.

"Chance?"

Scott calls out to me, halting his movement a respectful distance away, hesitant to invade the space around me and the graves of my family. I wait to answer, eager to savor the last vestiges of the solitude. I finally turn and give him an acknowledgment. He keeps his distance.

"Ella and I have been looking for you. We've been worried. Have long have you been here?"

"Long enough."

He comes closer and stands beside me. He, too, wears the same clothes as yesterday. We contemplate life together in silence. Rushing over here from the courthouse, I didn't take the time to get flowers for my wife and son. I'll come back soon with a batch of white roses, Amber's favorite. I read once that grave robbers these days steal cemetery flowers to sell for their own profit. At the time, I judged the perpetrators with Puritanical vigor, railing at the depths of human nastiness. Now I know that in the heart of every person lies the ingredients of a criminal. I have no stones left to hurl at other sinners. The rooster crows for the third time.

Scott asks, "Are you okay?"

"For the first time in years. Maybe my life."

Standing in the shadows, the chill of the morning hugs me close. But brightness is chasing the shade away, and the warmth of the sun is mere steps. On this morning, I cling to hope. Grace to oneself and to others transforms the dead into the living. My legs resist movement at first, battling with the hesitancy I feel about returning to a dark world. Except this time will be different. From the broken rise the redeemed.

I go forward and walk into the Light.

ACKNOWLEDGEMENTS

I am beyond thankful to a number of people whose invaluable input made *The Murder of Sara Barton* a much better book. First, Nancy Boren—or as she has been known to me since I was 15 years old, Mrs. Boren. Nancy Boren is living proof that teachers make a difference. In the two years she taught me high school English, Mrs. Boren pushed me to read Shakespeare, Hemingway, Steinbeck, Faulkner, Hawthorne, Charlotte Bronte, George Eliot, Orwell, Harper Lee, and Arthur Conan Doyle. More than any other person in my life, her influence nourished in me a hunger to be both an avid reader and a better writer. I would not be where I am today without her. Her specific contributions to *The Murder of Sara Barton* include catching my numerous grammar mistakes, providing invaluable input as a non-lawyer to ensure I didn't leave readers stuck in the legal weeds, and being frank when parts of the story simply didn't work. Her input improved the novel significantly.

Besides being a great law professor and delightful colleague, Browning Jeffries is a born editor. I knew she was an expert on writing, but her immense feel for subtlety and story nuance proved a blessing and paid huge dividends in the improvement of the narrative. Much like she has done with her writing students for over a decade now, Browning sent me back to the drafting table with invaluable feedback that forced me to confront some of the weaker parts of the work. Her suggestions were universally spot on and made for a better, tighter story. Her fingerprints are all over *The Murder of Sara Barton.*

Tom Lacy's real world experience as a trial lawyer was an immense help to my attempts to present the courtroom scenes with a reasonable degree of realism. Tom also made a key contribution to the story. His vigorous pushback on one particular plot point led me to reconsider a narrative element I had considered neatly wrapped up. The solution to the issue Tom raised turned into one of my favorite passages of the entire book. He is a great friend.

Joanna Apolinsky is a proofreading savant whose review of a late draft helped to clean up the final product. She even pulled up the menu from The Varsity to ensure that I had spelled "chili dogs" correctly. (I hadn't.) Joanna also provided two story observations that immediately made their way into the novel. I'm proud to call her a colleague.

The unconditional love and support of my parents, Jim and Peggy McMillian, has been a constant throughout my life. I am a first-generation college kid who owes his success to the sacrifices made by my parents to send me to the University of North Carolina, the London School of Economics, and the University of Georgia School of Law. My mom loves to read, and I'm proud that she can now read a novel written by her son. Sadly, my dad passed away before he had that chance. I miss him every day.

Writing is a lonely endeavor and the biggest thanks of all goes to my wife Carla for putting up with me over the years that I worked on this project. Authors are notoriously mercurial, and she tolerated me with great grace. Carla also made great contributions to the development of the story. After reading an early draft, her feedback led me to excise a number of story elements that dragged down the narrative. The finished product reflects her influence, and I'm a lucky man to have been married to her for over two decades now.

Finally, many thanks to my team at Bond Publishing for their encouragement and support—especially James and Emily.

All mistakes are mine alone.

ABOUT THE AUTHOR

Lance McMillian is a recovering lawyer who gave up the courtroom for the classroom. For over a decade, he has taught Constitutional Law and Torts to future lawyers at Atlanta's John Marshall Law School. Lance is married to Justice Carla Wong McMillian of the Georgia Supreme Court. *The Murder of Sara Barton* is his debut novel.

Lance loves to hear from his readers. You can connect with him via email (lancemcmillian@icloud.com), Twitter (@LanceMcMillian), or Facebook (fb.me/LanceBooks).

CPSIA information can be obtained
at www.ICGtesting.com
Printed in the USA
LVHW091022010920
664750LV00006B/33/J

9 781734 887723